T0109346

"Regarding your new book [*The Complete T*
hearing the turtle story many times from ma
the story and after reading many articles about such story, this is by far the
most entertaining, inspiring, extensive, and honest story of the turtles I have
ever read."

—Dr. Francisco J. Vaca
Vaca Capital Management LLC
Turtle Paul Rabar is a principal with Vaca Capital Management LLC

"*The Complete TurtleTrader*, Michael Covel's engaging and well-written account of the Turtles, covers not only the experiment, but a second generation of Turtles who were inspired by the Dennis/Eckhardt vision. One of the most interesting segments of the book covers Salem Abraham, who by chance met one of the original Turtles, took a 180 degree life turn, and began his own highly successful fund. It's a powerful illustration that, though markets have changed since the 1980s, the dynamics of success have not. Covel's book reads more like a piece of financial journalism than I expected, and I mean that as a compliment. It is this well-rounded perspective that makes *The Complete TurtleTrader* complete and a definitive contribution to the trading literature. He has clearly researched his topic and sources his quotes. He also casts a critical eye on his subjects, investigating why some Turtles found long-term success and why others didn't. A very enlightening portion of the book concerns Richard Dennis himself, the ending of the Turtle experiment, and the master's departure from his own trading rules and principles."

—Brett Steenbarger, Author

"I did enjoy the book...I hope it's doing well for you."

—Tom Shanks

"The book was wonderful..."

—Michael Shannon

"Liked it. Congratulations on a job well done."

—Jeff Gordon

"Book is very good...thank you for going for the truth and objectivity."

—Lucy Wyatt Mattinen

"Nice book."

—Russell Sands

"All in all, not bad. I wish it had never been done and I wish I were not in it, but I know that you were definitely going to do it, so I figured I would try to get the truth out as much as possible. By and large, it worked that way."

—Jim DiMaria

Also by Michael W. Covel

Trend Following:
How Great Traders Make Millions
in Up or Down Markets

The Complete
TurtleTrader

How 23 Novice

Investors Became

Overnight Millionaires

Michael W. Covel

HARPER

NEW YORK · LONDON · TORONTO · SYDNEY

HARPER

HarperCollins books may be purchased for educational, business, or sales
promotional use. For information, please e-mail the Special Markets Department at SPsales@harpercollins.com.

FIRST COLLINS TRADE PAPERBACK EDITION PUBLISHED IN 2008.

Designed by Joseph Rutt

The Library of Congress has cataloged the hardcover edition as follows:

Library of Congress Cataloging-in-Publication Data
Covel, Michael.
The complete turtletrader : the legend, the lessons,
the results / Michael Covel. — 1st ed.

p. cm.

ISBN 978-0-06-124171-0

1. Dennis, Richard (Richard J.), 1949– 2. Commodity trading advisors—
United States. 3. Commodity exchanges—United States 4. Speculation—
United States 5. Investment analysis—United States. I. Title.

HG6046.5.C68 2007
332.64'40973-dc22

2007023860

23 24 25 26 27 LBC 46 45 44 43 42

For Nina
Thank you for changing my life.

"Every morning in Africa a gazelle wakes up. It knows it must run faster than the fastest lion or it will be killed. Every morning a lion wakes up. It knows it must run faster than the slowest gazelle or it will starve to death. It doesn't matter whether you are a lion or a gazelle. When the sun comes up, you better start running."

African proverb

Contents

Preface

"Trading was more teachable than I ever imagined. Even though I was the only one who thought it was teachable . . . it was teachable beyond my wildest imagination."

Richard Dennis

This is the story of how a group of ragtag students, many with no Wall Street experience, were trained to be millionaire traders. Think of Donald Trump's show *The Apprentice*, played out in the real world with real money and real hiring and firing. However, these apprentices were thrown into the fire and challenged to make money almost immediately, with millions at stake. They weren't trying to sell ice cream on the streets of New York City. They were trading stocks, bonds, currencies, oil, and dozens of other markets to make millions.

This story blows the roof off the conventional Wall Street success image so carefully crafted in popular culture: prestige, connections, and no place at the table for the little guy to beat the market (and beating the market is no small task). Legendary investor Benjamin Graham always said that analysts and fund managers as a whole could not beat the market because in a significant sense they *were* the market. On top of that, the academic community has argued for decades about efficient markets, once again implying there is no way to beat market averages.

Yet making big money, beating the market, is doable if you don't follow the herd, if you think outside the box. People do have a chance to win in the market game, but he or she needs the right *rules* and *attitude* to play by. And those right rules and attitude collide head-on with basic human nature.

This real-life apprentice story would still be buried had I not randomly picked up the July 1994 issue of *Financial World* magazine, featuring the article "Wall Street's Top Players." On the cover was famed money manager George Soros playing chess. Soros had made $1.1 billion for the year. The article listed the top one hundred paid players on Wall Street for 1993, where they lived, how much they made, and in general how they made it. Soros was first. Julian Robertson was second, at $500 million. Bruce Kovner was fifth, at $200 million. Henry Kravis of KKR was eleventh at $56 million. Famed traders Louis Bacon and Monroe Trout were on the list, too.

The rankings (and earnings) provided a crystal-clear landscape of who was making "Master of the Universe" money. Here were, without a doubt, the top players in the "game." Unexpectedly, one of them just happened to be living and working outside Richmond, Virginia, two hours from my home.

Twenty-fifth on the list was R. Jerry Parker, Jr., of Chesapeake Capital—and he had just made $35 million. Parker was not yet forty years old. His brief biography described him as a former pupil of Richard Dennis (who?) and noted that he was trained to be a "Turtle" (what?). Parker was described as a then twenty-five-year-old accountant who had attended Dennis's school in 1983 to learn his "trend-tracking system." The article also said he was a disciple of Martin Zweig (who?), who just happened to be thirty-third on the highest-paid list that year. At that moment the name "Dennis" was neither more nor less important than "Zweig," but the implication was that these two men had made Parker extremely rich.

I studied that list intently, and Parker appeared to be the only one in the top hundred advertised as having been "trained." For someone like myself, looking for ways to try and earn that kind of money, his biography was immediate inspiration, even if there were no real specifics. Here was a man who bragged that he was a product of the "Virginia boondocks," loved country music, and preferred to keep as far away from Wall Street as possible. This was no typical moneymaking story— that much I knew.

The common wisdom that the only way you could find success was by working in eighty-story steel-and-glass towers in New York, London, Hong Kong, or Dubai was clearly dead wrong. Jerry Parker's office was absolutely in the middle of nowhere, thirty miles outside Richmond in Manakin-Sabot, Virginia. Soon after reading the magazine, I drove down to see his office, noting its lack of pretense, and sat in the parking lot thinking, "You have got to be kidding me. This is where he makes all that money?"

Malcolm Gladwell famously said, "There can be as much value in the blink of an eye as in months of rational analysis." Seeing Parker's country office was an electrical impulse for me, permanently dispelling the importance of location. But I knew nothing else at the time about Jerry Parker other than what was in that 1994 issue of *Financial World*. Were there more of these students? How did they become students? What were they taught? And who was this man Dennis who had taught Parker and others?

Richard Dennis was an iconoclast, a wildcatting Chicago trader not affiliated with a major investment bank or Fortune 500 firm. As the "locals" were fond of saying on Chicago trading floors, Dennis "bet his left nut." In 1983, by the time he was thirty-seven, he'd made hundreds of millions of dollars out of an initial grubstake of a few hundred. Dennis had done it on his own terms in less than fifteen years, with no formal training or guidance from anyone. He took calculated risks leveraging up huge amounts of money. If he liked a trade, he took all of it he could get. He lived the markets as a "betting" business.

Dennis figured out how to profit in the real world from an understanding of behavioral finance decades before Nobel prizes were handed out to professors preaching theory. His competitors could never get a handle on his consistent ability to exploit irrational market behavior throughout all types of markets. His understanding of probabilities and payoffs was freakish.

Dennis simply marched to a different drum. He eschewed publicity about his net worth even though the press speculated about it extensively. "I find that kind of gauche," said Dennis.[1] Perhaps he was reticent to focus on his wealth because what he really wanted to prove was that his earning skills were nothing special. He felt anyone could learn how to trade if taught properly.

His partner, William Eckhardt, disagreed, and their debate resulted in an experiment with a group of would-be apprentice traders recruited during 1983 and 1984 for two trading "classes." That "Turtle" name? It was simply the nickname Dennis used for his students. He had been on a trip to Singapore and visited a turtle-breeding farm. A huge vat of squirming turtles inspired him to say, "We are going to grow traders just like they grow turtles in Singapore."

After Dennis and Eckhardt taught novices like Jerry Parker how to make millions and the "school" closed, the experiment morphed into word-of-mouth legend over the years supported by few hard facts. The *National Enquirer* version of the story was captured in 1989 by a *Wall Street Journal* headline, "Can the skills of successful trading be learned? Or are they innate, some sort of sixth sense a lucky few are born with?"

Since the 1980s are long past, many might wonder if the Turtles' story still has relevance. It has more relevance than ever. The philosophy and rules Dennis taught his students, for example, are similar to the trading strategy employed by numerous billion-dollar-plus hedge funds. True, the typical stock-tip chaser glued daily to CNBC has not heard this story, but the players on Wall Street, the ones who make the *real* money, know.

The inside story has not been told to a wider audience until now because Richard Dennis is not a household name today, and because so much has happened on Wall Street since 1983. After the experiment ended, the characters, both teachers and Turtles, went their separate ways and an important human experiment fell through the cracks, even though what took place is as significant today as then.

The effort to get the real story out there started to gain momentum in 2004, when I was invited to visit Legg Mason's headquarters in Baltimore following the release of my first book, *Trend Following*. After lunch, I found myself in a classroom on the top floor with Bill Miller, the fund manager of the $18 billion Legg Mason Value Trust fund (LMVTX). Beating the Standard & Poor's 500-stock index for fifteen years straight put him in a similar league as Warren Buffett. Miller, like Dennis, had taken extraordinary calculated risks and more often than not been proven right.[2] On this day he was lecturing a roomful of eager trainees.

Out of the blue, Miller invited me to the lectern to address his class. The first questions, however, came straight from Miller and Michael Mauboussin (Legg Mason's chief investment strategist). They were, "Tell us about Richard Dennis and the Turtles." At that moment, I realized that if these two Wall Street pros wanted to know more about

Dennis, his experiment, and the Turtles, it was clear a much larger audience would want to hear the story.

However, as someone not there in 1983, I knew the task of telling a complete story from an objective vantage, with so many competing characters and competing agendas, was going to be a serious challenge. Getting those who lived the experience to talk, coupled with sleuth-like research to corroborate everything, was the only way to make this story really come alive. That said, behind the scenes the soap opera of those Turtles who worked hard to prevent this book's publication is a saga in itself.

Still, the biggest problem with a story like this is that most people don't want to actually understand how the real pros make big money. They want the road to riches to be effortless. Look at the collective public fascination with Jim Cramer—a man who is the polar opposite of Richard Dennis and Jerry Parker. Cramer is no doubt intelligent, but tuning into his extremely popular *Mad Money* TV show is like watching a traffic accident. There is a live studio audience that hoots and hollers at Cramer's fundamentally driven buy signals and wild prop-smashing antics. In one word: *bullshit*.

That said, a lot of people, many highly educated, believe that Cramer's way *is* the way to get rich. Instead of employing a statistical thinking toward market decisions, the general public keeps investing based on impulsive "feelings," letting an assortment of emotional bi-ases rule their lives. In the end, to their detriment, people are always risk-adverse toward gains, but risk-seeking toward losses. They are stuck.

The average newbie investor's method for success is not pretty. He gets in because his friends are doing it. Then the news media start up the stories of little guys doing well during a bull market. They all start to "invest" by picking stocks with "low" prices. As the market roars in their favor, thoughts of crashes never enter their mind ("With all the money in there, it could never go down!"). They never see their own slaughter coming, even though *their* market bubble is never different from past ones.

The media tell us that average investors now supposedly understand the concept of risk, yet worrying about possibilities while ignoring probabilities is at epidemic levels.[3] People gamble away fortunes on money-losing hunches or double down when logic says to fold. At the end of a lifetime they are never any closer to learning how to do it right. But outside of the herd there are the special few, who have the uncanny knack for knowing when to buy and sell, combined with an uncanny knack to properly assess risk.[4]

Richard Dennis mastered that uncanny knack by his early twenties. Unlike the general public wedded to their "feelings" to make decisions Dennis used mathematical tools to calculate risk and used it to his advantage. What he learned and what he taught students never resembled Jim Cramer barking stock tips. More important, Dennis proved that his ability to make money in the markets was not luck. His students, mostly novices, made millions for him and themselves.

What was the real story, and how did the Turtles learn their craft? What trading rules were they taught, and how can an average trader or investor use those insights today in his portfolio? What happened to them after the experiment, in the ensuing years? Finding the answers to those questions, with and without Dennis and his students' cooperation, has kept me passionately curious since 1994.

I am not alone in that curiosity. As author Steve Gabriel wrote on Yahoo! Finance recently, "The experiment has already been done that shows that we can all learn to trade for a living if we want to. That is why the 'Turtles' matter." The Turtles are an answer to the age-old question of nature versus nurture, the living proof of the single most famous Wall Street school for making money.

Acknowledgments

"Do not speak to me of rules. This is war! This is not a game of cricket!"

Colonel Saito,
from the movie The Bridge on the River Kwai

Justin Vandergrift assisted in bringing the Turtle trading rules to life, and also developed many of the accompanying charts. Celia Straus served as editor extraordinaire for the life of the project. Justin and Celia's value as sounding boards can't be stated strongly enough. A special thanks goes out to Shaun Jordan for finding me "access" and to Art Collins for all of his invaluable insights. Sara Sia, Tricia Lucero, and Maria Scinto provided help along the way. The following people also made significant contributions that allowed this book to come to life:

Mark Abraham, Salem Abraham, Jody Arlington, Christian Baha, Randy Bolen, Peter Borish, Ken Boyle, Sarah Brown, William Brubaker, Lindsay Campbell, Michael Carr, Michael Cavallo, Eva Cheung, Rebecca Clear, Jerome Covel, Johanna Covel, Jonathan Craven, Gary DeMoss, Sam DeNardo, Jim DiMaria, Adam Elend, Elizabeth Ellen, Charles Faulkner, Ethan Friedman, Michael Gibbons, Jeffrey Gordon, Roman Gregorig, Christian Halper, Martin Hare, Esmond Harmsworth, Larry Hite, Scott Houdek, Grace Hung, Withers Hurley, Ken Jakubzak, Ajay Jani, Erle Keefer, Peter Kline, Jeffrey Kopiwoda, Eric Laing, Charles Le Beau, Eleanor Lee, Jeff Marks, Howard Lindzon, Michael Martin, Michael Mauboussin, Bill Miller, Brian Mixon, Archie Moore, Robert Moss, Jerry Mullins, John O'Donnell, Robert Pardo, Jerry Parker, T. Boone Pickens, Paul Rabar, Barry Ritholtz, Chris Roberts, James O. Rohrbach, Tom Rollinger, Jay Rosser, Bradley Rotter, Mike Rundle, George Rush, Jack Schwager, Paul Scrivens, Ed Seykota, Tom Shanks, Michael Shannon, Mark Shore, Barry Sims, Aaron Smith, Larry Smith, Peter Sparber, Bob Spear, Celia Straus, Randall Sullivan, Gisete Tay, Irve Towers, John Valentine, David Wachtel, Sol Waksman, Robert Webb, Herschel Weingrod, Joel Westbrook, Paul Wigdor, Cole Wilcox, Thomas C. Willis, Thomas R. Willis, Rika Heidemann, Angie Lee, Paloma Martinez, Erica Nemmers, and Ben Steinberg.

Throughout *TurtleTrader* I have sourced material extensively. Material not sourced (i.e. assorted Turtle quotations and comments) was direct from interviews conducted specifically for this book.

1

Nurture versus Nature

"Give me a dozen healthy infants and my own specific world to bring them up in, and I'll guarantee to take any one at random and train him to become any type of specialist I might select—doctor, lawyer, artist, merchant, chef and yes, even beggar and thief, regardless of his talents, penchants, tendencies, abilities, vocations, and race of his ancestors."

John B. Watson,
early twentieth-century American psychologist

In the early 1980s, when Chicago's reigning trader king, Richard Dennis, decided to conduct his real-life social experiment, Wall Street was heating up. The stock market was at the start of a huge bull market. On the world stage, Iraq had invaded Iran. Lotus Development had released Lotus 1-2-3, and Microsoft had put their new word processing program ("Word") on the market. President Reagan, much to the liberally minded Dennis's chagrin, declared it "The Year of the Bible."

In order for Dennis to find his special breed of student guinea pigs, he circumvented conventional recruitment methods. His firm, C&D Commodities, budgeted $15,000 for classified ads in the *Wall Street Journal, Barron's,* and the *International Herald Tribune* seeking trainees during late fall 1983 and 1984. Avid job seekers saw this:

```
                Richard J. Dennis
               of C&D Commodities
     is accepting applications for the position of
             Commodity Futures Trader
      to expand his established group of traders.
```

Mr. Dennis and his associates will train a small group of applicants in his proprietary trading concepts. Successful candidates will then trade solely for Mr. Dennis: they will not be allowed to trade futures for themselves or others. Traders will be paid a percentage of their trading profits, and will be allowed a small draw. Prior experience in trading will be considered, but is not necessary. Applicants should send a brief resume with one sentence giving their reasons for applying to:

C&D Commodities
141 W. Jackson, Suite 2313
Chicago, IL 60604
Attn: Dale Dellutri

Applications must be received by October 1, 1984.
No telephone calls will be accepted.

Lost in the back pages of national dailies, the ad attracted surprisingly few respondents when you consider what Dennis was offering. But then, people don't usually expect the road to riches to be in plain sight.

The ad invited anyone to join one of Chicago's most successful trading firms, making "experience" optional. It was as if the Washington Redskins had advertised open positions regardless of age, weight, or football experience.

Perhaps most stunning was that C&D Commodities was going to teach proprietary trading concepts. This was unheard of at the time (and still is today), since great moneymaking trading systems were always kept under lock and key.

Dennis's recruitment process took place long before the chain-reaction flow of Craig's List ads that attract in thousands of résumés within hours for *any* job. However, it was 1983, and reaching out to touch the world with the flick of a blog post was not yet reality.

Potential students who were ultimately hired recall being stunned. "This can't be what I think it is" was a common refrain. It was, unbelievably, an invitation to learn at the feet of Chicago's greatest living trader and then use his money to trade and take a piece of the profits. One of the greatest educational opportunities of the century garnered responses ranging from a sentence written on a coconut to the mundane "I think I can make money for you." Let's face it, guessing what would make a wealthy, reclusive, and eccentric trader take notice of you in order to get to the next step—a face-to-face interview—had no precedent.

This casting of a wide net was all part of Dennis's plan to resolve his decade-long nature-versus-nurture debate with his partner William Eckhardt. Dennis believed that his ability to trade was not a natural gift. He looked at the markets as being like Monopoly. He saw strategies, rules, odds, and numbers as objective and learnable.

In Dennis's book, everything about the markets was teachable, starting with his very first prerequisite: a proper view of money. He didn't think about money as merely a means to go buy stuff at the mall, the way most people do. He thought of money as a way to keep score. He could just as easily have used pebbles to keep count. His emotional attachment to dollars and cents appeared nonexistent.

Dennis would say, in effect, "If I make $5,000, then I can bet more and potentially make $25,000. And if I make $25,000, I can bet that again to get to $250,000. Once there, I can bet even more and get to a million." He thought in terms of leverage. That was teachable in his book, as well.

On the other hand, William Eckhardt was solidly rooted in the nature camp ("either you're born with trading skills or you're not"). Dennis explained the debate, "My partner Bill has been a friend since high school. We have had philosophical disagreements about everything you could imagine. One of these arguments was whether the skills of a successful trader could be reduced to a set of rules. That was my point of view. Or whether there was something ineffable, mystical, subjective, or intuitive that made someone a good trader. This argument had been going on for a long time, and I guess I was getting a little frustrated with idle speculation. Finally, I said, 'Here is a way we can definitely resolve this argument. Let's hire and train people and see what happens.' He agreed. It was an intellectual experiment."[1]

Even though Eckhardt did not believe traders could be nurtured, he had faith in the underdog. He knew plenty of multimillionaires who had started trading with inherited wealth and bombed. Eckhardt saw them lose it all because they didn't feel the *pain* when they were losing: "You're much better off going into the market on a shoestring, feeling that you can't afford to lose. I'd rather bet on somebody starting out with a few thousand dollars than on somebody who came in with millions."[2]

The ramifications of Dennis and Eckhardt's intellectual experiment opened a Pandora's box of opinions and biases. Measuring and judging people by their IQ board scores, LSAT, GPA, degrees, or whatever other metric, is the way most of society operates. Yet if an IQ measure or test score was the only ticket needed for success, then all smart people would be loaded, which is obviously not the case.

Stephen Jay Gould, the late great American paleontologist, evolutionary biologist, and historian of science, was always quick to eschew society's misconceptions about intelligence: "We like to think of America as a land with generally egalitarian traditions, a nation conceived in liberty and dedicated to the proposition that all men are created equal."[3] However, Gould saw America slipping toward measures and ratios as a sole means of predicting life success and was appalled at the increasing predilection of Americans to use a hereditarian interpretation of IQ as a limiting tool.[4]

Dennis, like Gould, was not about to be taken in by a hereditary interpretation of IQ. His aim was to implant his mental software into the brains of his students, and then place them into his controlled environment to see how they would react and perform.

That someone of Dennis's stature and success would be so determined to prove nurture over nature that he would teach his proprietary trading methods to others was extraordinary. Certainly his partner was surprised that he was willing to put so much of his own money in the hands of amateurs.

With a dark beard and sideburns and a receding hairline, William Eckhardt bore an uncanny resemblance to Lenin and cut a sinewy, energetic figure, the polar opposite of the over-six-foot-tall rotund Dennis. Of the two, he was the true mathematician, with a master's in mathematics from the University of Chicago and four years of doctoral research in mathematical logic. But for the purpose of their nature-versus-nurture debate, Eckhardt was the unapologetic biological determinist, certain that his partner was a savant, an introverted genius with special genetic talents.

Today, there are plenty of people who would still argue against Dennis, insisting that "biological determinism," or the notion that genetics predicts the physical and behavioral nature of an organism, can't be overcome.[5] That's bad news for a potentially successful trader or entrepreneur in any field who doesn't have the so-called pedigree or right IQ score. The irony is that even though Dennis's experiment proved otherwise over twenty years ago, success in the markets is still perceived by many as a virtual IQ caste system.

Skeptics of Dennis's Turtle experiment have long rolled out barrages of excuses about how serendipitous answering that little ad was. They argue it would have been impossible for anyone, except insiders, to have known that ad was the ticket to cracking Wall Street's Top 100 paid traders (like Jerry Parker did). How could anyone know that an *ad* could potentially bypass what Warren Buffett has affectionately called "the ovarian lottery" and give a random group of people the chance to make millions? It's hard to accept that fact. It's too much like a Hollywood script.

It's a Small World

Richard Dennis wanted a mishmash of personalities, similar to MTV's *Real World* and their diverse casting calls. He selected both far-right-wing conservatives and bleeding-heart liberals. A high school graduate and an MBA were picked from the thousand-plus applicants who threw their hats into the ring. The wild cross-section of his final Turtle picks demonstrated Dennis's diversity desires.

There were college graduates from the State University of New York at Buffalo (business), Miami University in Ohio (economics), the New England Conservatory of Music (piano, music theory), Ferrum College in Virginia (accounting), Central Connecticut State University (marketing), Brown University (geology), the University of Chicago (Ph.D. in linguistics), Macalester College (history), and the United States Air Force Academy.

Others Dennis students had recently held jobs at Cushman/Wakefield (security guard), Caterpillar Tractor (salesperson), Collins Commodities (broker), the Ground Round Restaurant (assistant manager), A.G. Becker (phone clerk), Palomino Club (bartender), and Dungeons and Dragons (board game designer). One student simply declared his status as "unemployed." Earlier job histories of those who made the final cut were even more mundane: kitchen worker, teacher, prison counselor, messenger, accounting assistant, and waiter.

Dennis selected one woman from the ad, a rarity in the 1980s "all boys" world of Chicago trading. He also selected gay students, whether he knew their orientation at the time or not. His picks ran the gamut from mild-mannered, professional academics to regular-guy blue-collar types, to some with wildly volatile personalities.

There were certain things Dennis was looking for. He wanted students who showed a willingness to take calculated risks. Those who stood out from the herd in some kind of an unconventional way had a leg up. This wasn't a normal hiring process in the early 1980s, nor would it be normal now. Today, MBA types, for example, are geared to the intellectual rigors of running a company but are reluctant to get their hands dirty. They are the ones who think IQ and connections are all they need. They don't want to do the hard work. They don't want to really take a risk.[6]

Dennis didn't want those people. He was searching for people who enjoyed playing games of chance. He was looking for people who could think in terms of "odds." Think like a Vegas "handicapper"? You were more likely to get an interview. None of this was surprising to those who knew Dennis. Reacting to opportunities that others never saw was how he marched through life.

With a story like this, it's not hard to imagine the legend that has built up over the years. The experiment has inspired a cultlike reverence, often passed along by word of mouth. However, Charles Faulkner, a modeler of great traders, was instantly struck by the deeper meaning of Dennis's experiment. He wondered how Dennis *knew*, saying, "I would have sided with Bill's skepticism. Even if . . . it was teachable, it certainly should have taken more effort and a much longer time than Dennis allowed for learning it. The experiment, and more significantly the results, violated all of my beliefs around effort and merit and reward. If something was that easy to learn, it shouldn't pay so well and vice versa. I marveled at the range of thinking, awareness, and inference, this implied."

Dennis and Eckhardt taught their students everything they needed in only two weeks to trade bonds, currencies, corn, oil, stocks, and all other markets. Their students did not learn to trade from a screaming mosh pit on the trading floor with wild hand signals, but rather in a quiet office with no televisions, computers and only a few phones.

Each student received $1 million to trade after his classroom instruction. They were to get 15 percent of the profits, while Dennis got 85 percent. No surprise that he would get the lion's share; it was, after all, his money.

Dennis was honest about taking the majority of the profits when he said in November 1983, right before launching the experiment, that there would be no charity involved. He viewed the experiment as a way to diversify his portfolio. While he knew his "no experience necessary" students could be wiped out, he viewed it all as a way to gain more control of how his millions were being put to use, saying, "I'm tired of investing in someone else's condominium in Timbuktu."[7]

Replacing condo investment ideas with a group of surrogates was a smart move. Many of his students went on to make 100 percent or more per year over four years. That's monster moneymaking. Even more important than those successes from the early 1980s is the current track record of three of the participants. Long after the experiment's ending, Eckhardt, along with two of Dennis's former pupils, Jerry Parker and Paul Rabar, manage in excess of $3 billion in 2007. They still trade in a very similar fashion to how they did back in the day.

Beyond Turtles-related successes, there are hundreds of others, traders of big achievements, who owe a debt of gratitude to Dennis for sharing his knowledge and experience. Additionally, men considered to be trading peers of Dennis (not trained by him), men of similar macro trading backgrounds such as Bruce Kovner, Louis Bacon, and Paul Tudor Jones, are to this day regularly the highest paid on Wall Street.

Of course, the $3 billion traded by Dennis's trading progeny doesn't seem *that* large when headlines today scream out with stories of new hedge funds launched with billions out of the gate. When Jon Wood, formerly of UBS, started his new fund with more than $5 billion and when Jack R. Meyer, the former investment manager of Harvard University's assets, raised more than $6 billion for Convexity Capital, the $3 billion from Dennis's associates sounds less impressive.[8]

In fact, some argue that Dennis's "lack of pedigree" approach has been passed by. One recent story profiled a twenty-seven-year-old trader from Goldman Sachs. A "well-bred" product of Massachusetts's tony Deerfield Academy and Duke University, he was described as having all of the ingredients of a grade-A trader. One of his peers gushed. "He's smart, competitive, and a hard worker. Keep your eye on this kid."[9]

That praise has to be put into perspective. If a trader starts a career with a prominent investment bank, he becomes valuable by using Goldman Sachs's money, offices, and connections. The access he has sitting in the catbird seat at a top bank is a major secret of his success.

Investment banks were simply never the career paths of the great entrepreneurial traders. That is why Dennis brings hope. Independent-minded rebel traders, like him, never got to where they were by moving up bureaucratic ladders. They did not bide their time for twenty years engaging in office politics. Dennis and his peers were never part of a Fortune 500 hierarchy. They had one objective: to make absolute-return money trading the markets on their terms. It was high risk and high reward.

Dennis's Turtle experiment proved, all things being equal, that his students could learn to trade to make millions. However, all things being equal, after they learned the "right" trading rules to make those millions, if they did not exhibit, like Boston Red Sox slugger David Ortiz does in baseball, a "walk-off home run" mentality every day, they would fail. Great training alone was not enough to win for the long run. In the end, a persistent drive for winning combined with a healthy dose of courage would be mandatory for Dennis's students' long-term survival.

Before getting into what *really* happened with the Turtles, who the winners and losers were and why, it's crucial to get acquainted with what made Dennis tick in the first place. Knowing how a regular guy from the South Side of Chicago made $1 million by the age of twenty-five in the early 1970s and $200 million by the age of thirty-seven in the early 1980s is the first step toward understanding why nurture won out.

2

Prince of the Pit

"Great investors conceptualize problems differently than other investors. These investors don't succeed by accessing better information; they succeed by using the information *differently* than others."

Michael J. Mauboussin,
chief investment strategist of Legg Mason Capital Management

Nineteen eighty-six was a huge year for Richard Dennis. He made $80 million (about $147 million in 2007 dollars). That kind of money-making put him squarely at the center of Wall Street alongside George Soros, who was making $100 million, and then junk bond king Michael Milken of Drexel Burnham Lambert, who was pulling in $80 million.[1]

Profits like those for Dennis came with heartburn. He was down $10 million in a single day that year before bouncing back, a roller-coaster ride that would have made mere mortals lose serious sleep. Yet Dennis cockily said that he slept like a baby during all that volatility.[2]

His moneymaking style was about mammoth home runs and many smaller strikeouts. If there was a "secret," he knew that you had to be able to accept losses both psychologically and physiologically. Still, 1986 was a long time ago, and memories dull when an old pro starts talking about the benefits of taking "losses."

During his heyday in the 1970s, 1980s, and mid-1990s, Dennis was described in a number of ways by those who knew of him. There was Dennis the legendary floor trader, Dennis the trading system's trading guru, Dennis who started funds with investment bank Drexel Burnham, Dennis the philanthropist, Dennis the political activist, and Dennis the industry-leading money manager.[3] He was a difficult man to stereotype, and he liked it that way.

"Dennis the gambler" was the only label that offended him, because he never considered himself a gambler in the Las Vegas sense. He understood financial Darwinism (read: "odds") through and through. He always played the "game" knowing that everyone else was out to beat him. Financial futures pioneer Richard Sandor put Dennis in perspective: "The name of the game is survival when the markets are this chaotic. From that perspective, he may go down as one of the most successful speculators in the 20th century."[4]

Dennis's success started long before he launched the Turtle experiment. He grew up in Chicago during the 1950s, a street kid from the old South Side neighborhoods. There was no privileged childhood with wealthy parents and well-placed friends. He did not have a silver spoon or the right connections.

The teenage Dennis was introverted and wore thick glasses and polyester pants. His first stab at trading, while attending the all-boys' St. Laurence Prep School in Chicago, was to buy ten shares of a $3 "phonograph" stock. The company folded. While his first attempt at trading failed, he was a natural at poker, intuitively understanding the odds.

His teachers did not forget him. James Sherman, who taught theology and European history to Dennis, said that he never would take anything at face value. Dennis and his friends enjoyed the mental gymnastics of taking sides in an argument. Sherman added, "If somebody had said back then that Richard Dennis would become a very wealthy man as a commodity trader, I probably wouldn't have believed them." His former teacher would have predicted Dennis to be in front of the fire, with a sweater and a pipe, expounding on the cosmos.[5]

At seventeen, Dennis landed a summer job as a runner ($1.60 an hour) at the Chicago Mercantile Exchange. Each day the exchange floor was mobbed by hundreds of traders fighting and screaming to place their trades. They were exactly like auctioneers buying and selling their wares except that they were in a trading pit battling it out. An indoor game of tackle football would be a good description of the scene.

Dennis longed to be there, but to trade on the floor you had to be twenty-one. He found a way over that hurdle by talking his father into trading for him. A blue-collar worker for Chicago's city government, the father became a proxy guided by his son's hand signals from the sidelines.

Despite some trading success in his teens, Dennis headed off to college at DePaul University, where his passion for philosophy (after flunking out of an accounting class) from high school days was rekindled. He was most taken with British philosophers David Hume and John Locke, who had a relatively simple way of viewing the world. "Prove it to me" was their basic perspective.

Hume thought the mind a blank slate (*tabula rasa*) on which experience could be written. He believed that since human beings live and function in the world, they should try to observe how they do so. Discovering the causes of human belief was his key principle.[6] Locke, on the other hand, argued that there were no innate ideas. He asked the question, "How is the mind furnished?" He wanted to know where reason and knowledge came from. His answer was one word: "experience."

Both Hume and Locke belonged to the school of thought known as Empiricism. Empiricism is rooted in the notion that knowledge is derived from experiment, observation, and experience. Little nuggets of simple common sense from these two eighteenth-century British philosophers connected with an impressionable college student. They became his idols.

Dennis was not shy about his leanings, asserting, "I'm an empiricist, through and through. David Hume and Bertrand Russell. I'm solidly in the English tradition." Dennis saw Hume as ruthlessly skeptical. Hume took on the sacred cows of his generation, and Dennis loved that attitude.[7]

It wasn't only British philosophy that turned Dennis into a skeptic. Growing up in the late 1960s and early 1970s gave him an anti-establishment view of the world. He witnessed protesters being beaten by the Chicago police during the 1968 riots, right next to the venerable Chicago Board of Trade. It was a turning point in his life:

Trading has taught me not to take the conventional wisdom for granted. What money I made in trading is testimony to the fact that the majority is wrong a lot of the time. The vast majority is wrong even more of the time. I've learned that markets, which are often just mad crowds, are often irrational; when emotionally overwrought, they're almost always wrong.[8]

After graduating from DePaul University he received a fellowship to Tulane University graduate school, but promptly dropped out and returned to Chicago within days to start trading full time. Dennis bought a seat on the MidAmerican Commodity Exchange with money borrowed from his parents (part of it from a life insurance policy in his name). He still needed cash to trade, however. His initial war chest of $100 came from his brother Tom's earnings delivering pizzas.

This was not a family of market operators. Dennis was always honest about his father's "hatred" of the market, explaining, "My grandfather had lost all his money in the stock market in the Depression. The urge to speculate kind of skipped a generation." He knew his father's perspective would never work for him:

> You can't have a standard attitude about money and do well in this business. What do I mean by that? Well, my father, for instance, worked for the city of Chicago for 30 years, and he once had a job shoveling coal. So, just imagine coming from his frame of reference, and thinking about losing $50 in a few seconds trading commodities. To him, that means another eight hours shoveling coal. That's a standard attitude about money.[9]

It didn't take long for his father to recognize Dennis's unique abilities to make money. By the beginning of 1973, at twenty-four, Dennis had made $100,000. Around that time he cockily preached to the Chicago papers, "I just wanted to be able to get up and say, 'I once made $100,000 a year, and I still think you are an ass.' That rhetoric may not be wholesome motivation, but I do think it's part of what drives me."[10] He was making so much money fast that whatever the context or content of an interview, it was outdated in weeks or even days.

A rebel at heart, Dennis cultivated being a character from the outset. He was fond of saying that he never liked the idea of sharing a birthday with Richard Nixon—a gentle stab at all those conservative traders sur-rounding him in the pits on LaSalle Street. He was an anti-establishment guy making a fortune leveraging the establishment, while wearing jeans.

Society was splintered during the time Dennis earned his first big money. Nineteen seventy-four was a difficult year in which to focus. What with G. Gordon Liddy having been found guilty of Watergate charges and the Symbionese Liberation Army kidnapping Patricia Hearst, it was a wild time of constant turmoil. To top it off, Richard Nixon became the first President of the United States to resign from office.

Current events did not stop Dennis from leveraging a 1974 run-up in the price of soybeans to a $500,000 profit. By the end of the year, at age twenty-five, he was a millionaire.[11] Even though he downplayed his success, he couldn't hide it. When he showed up late one day to the soybean pit explaining that his beat-up 1967 Chevy had broken down, other traders gave him flack, knowing full well he could afford a new car hundreds of times over.

Not only was his persona different, his trading was different. Dennis read *Psychology Today* (no government economic or crop reports for him) to keep his emotions in check and to remind him of how over-rated intuition was in trading. He took delight in boasting, in contrast to most traders who got up early to read all they could from weather reports to daily Department of Agriculture assessments, that he stayed in bed until the last minute before getting to the exchange just as trad-ing started.[12]

At one point during this time, Dennis was in the middle of an in-terview with a reporter as he went to the bank to make a deposit. He was depositing a $325,000 check (in 1976, that represented two to three weeks of work for him). Depositing an amount like that in the mid-1970s was not normal. Dennis always got hassled when he tried to deposit checks that size.[13] He was oblivious to the fact that the teller was looking at a check that likely would exceed her total career earn-ings. Yet Dennis, probably younger than she was, couldn't sign his name straight.[14]

As his notoriety continued to grow, national newspapers like the

Chicago Tribune, the *New York Times*, and *Barron's* trumpeted his youth and success. This was not standard operating procedure in a tight-lipped world where the big Chicago traders typically kept silent.

Dennis enjoyed and even reveled in his upbringing and the unique perspective it afforded him:

> I grew up in an Irish-Catholic family on the South Side of Chicago. My institutional values were very strong, if somewhat confused. My holy trinity consisted of the Catholic Church, the Democratic Party, and the Chicago White Sox. I would describe my early value system as nourishing, if limited. When my father took me to Hurley's Tavern, I saw people falling off their bar stools—about what you'd expect from people who called whiskey "Irish pop."[15]

The Church, baseball, Democratic politics, and Irish drinking weren't only an influence on his youth:

> How much of my holy trinity informs me as an adult? In the White Sox I have a deep and abiding faith. In the Democratic Party I have shallow and fading faith, which is almost never rewarded. In the church, well . . . I fear 16 years of Catholic education left me a skeptic.[16]

Look at that 1976 *New York Times* photo of the then twenty-six-year-old multimillionaire, lounging on the couch with his dad seated to his left, seemingly oblivious to the photographer, and it is easy to see anti-establishment staring into the camera. The photo caption only reinforced Dennis's differences: "He drives an old, inexpensive car, he dresses in cheap knits; his money tends to pile up, unused."

However, all this press at such a young age left Dennis confronted by something he probably wasn't expecting: people with their hands out, asking for money. "Most of them were very sad," he recalled. "One person said, 'Help me to learn how to trade. I'm in debt.' Some people made it sound as if $5,000 or $10,000 were all they needed to make them happy. Those were the only letters worth answering—to explain that money won't really make a difference."[17]

Not many twenty-six-year-olds would have been mature enough to handle the press using such folksy wisdom. Yet Dennis never let the swirl around him interfere with what he was doing to make money. Quite simply, his trading technique was to trade seasonal spreads. In other words, he wanted to take advantage of seasonal patterns in markets like soybeans—his initial specialty. Dennis would hold "long" (bets to profit as the market increased) and "short" (bets to profit as the market decreased) positions in futures contracts simultaneously in the same or related futures markets.

The MidAm Exchange Experience

Once he had his MidAm seat (formerly called the Chicago Open Board), Dennis was off and running. Initially he had no clue what he was doing, but he was a fast learner who learned to think like a casino operator:

> When I started out, I had a system called "having no idea whatsoever." For four years, I was just taking edges. If someone was giving me a quarter cent edge to buy an Oat contract, I didn't think he knew anything either. I just knew that I was getting a quarter cent edge, and at the end of the day, the edges would approximately equal my profit. Obviously, on an individual basis that doesn't have to happen, but over a longer period of time, it will. I tried to be like the house in the casino. It wasn't that novel. People at the Board of Trade had been doing it forever. But for the MidAm, it was kind of revolutionary because no one would understand that you could balance your risk with a lot of volume. That's how I started.[18]

Dennis went from zero to sixty on the MidAm in record time, and no one knew how he learned to do what he was doing. He knew that traders had a tendency to self-destruct. The battle with self was where he focused his energies: "I think it's far more important to know what Freud thinks about death wishes than what Milton Friedman thinks about deficit spending."[19] Go down to Wall Street today after work with the hot-shot traders all earning $500,000 a year at the big banks and you'll find very few who talk about Freud being the ticket to making millions.

However, trading was harder than Dennis let on. The early ups and downs took a toll on him, but he learned the hard lessons within months. "You have to have mentally gone through the process of failure," he said. "I had a day during which I made every mistake known to modern man. I took too big risks. I panicked and sold at the bottom of every break. I had built my net worth up to about $4,000 coming into that day and I lost about $1,000 in two hours. It took me about three days to work through that experience emotionally, and I think it was the best thing that ever happened to me."[20]

It was about this time, in 1972–73, that fellow traders Tom Willis and Robert Moss met Dennis. They would go on to work together for years as close friends and business associates, with Dennis as their leader. The star did not wear a polished Armani suit, nor did his buddies. They sported used-car-salesman jackets, with muttonchops and bad hair, but their appearance disguised calculated gamers looking to beat the pants off their peers every day of the week.

Willis, like Dennis, was brought up in a working-class family. His father, who worked first as a milkman and then delivering bread, helped him buy a seat on the MidAm for $1,000 at age twenty-one. Willis had never heard of the exchange until he saw an article in the *Chicago Tribune* with the headline "Altruistic Grain Trader Successful." It was about 22½-year-old Richard Dennis.

Willis immediately identified with his peer's anti-establishment way of viewing the world. Dennis was not afraid to say that he had voted for Eugene McCarthy and didn't think that just because he had radical ideas he should be driving a cab. Years later, Dennis was even more direct, saying that "the market was a legal and moral way to make a living. Being a trader doesn't oblige one to be a conservative."[21]

Yet Dennis's political stance was not what first caught Willis's attention; it was his attitude about making money in a world where class and distinction were always barriers to entry. Without a second thought, Willis hopped in his Jeep and drove to the Fisher Building in the Chicago Loop to check out the exchange. When he arrived at the MidAm for the first time, his soon-to-be role model dominated the landscape: "Rich was in the pit. I knew him by the photo from the *Tribune*."

Willis started trading with his MidAm seat, but had no immediate contact with Dennis even though they were the two youngest traders in the pit. Nearly everybody else was sixty-five to eighty years old, and they actually had chairs and spittoons in the trading pit. A young Dennis, towering above a sea of old guys lounging on chairs, must have been a sight.

Situated only a few blocks from the Chicago Board of Trade, the MidAm was a bit player at the time. It was small, perhaps fifteen hundred square feet. While Willis didn't know how his start at the MidAm would unfold (he ended up building a thirty-plus-year trading career), he was certain Dennis saw a much bigger future.

Even then, big wigs from the Chicago Mercantile Exchange (CME) were coming over in their limos to pick young Dennis's mind. Ultimately, Dennis approached Willis most likely because he was good enough not to go broke and because they were both about the same age.

Dennis told Willis, "If you're buying wheat and it's strong and the beans are too low and the wheat is five higher, why don't you sell soybeans instead of selling the wheat you bought?" It was a very sophisticated insight. In fact, buying "strength" and selling "weakness" short still befuddles investors. It is counter-intuitive to buying low and selling high.

Dennis was already sharing his knowledge with other traders. He was a natural-born teacher. Dennis was teaching the young exchange members at either his or Willis's apartment. Willis would buy two hundred pieces of chicken and a barrel of potato salad. There were fifty or sixty guys in his one-bedroom apartment with Dennis holding court, explaining how to trade.

There was a practical need for this. The MidAm was selling new memberships to all kinds of traders, many with no experience. Dennis and Willis were teaching "liquidity." To give the market confidence in the viability of the MidAm exchange, there had to be a critical mass of buyers and sellers. This culture of education was creating a better exchange with better traders. And those better traders were starting to make money. It could all be traced to Dennis.

Craig and Gary Lacrosse, Ira Shyman, John Grace, Wayne Elliott, Robert Tallian, and David Ware are all Chicago traders who learned from Dennis. While they may not be household names, they became hugely successful in part because of the generosity of the young Dennis, who felt no compunction about sharing his skills with others.

After the apartment-training sessions everyone would go home, and they would meet the next day in the pits. During market hours they would ask Dennis, "Is this what you meant?" and he'd say, "Yeah." Dennis freely gave away his knowledge.

The Chicago Board of Trade

Great experiences and profits aside, it wasn't long before Dennis needed a bigger playing field than the minor-league MidAm. He was already plotting how to beat the big boys at the Chicago Board of Trade (CBOT), the world's largest futures exchange. Once at the CBOT, his placid demeanor contrasted sharply with the hoarse shouts and wild gestures of other floor traders, many of whom were millionaire traders with decades of experience. He was soon beating them at their own game with a "betting" style that was often so relaxed that his trading cards would literally slip out of his hand onto the floor.

Dennis's move to the CBOT was historic. Willis could hardly believe it: "Richard goes to the Board of Trade and knocks the cover off the ball. They've never seen anything like this. I mean this kid takes the whole pit off. Not because he can or not because he wants to show off, but corn is up, beans are up two and the corn is down three and they sell him a million bushels of soybeans up one and a half and the next thing you know they close up seven and they're talking about him, 'Who's this new kid?' " Willis refrained from divulging the names of old-timers that Dennis was beating the pants off when he first hit the CBOT, since many of those losing traders are still around today.

One of Dennis's students said that their teacher believed his physical attributes to be behind his pit-trading success: "You ever heard why he considered himself really successful? He is six feet something and the size of a freight train. He could see over people and more importantly, people could see him. People always knew that he was there. He honestly felt that's why he was successful."

Dennis's attributing his height and weight as the reason he was successful is not the full story. There was more to becoming a millionaire by twenty-five than being "six foot something" and three hundred pounds plus. Even with excess weight, his peers described him as having cat-quick reflexes on the trading floor.

The Move from the Pit

Trading on the floor, down in the pit, might have been exciting during this era, but today the Chicago Board of Trade floor is silent. That doesn't mean trading is dead today—far from it. Electronic trading outdated the old ways faster than anyone ever thought could happen.

However invigorating the trading floor may have been in the 1970s, the only way for Dennis to expand his trading success was to move *away* from it. The Chicago trading floors were designed with multiple pits and each pit traded a different market. To trade more than one market, he had to physically move back and forth across the floor to the various pits.

Dennis's solution allowed him to remain faithful to buying in strength and selling in weakness. He knew that if his system worked in soybeans and corn, then it would also work in gold and stocks and all other markets.

At the same time, he saw Wall Street changing, with new markets appearing fast and furiously as economies around the world opened and expanded. Fixed income futures were launched, and by 1975 the International Monetary Market (IMM) was allowing anyone to trade currencies the way they did stocks. Dennis knew what this would all mean.

To trade in that bigger world, Dennis moved into an office on the twenty-third floor of the CBOT, leaving the turmoil of screaming traders behind. Concurrent with his move, in November 1975, Dennis and Larry Carroll formed a partnership. Known simply by the first initial of their last names, C&D Commodities was born.

There is little public information on Larry Carroll (they did meet on the MidAm floor). And, although Dennis's "D" came second, theirs was not a partnership where the decisions and profits were split fifty-fifty. Dennis was always the man. Within short order, C&D Commodities became one of the largest independent trading firms in the world. They quickly rivaled such established institutional investors as Salomon Brothers and the Pillsbury Company.[22]

However, other traders who had seen him dominate the pits were shocked when Dennis left the floor. They thought he was crazy. To compete against the likes of Pillsbury and Salomon Brothers was considered suicide, because no one thought he could maintain that floor "edge." Dennis himself had always said the pit was the safest place to be.

The transition did almost sink Dennis. When he went off floor, he struggled. In the late 1970s, the markets were getting to him. Tom Willis saw the struggle and recalled, "He was a little disillusioned, a little off balance frankly." Both men went out to a bar to discuss the situation. Dennis was not throwing in the towel. He looked at Willis and said, "Tom, I got stuff that's so good that used off floor in the right hands it would make $50 million a year."

In today's terms, this would be like someone saying he has a way of trading that's so good he can make $200 million a year. Or think of some number that is fifty times more than is rationally achievable by any normal measure. With anyone else, Willis would have been skeptical: "If I didn't know Rich, I would have said, 'Gee, he really does sound a little more off balance than I'm even thinking.' Saying $50 million in 1979 is a crazy thing to do, but I believed it. And he did it. If an edge is good or the idea is good, let's get in front of the screen and trade them all. If it's that good, let's get in front of the screen and have 20 people do this. As a matter of fact, it's very, very consistent to expanding geometrically the ability to take advantage of this good idea."

The goal of trading every market he could and making more money in the process was reached within a year, just as Dennis had predicted. Yet making that much more money didn't change him one bit. His new office was not marble and glass. The outside hallway to the office had dingy brown paneling. On his office door was "C&D Commodities, Richard J. Dennis and Company." No flash. The men's room for the floor was next door.

Martin Hare, a nephew of Larry Carroll's, was sixteen and in high school when he was working for Dennis. Now an executive with Merrill Lynch in San Diego, he worked in Dennis's unconventional office environment from 1982 to 1989. Hare still gets enthusiastic when he thinks about his after-school job: "I cut out the Wall Street settlement prices for three summers. My weekly salary at C&D was $120. That was up from $90 the summer before. The C&D office was royal blue in color. There was a sleeping room for those that needed to nap, mostly for Rich, and a refrigerator full of the best beer."

Dennis may have physically disappeared from the trading floor, but the hermit-like trading wizard hovered over the markets like Zeus. Everyone knew he was there when a huge order came into the pits. Traders also knew not to get in front of his orders, or they could be potentially wiped out. Critics and regulators at times thought he was too big and moved markets unfairly. Dennis scoffed, "Sour grapes."

The criticisms were an excuse for people who had learned to lose. Dennis had no patience for people targeting his success. "I cringe a little when I'm identified as a millionaire," Dennis said after reading that his $250,000 contribution to Adlai Stevenson was the largest individual political gift ever in Illinois. "If somebody just had $100,000, he wouldn't be called a thousandaire, and if a pauper gave a dollar, they wouldn't say, 'Pauper gives his last buck.' "[23]

Although he grew wealthier by the day, he still kept an antinuclear poster hanging in his office and remained outside the chummy atmosphere of the exchanges. He was not prone to travel in the limelight. "We don't have much contact with him," remarked one Board of Trade player.[24]

While his peers collected vintage cars and mansions, Dennis kept wearing those out-of-date polyester pants hiked over an ever-expanding waist. He exercised by eating cheap hamburgers at noisy grills. Dennis in a short-sleeved shirt, no tie, religiously pouring over arcane baseball statistics from the Baseball Abstract, was a common sight. In fact, he would eventually buy a piece of the White Sox baseball team. Once he was an owner, his 1980s attempt to get White Sox management to see the benefits of Bill James–style "Moneyball" fell on deaf ears.

One of his students, Michael Shannon, watched his friends try to dress him up by moving him from his South Side studio apartment, and recalled, "Bill Eckhardt and others actually forced him to move into something that was a little bit more parallel to his station."

Money for Dennis was just a way to keep score in the game. He was frank about it: "Trading is a little bit like hitting a ball. If you're think-ing what your batting average should be, you're not concentrating on the right thing when you bat the ball. Dollars are the batting average of the trader."[25]

This original thinker and big-time baseball fan left a visual image on everyone. Several confidantes talked about Dennis's socks. One of his students smiled, "You need to make sure he's wearing a matched pair of the same color."

Bradley Rotter, a former West Point graduate and often called Dennis's first investor, witnessed his eccentricity: "I was at his house for a Fourth of July tennis party and Richard Dennis couldn't be found . . . at the end of the party he came out of his house wearing a white tennis shirt, white tennis shorts, and black shoes and black socks. I'll never forget that picture."

Rotter was not mocking Dennis. He respected Dennis's testicular fortitude to trade trends no matter what. In baseball, testicular fortitude means everyone can talk about the game, but if you're going to get into the game, you must swing the bat. Dennis swung and swung hard. No singles. His was Babe Ruth, home-run, swing-for-the-fences-style moneymaking.

However, the Babe Ruth of trading was near oblivious to the basics of everyday life. Mail and personal bills were handled by C&D's back office because of his inattention. His office would even send over toilet paper to his apartment. The weight room in his Gold Coast condo was virtually unused. "I pat the weights once in a while." said Dennis.[26] He enjoyed using a third of his time to do absolutely nothing.

Another Dennis student, Erle Keefer, went beyond his eccentrici-ties: "Rich is probably the greatest trigger puller that I personally have ever known: he has the ability under tremendous pressure to stand there with his own money and pull the trigger when other people wilted. And when he was wrong, he could turn on a dime. That's amaz-ing—that's not trading, that's genetic." The genetic line was debatable; after all, that was the point of his Turtle experiment.

Political Ambitions

Dennis's success eventually caused more serious problems. In the mid-1980s, critics accused him of strong-arming the market. They blamed him for too much market volatility. Words like "collusion" were thrown around. Dennis was not buying it. He said, "One man's volatility is another man's profit."[27]

When Dennis was a guest on a radio show in 1984, a caller assured him that if he traded long enough, he would give it all back.[28]

You could feel the anger. Some people simply did not want to hear about a young guy making millions. Even though everyone knew exchanges needed speculators, too many people didn't want those same risk-takers to make a profit. Dennis himself appeared before Congress as they investigated the "efficiency of the markets"—unable to define what that phrase meant. His detractors were silenced after government regulators testified that the total buying and selling by Dennis did not breach exchange limits.

Soon, Dennis would join the political fight at a whole new level. He became one of the largest Democratic donors in the country, often focusing his generosity on standard politicians and assorted underdogs. From donating millions to battered women's shelters to the decriminalization of marijuana, causes without wide publicity appealed to him (he would give away 10 percent of his earnings every year). While calling himself a liberal libertarian, he once donated $1,000 to former Black Panther Bobby Rush.

Dennis did more than just write checks. He became good friends with Bill Bradley and supported Walter Mondale (1984) and Bruce Babbitt (1988) for President. He lobbied hard against conservative stalwart Robert Bork. There was a rational justification in Dennis's mind for his political ideals: "If it's something everyone hates but you think is right, those are the important things to do because no one else is going to do them."[29]

However, becoming a successful politician on the basis of supporting the have-nots of society was not as easy as trading to make millions. It wasn't enough merely to fund his causes; Dennis also wanted to "work" them, and immediately ran into roadblocks. Politics was not a zero-sum game, and he got frustrated. "Politicians, at worse, are mind-less replicas of what their constituents think. People . . . don't want to hear painful truths."[30]

When invited to participate in the diplomatic dances that made up Washington politics, he stepped on toes, and seldom refrained from voicing his opinions. Former Federal Reserve chairman Paul Volcker was once introduced to Dennis. He told Dennis that he didn't "like those casinos you have out there in Chicago."[31]

Dennis was well aware that he was being indulged because he was rich and would be listened to only if he had something significant to say. Soon after he founded his new 1982 think tank, the Roosevelt Center for American Policy Studies in Washington, D.C., it began to flounder.

Washington was a tough market no matter how many millions you had. And now Democrats were frustrating him, too. He said, "My principal irritation with liberals in general: they don't understand how it can possibly be true that you make the poor richer by making every-one richer. I don't understand that they don't even consider that pos-sibility."[32]

The problem in a political world was that Dennis couldn't work the floors of Congress the way he had the Chicago trading floors. It was one thing to own one of the six original copies of the U.S. Constitution (which he did) and an entirely different thing to try to influence mod-ern political leaders. He was impatient.

Ultimately, over time he would become a board member of the libertarian Cato Institute, serving with such notable peers as John C. Malone, chairman, Liberty Media Corporation, and Frederick W. Smith, chairman and CEO, FedEx Corporation. He also joined the board of the Reason Foundation, another libertarian think tank.

Dennis's political forays were never easy. One political critic of his thought Dennis was a bully because he didn't adjust his thinking to accommodate others.[33] Dennis saw that criticism as coming from a typical Washington careerist being afraid to rock the boat.

His stance on the decriminalization of narcotics best illustrated what made him tick. He knew the "drug czar" of the day, Bill Bennett, would never defeat drug violence with his "just say no" approach.

Dennis thought people should be allowed to do what they wanted to do, even if they injured themselves, as long as they did not hurt others. He commented:

> The drug war violates the Golden Rule of doing unto others as you would have them do unto you. None of us is free of vice or temptation. Does any one of us really want to be jailed for our moral shortcomings? If our teenaged child is arrested for drug possession—a distinct possibility, since 54 percent of teenagers admit trying illicit drugs—do we really want him or her sent to prison for falling victim to the curiosity of youth?[34]

Here was a man making millions in the pits by winning as much money from others as possible, but at the same time he was clearly worried about others' well-being. He was a mass of contradictions.

Rough Seas

Dennis had some severe down periods before that banner year of 1986. Perhaps his political ambitions had caused a loss of focus. Adding to his responsibility, by this time he had moved beyond trading only his own money. He was trading for others, and managing their money was not his strongest suit. He said, "It's drastically more work to lose other people's money. It's tough. I go home and worry about it."[35]

This was not what his clients wanted to hear. In 1983, when his assets under management peaked at over $25 million, his accounts for clients hit turbulence. After a 53 percent rise in January, accounts dropped 33 percent in February and March. That drop was enough to prompt George Soros to yank the $2 million he had invested with Dennis only two months earlier. After a partial rebound in April and May, Dennis's funds dived another 50 percent in value. His 1983-era computer that cost $150,000 did little to console nervous clients.

It took many of his investors more than two years to get back to even with their investment. Most didn't stick around, and Dennis closed down some accounts in 1984. He rebated all management fees to losing accounts and conceded that trading client money as aggressively as his own money was not something clients could psychologically handle.[36] What did that aggression look like on a month-by-month basis?

Table 2.1: Richard Dennis Trading Performance:
July 1982–December 1983.

Date	VAMI	ROR	Yearly ROR	Amount Size
Jan-83	3475	53.33%		
Feb-83	3284	–5.49%		
Mar-83	2371	–27.82%		$18.7M
Apr-83	3058	29.01%		
May-83	3184	4.11%		
Jun-83	2215	–30.42%		$19.0M
Jul-83	1864	–15.88%		
Aug-83	1760	–5.57%		
Sep-83	2057	16.87%		$14.6M
Oct-83	2671	29.89%		
Nov-83	2508	–6.10%		
Dec-83	2160	–13.90%	–4.70%	$13.5M

VAMI (Value Added Monthly Index): An index that tracks the monthly performance of a hypothetical $1,000 investment as it grows over time.
ROR: Rate of return.
Source: Barclays Performance Reporting (www.barclaygrp.com).

Dennis was famous for those big returns, and that was what his clients wanted—to become *rich like Rich*. They got on board knowing full well the voyage would get rocky, but conveniently forgot that fact when rough sailing made them seasick. At the first sign of troubled waters, when they were puking losses, they cut short the voyage and blamed Dennis. He was learning the hard way about people's irrational expectations.

In 2005, Dennis looked back on his troubled times in the fund management arena:

I think the problem is that a money manager very rarely ever sits down with the person whose money it is. There's always a representative of a firm of a firm of a firm. When you have customer money, you generally try to please the people who want "passable," whereas you might be able to explain it to the ultimate end user whose money it is that "this might look brutal, but we're trying for something spectacular."[37]

However, at that time in 1983, Dennis needed a way out of the customer rat race. He wanted to divert even more attention to big-picture strategies, from philosophizing to an even greater focus on decriminalization of pot to anything but being beholden to impatient and uninformed clients.

In many ways his Turtle teaching experiment was his second act, and he knew it. He said, "You shouldn't, I suppose, live in your trading children's reflective glory, but I am. I think [training the Turtles] is the single best thing I've done in commodities."[38] Yet there was no way he could have known at the time that the single best thing he would do would change his life and the history of speculative trading in ways never imagined.

Glory and legend aside, in 1983, with a clear plate, Dennis's most immediate task was to select his Turtle students from the thousands who responded to his want ad.

3

The Turtles

"How much of a role does luck play in trading? In the long run, zero. Absolutely zero. I don't think anybody winds up making money in this business because they started out lucky."

Richard Dennis

Over the years, almost every time the subject of Dennis's training experiment (starting in winter 1983) comes up, those people who have heard of it invariably compare it to the spring 1983 classic movie *Trading Places*, staring Eddie Murphy and Dan Aykroyd. Millions have seen the movie over the last twenty years, either in the theater or on television.

The idea for the movie appears to have sprung from Mark Twain's 1893 short story "The £1,000,000 Bank Note." Twain's famous story speculated on what would happen if a perfectly honest American visitor was turned loose in London with nothing but a million-pound bank note in his pocket and no explanation of how it got there.

In *Trading Places*, ultra-rich commodity brokers, brothers Mortimer and Randolph Duke, make a bet that they can turn a blue blood (Aykroyd, as Louis Winthorpe III) to crime and turn a street hustler (Murphy, as Billy Ray Valentine) into a successful trader. In the movie Mortimer, arguing against Hume and Locke, exclaims, "With his genes, you could put Winthorpe anywhere and he's going to come out on top. Breeding . . . same as in race horses. It's in the blood."[1]

When I was trying to nail down with 100 percent certainty that the screenplay came before Dennis's Turtle training experiment, the film's screenwriter, Herschel Weingrod, shed some light. He flatly said that he had never heard of Richard Dennis when his script was completed in October 1982. He was researching and writing a script in the early

1980s about Chicago trading and didn't immediately hear of Richard Dennis? That seemed implausible.

Yet it's very plausible to assume the movie's basic premise had an influence on Dennis's experiment. I wasn't alone in that view. Mike Carr, one of Dennis's students, often received the same reaction when the subject of the experiment came up: "Whenever you describe the program to anybody, they say, 'Oh it's like *Trading Places*,' and of course, that's a logical parallel. I think you'd have to ask Rich and Bill, but I never viewed it as anything other than coincidental."

It is easy to see why Carr would say that; Dennis was an empiricist before the movie was on the drawing board. But at a bare minimum the movie must have been a catalyst, the trigger for him to take action. When he was asked whether his training experiment was inspired by *Trading Places*, Dennis denied it: "Oh God, no! Actually I think the movie came after. I certainly hope that's true! I did like that movie more than I wanted to. We did [the experiment] because everyone believed in intuition including Bill who is a very logical guy. And I thought about intuition and about trading and it didn't seem right."[2]

A third student of Dennis's Mike Shannon, with respect for Dennis in his voice, disagreed wholeheartedly with Carr: "Let me put it this way, and bluntly, you bet your ass it had a freaking role in [the experiment]. It absolutely did. Whether he denies it or not, of course it did."

Despite Dennis's denial, the parallels seem to be too close to be coincidental. Dennis was watching Randolph and Mortimer play out *his* debate on the big screen. Randolph was convinced Eddie Murphy's character was the product of a poor environment; Mortimer thought that view was babble.

Unlike the movie, the exact nature of Dennis and Eckhardt's wager, if any existed, is not known. However, the movie *Trading Places* did gross over $100 million *before* the training experiment was even on the drawing board.

Dennis was about to become the new Willy Wonka. He was about to let people into his "factory," C&D Commodities, just like Wonka let kids into his chocolate factory. There were risks for him. His students might let him down or, worse, steal his secrets. He was undeterred: "Some people tell you 'no,' but I think it [trading] is transferable. It seemed to me so clear that it is transferable, that there are no mysteries.

If it isn't a mystery, then I ought to be able to get people to do that. I don't want to spend so much time working anymore and also I want to prove to people that there's no great mystery to it."[3]

Life Is Random . . . Sometimes

People were willing to do just about anything to get Dennis's attention. Of all the approaches his students took to get themselves admitted to his trading school, Jim Melnick's was the most extreme and inventive. He was an overweight, working-class guy from Boston who was living over a saloon in the Chicago suburbs. However, Melnick was determined to get as close to Dennis as possible. He actually moved to Chicago just because he'd heard about Richard Dennis. He ended up as a security guard for the Chicago Board of Trade and every morning would say, "Good morning, Mr. Dennis" as Dennis entered the building. Then, boom, the ad came out and Melnick got selected.

Dennis, who was loaded with millions and power, took a guy off the street and gave him the opportunity to start a new life. The story of Melnick is pure rags-to-riches. How did he know that getting that close to Dennis could lead to something? He didn't, of course, but he hoped it would. His self-confidence was prophetic.

Another of Dennis's students described Jim's "everyman" qualities: "He reminded me of a truck driver and like magic became a 'Turtle' and he still couldn't believe why or how . . . as far as where he is today, I have no clue at all."

Mike Shannon, a former actor who had left school at the age of sixteen, made it to Dennis's door, too. He recalled, "I was working as a broker, and I was a very bad commodity broker." Through a bunch of floor brokers Shannon found out about the ad, but he knew his résumé was problematic. He had a solution to that: "I made up a phony resume, and I sent it off to Richard Dennis. I used the school of audacity to get the job." People get fired or, at the very least, don't get hired because of falsifying a résumé, but that was not how it worked with the eccentric head of C&D Commodities.

On the other hand, Jim DiMaria, a Notre Dame graduate and family man straight from the *Ozzie and Harriet* back lot, was already on the trading floor working for Dennis when he applied. DiMaria remembered that every now and again there would be a "1,000 lot" (jargon for a huge order of one thousand futures contracts) that would come through on the trading floor. Finally, he said, "Who is this client with the enormous orders?" He thought he'd heard it was a rich dentist, which was plausible since doctors often dabbled in trading. Eventually he put two and two together, realizing that *Rich Dennis* was the "rich dentist."

Dennis, however, was not looking solely for doormen and floor traders. He went after the highly educated, too. Michael Cavallo had a Harvard MBA. With a mop of brown hair and wire-rimmed glasses, he was a preppy corporate warrior working in Boston when he caught wind of the ad that would change his life.

When he saw the ad, Cavallo had already heard of Dennis. He recalled, "I nearly fell out of my seat when I saw it. He was looking for starting shortstop. I couldn't believe it. This is sort of a dream job for me. I immediately responded."

There was plenty of serendipity as other potential students learned of the experiment. Former U.S. Air Force pilot Erle Keefer's path to Dennis was pure coincidence as well. He was sitting in a New York City sauna when he picked up a newspaper and spotted the Dennis ad.

At that moment the female star of the movie *Trading Places*, Jamie Lee Curtis, was sitting in the same sauna with her boyfriend. Keefer was sitting there reading *Barron's*. "I am looking at this ad and I knew who Rich was. I said, 'Wow! This guy did it.'" Keefer thought there was little chance he would get accepted.

In the strictly man's world of commodities trading in the early 1980s, women did apply. Liz Cheval, the diminutive and flamboyant Katie Couric look-alike, was one of them. She must have known that she would stand out from other applicants by being female. At the time she was actively considering a career in filmmaking, even though she was working for a brokerage firm as a day job.[4]

Cheval's former boss, Bradley Rotter, knew the offer was a big deal: "Dennis had already been managing money for me, and I did very well. Liz came to me and said she was thinking about applying and asked whether or not she should do it and I said absolutely. It was an opportunity of a lifetime."

Jeff Gordon, an attorney and small business owner at the time, just happened to be thumbing through the newspaper and saw the ad. Gordon, five foot eight, a slender man who could have been a former member of the *Revenge of the Nerds* cast, knew the opportunity could be huge: "Everybody wanted to be able to trade, to make money like Richard Dennis." Firing off a résumé was a coincidental and fortuitous life-changing decision that Gordon made in a heartbeat.

Given Dennis's eccentric personality, it was no shock that Jiri "George" Svoboda, an immigrant from then communist Czechoslovakia and a monster underdog in most people's eyes, was selected. He was a master blackjack player beating Las Vegas like a drum long before *Breaking Vegas* and 1990's famed M.I.T. blackjack team.

Dennis also selected Tom Shanks. Handsome, dark-haired, and smooth with the ladies, Shanks was working as a computer programmer for Hull Trading as his day job and beating Vegas at night with his blackjack skills.

Shanks and Svoboda knew each other from the blackjack underground. When they bumped into each other in Chicago, Svoboda said to Shanks, "Hey, I'm here for an interview with Richard Dennis. Have you heard?" Shanks had no clue, but said, "You've got to get me an interview!" They both ended up getting hired that same afternoon.

Erle Keefer knew about their wild backgrounds. He said, "George ran the Czech team, and Tom was essentially with the computer in a boot." Shanks used to say, "I never want to see another boot in my life." He had to learn how to take it apart to put the computer in and was mighty sick of boots after a while. Other inventions allowed Shanks to be almost dead accurate as to the sequence of cards as they were dealt.

How could Dennis *not* hire a guy who had put a computer in a boot during the 1970s? That effort just screamed, "Do anything to win."

Mike Carr, on the other hand, had built a name for himself at the role-playing game firm Dungeons and Dragons, where he developed a cult following with his "wargaming" authorship. He had also developed a board game, "Fight In The Skies," which modeled World War I–style air combat. He just happened to pick up the *Wall Street Journal* for the first time in six months and saw the ad. He called it "Divine Providence."

Jerry Parker, who would make the cut, knew the potential life-changing ramifications of being selected. The unassuming accountant and evangelical Christian, with a proper side part to his hair, was not headed down the trading path prior to seeing the C&D ad. He said, "I was a small town person [from Lynchburg, Virginia] and Richard Dennis rescued me from leading a normal life."[5]

Before any of the average-Joe pupils were officially "rescued," as Parker had so aptly phrased it, they had to continue through the selection process. After sending in their résumés, applicants who made the first cut received a letter and a test.

The letter was formal and utilitarian. It reflected none of that Dennis "energy and spirit." In by-the-book attorney-speak, it said if selected, Turtles would get 15 percent of the profits as salary after they completed a short training period and then a short trial trading period. All potential students were told that they would have to relocate to Chicago. Prospective students at this stage of the process were asked for their college entrance exam scores. If they didn't have those, they needed to explain why.

There was more. Candidates had to complete a 63-question true–false test. The true–false questions all appeared to be easy at first glance, but perhaps tricky on second thought. A cross-section of true-false questions included:

1. Trade long or short, but not both.

2. Trade the same number of contracts in all markets.

3. If you have $100,000 to risk, you should risk $25,000 on every trade.

4. When you enter, you should know where to exit if a loss occurs.

5. You can never go broke taking profits.

6. The majority of traders are always wrong.

7. Average profits should be about 3 or 4 times average losses.

8. A trader should be willing to let profits turn into losses.

9. A very high percentage of trades should be profits.

10. Needing and wanting money are good motivators to good trading.

11. One's natural inclinations are good guides to decision making in trading.

12. Luck is an ingredient in successful trading over the long run.

13. It's good to follow hunches in trading.

14. Trends are not likely to persist.

15. It's good to average down when buying.

16. A trader learns more from his losses than his profits.

17. Others' opinions of the market are good to follow.

18. Buying dips and selling rallies is a good strategy.

19. It's important to take a profit most of the time.

Just as on college entrance exams, there were also essay questions to answer. On the back of the true–false answer sheet, prospective students had to answer these essay questions with one sentence:

1. Name a book or movie you like and why.

2. Name a historical figure you like and why.

3. Why would you like to succeed at this job?

4. Name a risky thing you have done and why.

5. Is there anything else you'd like to add?

Dennis also listed essay questions that asked what good or bad qualities students might have and whether those would help or hurt in trading. In addition, he wanted to know whether prospective students would rather be good or lucky. There was seemingly no primer to answer these questions!

The answers to the fourth essay question ranged from a prospective student who drove an hour to a basketball game without having a ticket to someone who drove around Saudi Arabia for several months with whiskey in his car trunk—not exactly something you should do in that part of the world. The person without the basketball ticket was hired, but the person who took a risk for the sake of risk-taking was not.[6]

Dale Dellutri, who was Dennis's programmer at C&D and ended up as the day-to-day manager of the students, said the hiring strategy had a "wing-it mentality," adding, "We were looking for smarts and for people who had odd ideas. There was some experimental part to it."[7]

Dennis, however, was clear about what he was looking for. He wanted people who had high math aptitude and high ACT (American College Testing) scores. He wanted people with some interest in computers or market methods. Those who worked to systematize things had an advantage. Dennis added, "The majority of people we wound up hiring had some interest in games. They were chess players or backgammon players, enough so that they would even mention it on a resume."[8]

Math ability was not the sole determinant for hiring by any stretch. Dennis and Eckhardt knew long-term trading success did not correlate one-to-one with high IQs. They were trying to assess the applicants' ability to think in terms of odds—the same kind of thinking needed to win at blackjack in Las Vegas. And they wanted applicants with the emotional and psychological makeup to treat money abstractly so they could focus on how to use it as a tool to make tons more.

More than anything, Dennis was interested in choosing people who could subsume their egos. None of the chosen few ever would have wanted to be on the cover of *Time* magazine (at least, that is, when they were chosen). He ultimately chose people who he thought had the ability to accept learning. While they were with Dennis, they had to be *tabulae rasae*—blank slates.

It is worth repeating: The selected students were a seriously eclectic bunch. The group was as culturally, sociologically, sexually, and politically diverse as you could assemble. Walt Disney and his famed "It's a Small World" would have been proud of Dennis's open-arms approach.

The Interview of Your Life

Those candidates who passed the test were then asked to interview in person at C&D Commodities' offices during the Chicago winter. The process was the same across the board. Dale Dellutri escorted them in and out of the room, and both Dennis and Eckhardt interviewed everyone. Interviewees were struck by how informal and, in most cases, friendly their interviewers were.

Mike Shannon, the candidate with the padded résumé, did some serious research in advance of his interview. He went down to the *Chicago Tribune* basement to learn everything he could about Dennis. He later discovered, "Over 90 percent of the answers to the questions on the test were in those articles." Shannon had even researched what Dennis liked to wear: "I knew that he didn't like to wear shoes. He hated suits and all that. I just wore a beat-up old sport coat, pair of jeans, and pair of topsiders with *no socks*."

It turns out Dennis and Shannon had one thing in common: They both grew up playing the board game Risk. Shannon said, "I knew he played when he was a teenager. I think that kind of helped and that definitely broke the ice."

For those unfamiliar with Risk, it is a game of world domination, where the object is to conquer the world. To win, you must attack and defend—attacking to acquire territory, and defending to keep it from your opponents. Dennis may have been quirky, but he lived to win. That was exactly what playing Risk meant: Beat the other guy and win.

Paul Rabar, another student candidate, just happened to have been the most experienced trader of all student hires. Rabar had dropped out of UCLA Medical School. Before that, he was a classically trained pianist. However, before being hired by Richard Dennis, he was trained and mentored by Chuck Le Beau. In the late 1970s and early 1980s, Le Beau was a regional director for the E. F. Hutton & Co. brokerage on the West Coast. It was there that he taught Rabar.

In one of those small-world stories, their E. F. Hutton office ended up handling some brokerage for the infamous Billionaire Boys Club (BBC) during the early 1980s. The BBC was started by Joe Gamsky (who later renamed himself Joe Hunt, and became the focus of several

TV movies). Gamsky was trading serious-sized money across the Chicago Mercantile Exchange from 1980 to 1984, making a big name for himself. Before he was exposed as a con, Gamsky was getting Dennis-like attention on the Chicago trading floors and in the press. He, too, was called a boy wonder.

Le Beau and Rabar, however, did nothing wrong. They were simply brokers placing trades for an assortment of clients. Still, was it possible that Dennis was interested in going through the interview process with Rabar just to see what he may or may not have known about Gamsky's trading? That's the kind of opposition research of which Dennis was certainly capable.

Rabar's interview did evolve into a discussion of the finer points of trading. At one point Dennis asked a trick question: "What if you get bounced out of the same 'long' trade five times in a row?" Rabar was cocksure: "If it goes up again, I will buy it again." Rabar's knowledge had a lot to do with his hiring, but he was the exception. Dennis didn't want a room full of Rabars.

Erle Keefer, on the other hand, started talking about British empiricism with Dennis. They were discussing "what is reality?" and quickly dove into a deep debate about George Berkeley's book *Hylas and Philonous*. Keefer later learned that one of the things Dennis was looking for was the ability to suspend your belief in reality.

Then, quickly, Eckhardt changed the subject from philosophy in order to test Keefer. He asked, "Do you believe in the central limit theorem?" Keefer replied, "I believe the central limit theorem is like a stop clock, which is right twice a day." He later said, "Little did I realize the game we were going to play."

Eckhardt was signaling that their trading strategy relied upon the idea that if you were tossing dice, a string of 6 sixes in a row happens more often than people know or expect. In other words, Eckhardt was saying that they were not mean reversion traders. Mean reversion traders make bets that markets stay in tight ranges and that if they veer out of the range, they typically revert to the average or mean. He was saying in plain terms that markets trend, and those trends come unexpectedly. Keefer knew it meant that they were not options traders.

Michael Cavallo had a different vantage on the interview. He said it was the only job interview that he ever truly enjoyed. He didn't care whether or not he got the job because he had "this great conversation with people who were incredibly intelligent." Dennis and Eckhardt peppered Cavallo with questions. They asked him how much he knew about markets, on a scale of a zero to one hundred. He recalled, "I answered, 'sixty,' being not just an interview gamesmanship response, just the kind of response where I thought I was at."

Later, Dennis liked to tell the story that he had asked that question of everybody and that Curtis Faith had replied "ninety-nine" and Liz Cheval had replied "one." Dennis always fondly said, "I hired both of them because that way I figured I had everything that you could know about commodities."

There was obviously no way you could second-guess what answers Dennis was looking for. And let's face it; The odds were stacked *against* potential students if they gave pat "Harvard Business School graduate" responses. Cavallo knew in the Fortune 500 world that people would not get a job answering the way Faith and Cheval did. As he commented, "A lot of places would say, 'Oh well, this guy is too arrogant and he thinks he knows more than he does and he's headed for a fall.' And they might say, 'She's too timid.' But in fact, certain things that they liked most other places wouldn't necessarily like."

On the other hand, Mike Carr's answer to Dennis's question about what person he admired the most could easily have been interpreted as politically incorrect. Carr recalled, "I remember Rich asking me, 'Why Rommel?' I was the only one who cited Field Marshal Erwin Rommel, the famed 'Desert Fox,' as the person from history I most admired. Despite being a German general during the Second World War, he was not a Nazi. Most telling of all, he was highly respected by military men on both sides, as a general and as a man."

After the interview was over, Mike Cavallo was the only Turtle to mention that he was on to the clever ploy that the interview didn't end after he left the room. After the interview, Dale Dellutri took Cavallo to the elevator and said, "Well, how did it go?" Cavallo told him how great he thought the interview was, but he quickly realized that question was part of the interview itself: "I said I liked Rich and Bill so much. Whereas other people might have said, 'Oh God, they really put me through the ringer' or something like that."

The Dennis brain trust was showing their hand. You had to play their "game." The elevator filter must have eliminated students from the process who otherwise would have made it. That's brutal. Perhaps, as they read this, former interviewees who did not make the cut will realize that when they said something foolish to Dale Dellutri at the elevator, it was at that point that they were eliminated from the candidate pool. No one ever said life was fair.

Mike Cavallo was under no false illusion and knew that obvious candidates with his type of résumé were not what Dennis had in mind. He was surprised that he was even in the running. At the end of the day, Dennis and Eckhardt figured too many Cavallos and Rabars would have too many bad habits to unlearn.

Those who think a Harvard MBA is the only ticket to business success, wake up. Cavallo was the exception, not the rule. Dennis and Eckhardt clearly believed that hiring all Harvard MBAs would have been a bust.

All these potential students saw the interview process from different vantage points. Jeff Gordon thought the selection process came down to a "games" aptitude: "I didn't have a résumé at the time so I wrote him a letter that indicated that I had spent more time playing chess than attending law school. The funny thing is my girlfriend read the letter and said, 'You can't say that!' I said, 'No, that's not true, Rich Dennis is a different kind of guy, I think he'll be looking for people who are a little bit different.' "

During his interview, Gordon was logically assuming that he had a lot to learn from Dennis and Eckhardt, but they said to him. "Well, you might actually be disappointed." Dennis was worth hundreds of millions at the time, yet he was self-deprecating and humble.

Mike Carr's previous job for Dungeons and Dragons may have been the key to convincing the C&D brain trust to hire him because both Dale Dellutri and William Eckhardt said their sons enjoyed playing the game and, as Carr commented, "I knew that couldn't hurt!" That said, Carr had no real idea of Dennis's style of trading and fumbled through parts of the interview. He recalled, "Richard Dennis was renowned as a technical trader, but I wasn't aware of that at the time." During the interview, he had asked Dennis, "Do you trade technically or fundamentally?" Dennis replied, "We trade technically." Carr then said, "Is fundamental trading dead?" Dennis sarcastically shot back, "We hope not."

Jim DiMaria, the relative insider already working for Dennis as a broker, knew the importance of his hometown for his trading ambitions: "It's just part of the fiber of Chicago. If I were from Baltimore or Los Angeles. I probably would never have done anything like this."[9] But before DiMaria was ever picked for the experiment, he knew he ultimately wanted to be the person making the trading decisions, not just someone else's floor broker.[10] He had to find a way to get there, and Dennis's experiment was it. DiMaria, however, was completely bamboozled by the selection process: "For whatever reason I was selected. I don't know if anyone knows why they were selected. I've heard that some of the people from Rich's entourage were selected as a control group. Like let's just grab this guy. Like maybe me? I don't know."

All the prospective students knew the chance of a lifetime was staring them in the face whether or not they understood exactly what they were getting into. For example, near the end of her interview, when she realized she might be making a good impression, Liz Cheval's knees went weak: "I couldn't have gotten through the interview, had I known [it might work out; it was] like winning the job lottery."[11] She was confident in the interview because she couldn't believe she had gotten that far. She knew her worst-case scenario if selected was that her résumé would be enhanced by even a few weeks spent under Dennis's tutelage. There was nothing to lose.

All in all, the hiring process was far from headhunter precise. Dennis and Eckhardt had no formal training in job recruitment or in developing questionnaires designed to select those people most able and ready to learn. It was one thing for them to trade and make fortunes, but it was a very different thing to execute a "nature versus nurture" experiment with live human beings.

The Turtle Contract

Once accepted into Dennis's program, Turtles had to adhere to a strict confidentiality agreement. It was titled "Synopsis of Contract for Trading Advisor Trainees" and said in part that each participant would have a five-year contract, which could be terminated without notice by Dennis at any time. There was no assurance of staying in the program, but the agreement did clearly state students would not be held accountable for losses that they might generate trading Dennis's money: "The trainee will not be obligated to repay advances, which are not covered by earned performance fees, nor will the trainee be liable for losses due to adverse trading performance." And for those students thinking ahead about how to get-rich-quick now that they had Dennis's "secrets," the agreement had no flexibility. During the term of the contract they were prohibited from trading for their own account and prohibited from trading for anyone other than Dennis. The agreement went on to clearly preclude competing against Dennis or disclosing any confidential or proprietary information the participants might learn. Lastly, at the end of the agreement all students were prohibited from disclosing Dennis's proprietary trading methods for another five years.

For those with a legal background, this agreement could have been a deal-breaker. That said, no one declined to join the Turtle program even though there were no real guarantees and many potential restrictions on their future activity. Once the agreement was signed, the Turtles headed off to class.

Chicago was a different place when the Turtles entered class in January 1984. Harry Caray was the announcer at Wrigley Field, and Ryne Sandberg's rookie year was underway. The Apple Macintosh had just been introduced, and Hulk Hogan defeated The Iron Sheik for the World Wrestling Federation Championship. Politically, Dennis would be very unhappy with Reagan heading toward a landslide defeat of Mondale.

In the context of that world, the lucky few chosen to learn how to trade for big money still had to absorb trading rules that would have made investors like Warren Buffett cringe. There would be no buying and holding, or buying low and selling high. What they were about to learn was the antithesis of what was and still is taught in finance departments at the world's finest universities. Run this story by a college finance professor today and take note of his reactions.

The Classroom

If Dennis had been worth only $100,000 at the time of the experiment, would the Turtles have listened as intently? No. Dennis knew the Turtles were the "dumb stumps" and that the only reason that they bought into everything was that he had made $200 million.

If he said, "On Monday, you will buy the S&P 500 stock index when it's up exactly 35 ticks no matter what', all of the Turtles would have gone over a cliff to follow orders. One Turtle said that when a guy has made $200 million and he says, 'You can walk on water', people are going to say, 'Okay I can walk on water.' You have just crossed that unbelievable emotional *hump* that we all have in our brains."

Crossing the "emotional hump," whether in trading or baseball, is reaching that point at which you are intellectually and emotionally challenged and respond by saying, "I can do it." Between Dennis's reputation and the self-confidence that came from being chosen from over a thousand applicants, the Turtles crossed that hump with ease. The bottom line was that two trading superstars had selected *them* as students. Motivation was a given.

That same kind of aura surrounded Jim Leyland, manager of the 2006 pennant-winning Detroit Tigers baseball team. This was a team that only a few years prior had lost over a hundred games in one year—a horrendous record. But now they had a manager, Leyland, in whom everyone believed. There wasn't a Detroit Tiger who didn't suddenly feel like he could deliver in the clutch. "If I walk in there tomorrow and find my name and I'm batting cleanup, I'd expect to get a hit," pitcher Todd Jones said. And, of course, pitchers are not counted on to hit!

The Turtles had the same attitude. The two weeks of training consisted of Dennis and Eckhardt figuratively yelling "jump" and the Turtles responding, "How high?" However, years of legend-building have made the entire process of the Turtles' training sound a great deal more elegant and sophisticated than it really was.

They were put up in the Union League Club in downtown Chicago. Mike Cavallo described it as "sort of one of those old-fashioned fancy clubs where there were elderly people dozing under their newspaper."

He was not exaggerating. Tom Willis and I tried to have lunch there in 2006, but were asked to leave because I was wearing jeans. The Union League Club remains an old-world bastion for those who made their market fortunes way back when. With dark wood paneling, worn Oriental carpets, and leather-upholstered furniture, and staffed by elderly union workers moving in slow motion, it is well past its prime.

Clearly, not much had changed at the club since the Turtles walked in the door. That Richard Dennis should belong to such a club in 1983 was amusing given how anti-establishment he was. However, he was simply being practical, because the club was close to the Chicago Board of Trade and C&D Commodities' offices.

The Turtles spent their two weeks of training at the Union League Club as well. They all had to wear a jacket and tie at all times—including Dennis. Only half of the more than two dozen students in the training room were Turtles, if you defined Turtles as those students who would trade only Dennis's money. It was HBO's hit show *Entourage* for sure.

Right before training began the Turtles attended a welcoming party, since Dennis liked to throw lavish cocktail parties during the Christmas holidays. The newcomers got a glimpse of what passed for Dennis's Chicago social scene and had the chance to meet each other. But the party did little to assuage the jitters. The first day of training had many feeling the stomach clutch of starting grade school all over again. They walked into the classroom fully unnerved.

Richard Dennis, William Eckhardt, and Dale Dellutri handled the training the same way they had managed the interview process. It turns out that the C&D Commodities brain trust had met each other at St. Laurence Catholic High School. As fate would have it, they became close friends only because they were seated in alphabetical order.

On the first day of Turtle class you could hear a pin drop. Palpable excitement was in the air. The possibility of making money like Dennis had everyone jacked. The first hours consisted of Dellutri discussing how things would work procedurally and laying out "housekeeping" matters for people who had never traded.

Dellutri was assigned the role of Turtle "team mom." He encouraged the Turtles to ask questions during class, but few did at the outset. To everyone's disappointment, Dennis was not there during that first class. Instead, it was Eckhardt who launched into the challenge of "managing risk" as the first topic.

Managing risk was not what new traders would assume as a logical starting point. That Eckhardt would choose to begin with risk management was the first indication that the Turtles were starting an unconventional journey. Instead of introducing the course with a lecture on making money, he was laying the foundation for what the students had to do when they *lost* money.

Another C&D colleague, Robert Moss, was brought in on several occasions to discuss order execution. He wanted the class to understand what really was going on in the pit when their orders went in. "I think Bill and Rich wanted them to have a pretty good understanding given that some of them had never really been involved in the industry before," he said.

Once the students were past the initial jitters there was some give and take, with questions and discussion. However, the class was primarily a lecture with note-taking. The Turtles with experience quickly realized that Dennis and Eckhardt knew far more than they did. Mike Cavallo said, "A lot of the stuff that they were talking about I knew, but I had no idea they weighted some stuff at so much more importance."

Contrary to popular belief among those familiar with the Turtle experiment, Dennis's absence that first day of class was not an aberration. William Eckhardt taught the Turtles a great deal of what they learned during those two weeks in the classroom (there was only one week of training the second year).

The irony is that while it was Eckhardt who bet *against* people being able to learn how to trade, in the classroom he taught much of "the meat and potatoes." It was Dennis who added a succession of trading war stories and anecdotes.

To those who saw them up close, Dennis had the capacity to make an observation in an instant that would take someone else weeks of painstaking math to figure out. Even Eckhardt marveled as Dennis's knack to intuitively see "it": "Look what this means. Look at the deep axiom in here. It works." That said, Eckhardt was the mathematical genius. He was the master of probability. Combining their observations was the magical mixture.

Mike Shannon saw the importance of their symbiotic relationship:

"In fact, a lot of the system development wasn't Richard Dennis. It was indeed Bill Eckhardt. They both hatched it up between them and they're both certainly responsible for it."

To many it seemed Eckhardt was along for the ride, appreciating the Turtle experiment from a psychological point of view, but he definitely wanted his credit for the Turtles after it was over. Today, his regulatory disclosures emphasize that he "co-developed" the systems "co-taught" to the Turtles. Without Eckhardt, there would have been no Turtles.

Mike Cavallo thought there was a more important, though subtle, aspect in their collaboration: "Bill did a lot of the real mathematical work on developing the systems. I think he didn't have Rich's trading genius, which is why I think in their discussion, he thought the trading genius was the main part whereas Rich thought the system was the main part."

To this day, Eckhardt has had a terrific trading career. He has arguably achieved much greater wealth over the long term than Dennis. His hedge fund is now near $800 million USD. Yet when Eckhardt and Dennis first started working together, Dennis was the one who had made the fortune trading and Eckhardt was the original Turtle learning from him.

It was clear to Mike Shannon that Dennis had a massive head start over Eckhardt in terms of wealth and trading experience. He said, "Bill was more inclined at the time to intellectually pursue the concept of trading more so than he was in it for serious financial gain." Over time, Eckhardt realized that he had to strike a balance between the business end and the actual trading. Shannon added, "I think Bill probably is worth more, but once you get over being worth a quarter of a billion dollars . . ."

Eckhardt always good-naturedly admitted that he had lost the nurture-versus-nature battle, in which he had taken the point of view that their systems could not be taught to kids off the street: "I assumed that a trader added something that couldn't be encapsulated in a mechanical program. I was proven wrong. By and large, [the Turtles] learned to trade exceedingly well. The answer to the question of whether trading can be taught has to be an unqualified yes."[12] He also scoffed at the argument that the Turtles' success was based on sheer luck: "The probability of experiencing the kind of success that we have had and continue to have by chance alone has to be near zero. The systems worked for us year after year. We taught some of these systems to others, and it worked for them. They then managed other people's money, and it worked again." He acknowledged the possibility that their achievement *could* have been the result of luck, but he saw the probability of that being infinitesimally small.[13]

Nor did Eckhardt buy into the infinite monkey theorem that says out of the millions of monkeys in the world, one, simply by randomly hitting the keyboard, would eventually produce the collected works of Shakespeare. To this day, many regularly push the notion that successes such as Eckhardt and the Turtles were simply the lucky survivors from the whole monkey population.

Some critics have attempted to explain away the Turtles as a careful selection of very smart students. Michael Cavallo, after all, could play five people at once at chess while blindfolded and beat them fast. He exemplified the fact that brainpower wasn't lacking in the C&D office. Eckhardt disagreed, saying that he had not seen much correlation between good trading and intelligence:

Some outstanding traders are quite intelligent, but a few aren't. Many outstandingly intelligent people are horrible traders. Average intelligence is enough. Beyond that, emotional makeup is more important. This is not rocket science. However, it's much easier to learn what you should do in trading than to do it.[14]

Eckhardt was saying that, as with anything in life, most people know what the right thing to do is but fail to do it. Trading is no different.

Dennis's partner and right-hand man personally learned how hard it was to do the right thing as an early acolyte of Dennis—just like the many other young traders in Chicago during the 1970s. His galvanizing experience with Dennis was on the morning of November 1, 1978. President Carter was trying to halt a sinking U.S. dollar. It was a lesson in "emotional fortitude" forever etched in Eckhardt's memory.

There was a rate hike and intervention in the currency markets—not good news for Dennis and Eckhardt, who held large long positions in gold, foreign currencies, and the grains. The markets collapsed on the open. Gold opened below the $10-an-ounce trading limit, so they could not exit. Silver, though down sharply, was still trading. The Comex in New York told them they could still trade it. So they started selling silver "short," aiming to profit as it decreased in order to protect themselves against further losses from the gold. But they were also concerned that silver might rally. Decisions had to be made, and fast. There was a lot at stake.[15]

Dennis asked Eckhardt calmly, "What should we do?" Eckhardt panicked and froze at the controls. Dennis shorted silver and seconds later it was limit down, too (a big winner). Eckhardt enthused, "In my book that was Rich's best trade ever because he did it under maximum duress. If he hadn't done it, we both would have been bankrupted by the subsequent slide in gold."[16]

One Turtle gushed in awe that Dennis still had the "balls" to execute that trade "when they were dumb, deaf, and broke": "They were going the wrong way and for Dennis to just totally cover and totally reverse was amazing. He was one of the few people who could pull the trigger on big numbers and pull the trigger intelligently. There are some people that just go nuts and they melt down. Especially when they're on the wrong side of the trade and it's going to send them to the poor house."

Many people can trade small amounts day in and day out and not worry about losing money. But as the size of their trading is increased, say by 100 percent, their trading decisions become more significant and problematic. They begin to think about how much they're winning or losing, and it becomes harder to keep a level head about trading "big." Emotions rise to the surface, and objectivity becomes harder and harder to maintain. Disassociating the dollars from the trading was a huge part of what was instilled in the Turtles.

Robert Moss saw the qualities in Dennis that allowed that silver trade to happen: "There are some people who can trade one lot or two lots or a five lot and handle that position and perform not thinking about the money." Moss had never seen anybody better. Tom R. Willis, the son of Tom Willis and close enough to Dennis to consider him an uncle, said that Dennis simply had a sense of proportion that was different from the rest of the world's: "When he perceived that he had an edge, he would go all into a position with mammoth trading size."

Dennis may have been able to pull the trigger, but that disastrous first year came close to wiping him out. He lost $2 million that first day of November. It was touch-and-go for a while. The experience forced Dennis and Eckhardt to reevaluate everything they had learned about trading. They began to test by computer "every idea or piece of conventional wisdom that had ever passed their way. The successful trader is the one who codifies, the one who turns things into rules. Every idea that's market-worthy must then be tested."[17]

Don't discount this story by saying, "It was $2 million; this is a game for rich people, not me!" That is the dead wrong view. There will always be someone with more or less money than someone else. If you have $100 million and you lose $2 million, that is not a big deal. If you have $50,000 and you lose $1,000, that is not a big deal. Both losses are 2 percent.

That is not to say losses are easy to accept, but Dennis and Eckhardt taught the Turtles *not* to consider their trading in terms of amounts of money. They wanted them to think of money as a variable, because in that way, regardless of account size, they could make the correct trading decisions at all times.

However, first and foremost Dennis and Eckhardt wanted the Turtles to understand that their kind of speculation had virtually no external limits. It took place in a limitless environment. They could bet any amount on any potential market movement at any time, but if the Turtles entered this no-limit environment and didn't protect their scarce capital, then sooner or later the probabilities would catch up with them.[18]

The lessons they put forward in the classroom solved the dilemma of "speculation." Since the markets are a zero-sum game, the Turtles learned that even a marginally profitable trader must win money from other market players. By definition, they must use different methods than everyone else in the game.[19]

What this means is that only when "good" trades, not necessarily profitable trades, are consistently made over the long run, the chances of profitable results increase dramatically. A bad month, a bad quarter, or even a bad year does not mean much in the grand scheme. The

Turtles learned that the most important thing was to have a sound trading approach tested in the real world.[20]

Dennis and Eckhardt had that real world of making money figured out. Their philosophy and rules taught in the Turtle classroom were the equivalent of a two-week seminar on how to fly a plane without ever getting in the plane.[21]

4

The Philosophy

"... when you have eliminated the impossible, whatever remains, however improbable, must be the truth."
Sir Arthur Conan Doyle (Sherlock Holmes)

Dennis and Eckhardt's two weeks of training were heavy with the scientific method—the structural foundation of their trading style and the foundation on which they had based their arguments in high school. It was the same foundation relied upon by Hume and Locke.

Simply put, the scientific method is a set of techniques for investigating phenomena and acquiring new knowledge, as well as for correcting and integrating previous knowledge. It is based on observable, empirical, measurable evidence, and subject to laws of reasoning.[1] It involves seven steps:

1. Define the question.

2. Gather information and resources.

3. Form hypothesis.

4. Perform experiment and collect data.

5. Analyze data.

6. Interpret data and draw conclusions that serve as a starting point for new hypotheses.

7. Publish results.[2]

This is not the type of discussion you will hear on CNBC or have with your local broker when he calls with the daily hot tip. Such pragmatic thinking lacks the sizzle and punch of get-rich-quick advice.

52

Dennis and Eckhardt were adamant that their students consider themselves scientists first and traders second—a testament to their belief in doing the "right thing."

The empiricist Dennis knew that plugging along without a solid philosophical foundation was perilous. He never wanted his research to be just numbers bouncing around in a computer. There had to be a theory, and then the numbers could be used to confirm it. He said, "I think you need the conceptual apparatus to be the first thing you start with and the last thing you look at."[3]

This thinking put Dennis way ahead of his time. Years later, the academic Daniel Kahneman would win a Nobel Prize for "prospect theory" (behavioral finance), a fancy name for what Dennis was actually doing for a living and teaching his Turtles. Avoiding the psychological voltage that routinely sank so many other traders was mandatory for the Turtles.

The techniques that Dennis and Eckhardt taught the Turtles were different from Dennis's seasonal spread techniques from his early floor days. The Turtles were trained to be trend-following traders. In a nutshell, that meant that they needed a "trend" to make money. Trend followers always wait for a market to move; then they follow it. Capturing the majority of a trend, up or down, for profit is the goal.[4]

The Turtles were trained this way because by 1983, Dennis knew the things that worked best were "rules": "The majority of the other things that didn't work were judgments. It seemed that the better part of the whole thing was rules. You can't wake up in the morning and say, 'I want to have an intuition about a market.' You're going to have way too many judgments."[5]

While Dennis knew exactly where the sweet spot was for making big money, he often fumbled his own trading with too many discretionary judgments. Looking back, he blamed his pit experience, saying, "People trading in the pit are very bad systems traders generally. They learn different things. They react to the [price] 'tick' in your face."[6]

Dennis and Eckhardt did not invent trend following. From the 1950s into the 1970s, there was one preeminent trend trader with years of positive performance: Richard Donchian. Donchian was the undis-

TurtleTraderThePhilosophy

puted father of trend following. He spoke and wrote profusely on the subject. He influenced Dennis and Eckhardt, and just about every other technically minded trader with a pulse.

One of Donchian's students, Barbara Dixon, described trend followers as making no attempt to forecast the extent of a price move. The trend follower "disciplines his thoughts into a strict set of conditions for entering and exiting the market and acts on those rules or his system to the exclusion of all other market factors. This removes, hopefully, emotional judgmental influences from individual market decisions."[7]

Trend traders don't expect to be right every time. In fact, on individual trades they admit when they are wrong, take their losses, and move on. However, they do expect to make money over the long run.[8] In 1960, Donchian reduced this philosophy to what he called his "weekly trading rule." The rule was brutally utilitarian: "When the price moves above the high of two previous calendar weeks (the optimum number of weeks varies by commodity), cover your short positions and buy. When the price breaks below the low of the two previous calendar weeks, liquidate your long position and sell short."[9]

Richard Dennis's protégé Tom Willis had learned long ago from Dennis why price, the philosophical underpinning of Donchian's rule, was the only true metric to trust. He said, "Everything known is reflected in the price. I could never hope to compete with Cargill [today the world's second-largest private corporation, with $70 billion in revenues for 2005], who has soybean agents scouring the globe knowing everything there is to know about soybeans and funneling the information up to their trading headquarters." Willis has had friends who made millions trading fundamentally, but they could never know as much as the big corporations with thousands of employees. And they always limited themselves to trading only one market. Willis added, "They don't know anything about bonds. They don't know anything about the currencies. I don't either, but I've made a lot of money trading them. They're just numbers. Corn is a little different than bonds, but not different enough that I'd have to trade them differently. Some of these guys I read about have a different system for each [market]. That's absurd. We're trading mob psychology. We're not trading corn, soybeans, or S&P's. We're trading numbers."[10]

"Trading numbers" was just another Dennis convention to reinforce *abstracting* the world in order not to get emotionally *distracted*. Dennis made the Turtles understand price analysis. He did this because at first he "thought that intelligence was reality and price the appearance, but after a while I saw that price is the reality and intelligence is the appearance."[11]

He was not being purposefully oblique. Dennis's working assumption was that soybean prices reflected soybean news faster than people could get and digest the news. Since his early twenties, he had known that looking at the news for decision-making cues was the wrong thing to do.

If acting on news, stock tips, and economic reports were the real key to trading success, then everyone would be rich. Dennis was blunt: "Abstractions like crop size, unemployment, and inflation are mere metaphysics to the trader. They don't help you predict prices, and they may not even explain past market action."[12]

The greatest trader in Chicago had been trading five years before he ever saw a soybean. He poked fun at the notion that if "something" was happening in the weather, his trading would somehow change: "If it's raining on those soybeans, all that means to me is I should bring an umbrella."[13]

Turtles may have initially heard Dennis's explanations and assumed he was just being cute or coy, but in reality he was telling them exactly how to think. He wanted the Turtles to know in their heart of hearts the downsides of fundamental analysis: "You don't get any profit from fundamental analysis. You get profit from buying and selling. So why stick with the appearance when you can go right to the reality of price?"[14]

How could the Turtles possibly know the balance sheets and assorted other financial metrics of all five hundred companies in the S&P 500 index? Or how could they know all the fundamentals about soybeans? They couldn't. Even if they did, that knowledge would not have told them when to buy or sell along with how much to buy or sell.

Dennis knew he had problems if watching TV allowed people to predict what would happen tomorrow—or predict anything for that matter. He said, "If the universe is structured like that, I'm in trouble."[15] Fundamental reporting from CNBC's Maria Bartiromo would have been called "fluff" by the C&D Commodities teaching team.

Michael Gibbons, a trend-following trader, put using "news" for trading decisions in perspective: "I stopped looking at news as something important in 1978. A good friend of mine was employed as a reporter by the largest commodity news service at the time. One day his major 'story' was about sugar and what it was going to do. After I read his piece, I asked, 'how do you know all of this?' I will never forget his answer; he said, 'I made it up.' "

However, trading à la Dennis was not all highs. Regular small losses were going to happen as the Turtles traded Dennis's money. Dennis knew the role confidence would play. He said, "I suppose I didn't like the idea that everyone thought I was all wrong, crazy, or going to fail, but it didn't make any substantial difference because I had an idea what I wanted to do and how I wanted to do it."[16]

The Turtles' core axioms were the same ones practiced by the great speculators from one hundred years earlier:

"Do not let emotions fluctuate with the up and down of your capital."

"Be consistent and even-tempered."

"Judge yourself not by the outcome, but by your process."

"Know what you are going to do when the market does what it is going to do."

"Every now and then the impossible can and will happen."

"Know each day what your plan and your contingencies are for the next day."

"What can I win and what can I lose? What are probabilities of either happening?"

However, there was precision behind the familiar-sounding euphemisms. From the first day of training, William Eckhardt outlined five

TurtleTraderThePhilosophy

questions that were relevant to what he called an optimal trade. The Turtles had to be able to answer these questions at all times:

1. What is the state of the market?

2. What is the volatility of the market?

3. What is the equity being traded?

4. What is the system or the trading orientation?

5. What is the risk aversion of the trader or client?

There was no messing around in Eckhardt's tone, as he suggested that these were the only things that had any importance.[17]

What is it the state of the market? The state of the market simply means. "What is the price that the market is trading at?" If Microsoft is trading at 40 a share today, then that is the state of that market.

What is the volatility of the market? Eckhardt taught the Turtles that they had to know on a daily basis how much any market goes up and down. If Microsoft on an average trades at 50, but typically bounces up and down on any given day between 48 and 52, then Turtles were taught that the volatility of that market was four. They had their own jargon to describe daily volatilities. They would say that Microsoft had an "N" of four. More volatile markets generally carried more risk.

What is the equity being traded? The Turtles had to know how much money they had at all times, because every rule they would learn adapted to their given account size at that moment.

What is the system or the trading orientation? Eckhardt instructed the Turtles that in advance of the market opening, they had to have their battle plan set for buying and selling. They couldn't say, "Okay, I've got $100,000; I'm going to randomly decide to trade $5,000 of it." Eckhardt did not want them to wake up and say, "Do I buy if Google hits 500 or do I sell if Google hits 500?" They were taught precise rules that would tell them when to buy or sell any market at any time based on the movement of the price. The Turtles had two systems: System One (S1) and System Two (S2). These systems governed their entries and exits. S1 essentially said you would buy or sell short a market if it made a new twenty-day high or low.

What is the risk aversion of the trader or client? Risk management was not a concept that the Turtles grasped immediately. For example, if they had $10,000 in their account, should they bet all $10,000 on Google stock? No. If Google all of a sudden dropped, they could lose all $10,000 fast. They had to bet a small amount of the $10,000, because they didn't know whether or not a trade was going to go in their favor. Small betting (for example, 2 percent of $10,000 on initial bets) kept them in the game to play another day, all the while waiting for a big trend.

Class Discussion

Day after day, Eckhardt would emphasize comparisons. Once he told the Turtles to consider two traders who have the same equity, the same system (or trading orientation), and the same risk aversion and were both facing the same situation in the market. For both traders, the optimal course of action must be the same. "Whatever is optimal for one should be optimal for the other," he would say.[18]

Now this may sound simple, but human nature causes most people, when faced with a similar situation, to react differently. They tend to outthink the situation, figuring there must be some unique value that they alone can add to make it even better. Dennis and Eckhardt *demanded* that the Turtles respond the same or they were out of the program (and they did end up cutting people).

In essence Eckhardt was saying, "You are not special. You are not smarter than the market. So follow the rules. Whoever you are and however much brains you have, it doesn't make a hill of beans' difference. Because if you're facing the same issues and if you've got the same constraints, you must follow the rules." Eckhardt said this in a far nicer, more professorial and academic way, but that was what he meant. He did not want his students to wake up and say, "I'm feeling smart today," "I'm feeling lucky today," or "I'm feeling dumb today." He taught them to wake up and say, "I'll do what my rules say to do today."

TurtleTraderThePhilosophy

Dennis was clear that it would take stick-to-itiveness to follow the rules day to day and do it right: "To follow the good principles and not let fear, greed and hope interfere with your trading is tough. You're swimming upstream against human nature."[19] The Turtles had to have the confidence to follow through on all rules and pull the trigger when they were supposed to. Hesitate and they would be toast in the zero-sum market game.

This motley crew of novices quickly learned that of the five questions deemed to be most important by Eckhardt, the first two, about the market's state and the market's volatility, were the objective pieces of the puzzle. Those were simply facts that everyone could see plain as day.

Eckhardt was most interested in the last three questions, which addressed the equity level, the systems, and the risk aversion. They were subjective questions all grounded in the present. It did not make a difference what the answers to these three questions were a month ago or last week. Only "right now" was important.[20]

Put another way, the Turtles could control only how much money they had now, how they decided to enter and exit a trade now, and how much to risk on each trade right now. For example, if Google is trading at 500 today, Google is trading at 500. That's a statement of fact. If Google has a precise volatility ("N") today of four, that's not a judgment call.

To reinforce the need for objectivity on issues such as "N" Eckhardt wanted the Turtles to think in terms of "memory-less trading." He told them, "You shouldn't care about how you got to the current state but rather about what you should do now. A trader who trades differentially because of swings in confidence is focusing on his or her own past rather than on current realities."[21]

If five years ago you had $100,000 and today you have only $50,000, you can't sit around and make decisions based on the hypothetical $100,000 you used to have. You have to base your decisions on the reality of the $50,000 you have now.

How to handle profits properly is a separation point between winners and losers. Great traders adjust their trading to the money they have at any one time.

TurtleTraderThePhilosophy

If crude oil had just traded above $40 for the first time, the Turtles were not to sit around and kibitz about it. They were to take action if it hit their S1 or S2 entry or exit signals. Why or how it got to $40 was irrelevant. Eckhardt threw out the examples fast and furious.

He started with a commonplace idea that most people are willing to accept. If you make some profits with your original money, you can take more risks, because now you're playing with *their* money. He said, "It's certainly a comforting thought. It certainly can't be as bad to lose their money as yours. Can't it? Why should it matter whom the money used to belong to? What matters is whom it belongs to now (you) and what to do about it now."[22]

For instance, assume you start with a $100,000 account, quickly making another $100,000. You now have $200,000. Although you made a profit, you can't say, "I can now take crazier risks with that $100,000."

Why would you view your money as funny money or lucky money? The Turtles were taught to treat that additional $100,000 as they did their original $100,000. They had to use the same concern, care, and discipline. The five questions didn't change, even if their account balances did.

Traders who face the same opportunity must trade the same. Personal feelings can't interfere.

Pretend there are two traders, John and Mary. John and Mary are exactly alike in all respects. They have the same risk aversion and the same system. There is one small difference between the two: John has 50 percent more money. John then decides to go on vacation and while he's away having fun at South Beach, Mary makes 50 percent. Now they have exactly the same amount of money. How or why they got to the point of having the same amount of money is not relevant. The correct course for John is the correct course for Mary.[23]

Eckhardt did not want the Turtles to say. "I had a period where I made some money, so now I can do something different." They had to take the same steps regardless.

Logically, upon first hearing that Mary had just made 50 percent more, most people might want to debate Eckhardt's contention that they should trade the same way. The rule was designed to keep traders with a big profit run-up in their trading account from acting irrationally or breaking a rule. Many people with a big profit run-up don't want to lose those paper gains. They are anxious to take their profits off the table so they can *feel* secure.

Eckhardt slammed home the point that the security craved by humans was bad for proper trading: "The distinction between open trade equity and closed-out trading profits is completely vacuous. How much do you have in open trade equity? How much do you have in closed-out equity? This is a bookkeeper's artifact. It has absolutely no relevance to correct trading."

While it might have zero relevance, people go the wrong way all the time. Instead of trading as they should today, based on their money now and their rules, they trade based on the money they once had. They are clearly trying to recoup. "How much money you use to have has no significance. It's how much money you have now," implored Eckhardt.[24]

If the Turtles started with $100,000 but now had $90,000, they still had to make trading decisions based on what they had now. If the Turtles were supposed to risk 2 percent of their trading capital, then they had to risk 2 percent of their current $90,000, not 2 percent of their original $100,000.

If the Turtles lost money in a market, they had to move on. Accepting and managing losses are part of their game.

The whole notion of holding on to the past was a big issue for the team at C&D Commodities. Eckhardt was stern about the mistake losing traders make when they look backward in time. The losing trader is trying to make money back in the same market and on the same position. Eckhardt described it as a "market vendetta."

Suppose John lost money in Cisco. That market "hurt" him. Instead of focusing on what the best opportunity might be now, he only wants his money back in Cisco. All John can think about is his Cisco position, and in turn his loss just keeps growing. According to Eckhardt, this is the kind of personal memory mistake that always leads to disaster.[25]

The Turtles were taught not to fixate on what particular market made money that month or year or what market lost money. They learned to be agnostic and accept whatever trending market created opportunity.

The same principle was seen with "losses." For example, when the Turtles were taught that they had to exit with a small loss, because they don't know how far it could drop, they got out. What they didn't want to do was look at the initial small loss and say, "I had $100,000 of Microsoft and now I have $90,000, so I'm going to put another $10,000 of my money into MSFT because now it's cheap."

Dennis said that to add to a losing position was like being the kid who's been burned on a hot stove once already but puts his hand back on the stove just to prove it was the stove that was wrong.[26] However, that said, if after taking a small loss the Turtles got a signal to get into the market again, they got back in. An example using legendary hedge-fund manager Paul Tudor Jones best explains the point.

In one of Jones's best trades, he got an entry signal. He got in. The trade went against him and he lost 2 percent, forcing him to get out. All of a sudden, the entry signal came right back as the market moved in his favor again. He could not debate it. He had to get back in. Then it went against him again for another 2 percent loss, forcing him to get out again. He went through this process ten or so times in a row until he got a position that actually kept trending. That final big trend made enough money to pay for all those false starts and then some, but to get there in the first place he had to follow his rules religiously.

The same lesson is seen in sports. Even though Larry Bird was one of the best basketball three-point shooters ever, he wasn't perfect. Let's say on an average he hit 40 percent of his three-point shots. But if all of a sudden he went on a streak where he missed fifteen in a row, what did that mean? Could Bird afford to stop taking three-point shots? No. That was what Dennis and Eckhardt were teaching.

Another great example of the statistical mindset Dennis and Eckhardt were teaching the Turtles can be found in baseball. Assume you bat .300 for ten years straight. All of a sudden you go 0 for 25. Does that mean you are no longer a .300 batter? No. It means you still have to go up to the plate and swing like you've always swung, because that's the discipline of being a .300 hitter. The Turtles played the odds for the long haul.

The Turtles were taught not to fixate on when they entered a market. They were taught to worry about when they will exit.

Pretend again there are two traders, John and Mary. They are exactly the same except in the amount of trading capital each of them has. Assume John has 10 percent less money, but enters a trade before Mary. By the time Mary gets in her trade, they both have the same amount of money. Eckhardt clarified, "What this means is that once an initiation is made, it should not matter at all to subsequent decisions what the initiation price was." He wanted the Turtles to literally trade as though they didn't know what their entry price was.[27]

Dennis kept bringing his teachings back to losses "The trader who is averse to losses is in the wrong business."[28] The "secret" was what he did with the wrong positions, not with the right ones.[29] Managing the losing trades (what Dennis called the "wrong positions") allowed traders to wait for the right ones (big trends). This is why the entry price was only so important.

What Dennis and Eckhardt were teaching was the exact opposite of Warren Buffett's buying "value." The Turtles were supposed to say, "I want to buy or sell short markets that are in motion, moving up or down, because markets in motion tend to stay in motion." If markets are moving higher, that's a good thing. If markets are moving lower, that's a good thing, too. Dennis and Eckhardt wanted the Turtles to profit from both.

Dennis was pushing his students go against basic human nature. He said, "The single hardest thing I have to do to make people understand how I trade is to convince them how wrong I can be about things, how much of a guess it is. They think that there's some magic involved and that it's not just trial and error."[30]

C&D's trading inspired a great deal of mystification, but in reality they were a mass merchandiser who sold 90 percent of their products as loss leaders so they could make a gigantic profit on the remaining 10 percent. Sometimes they had to wait a long time for good things to happen. Most people can't psychologically handle the wait.[31]

Look at this logic from a media company perspective. Like Dennis and Eckhardt, movie producers and publishing executives know they

TurtleTraderThePhilosophy

will have "losers." A movie studio will fund ten movies. A book publisher will fund ten books. In both cases, the producers or publishers often have no idea which one exactly of the ten is going be successful. In fact, they might be lucky if one of the ten is successful. Since they don't know which one is going be successful, they still have to fund all ten. If nine of those books aren't successful, well, the publisher is only going to print a small batch to begin with—that equals a small loss. If those movies or books don't do well, fine. They're done. The companies cut their losses and get out. However, the movie or book that does really well, the tenth one, pays for the losses from the nine losers.

The Turtles were taught to think of themselves as the publisher, the movie studio, or the casino "house."

Don't try to predict how long a trend either up or down will last. It is impossible.

Eckhardt gave the Turtles an example of a market moving rapidly through the point where they were supposed to buy, but for whatever reason had missed. Now they are sitting there waiting for a "retracement." While they wait for the cheap place to buy, the market keeps racing higher and higher. Eckhardt said there was "a great temptation to reason that now it's too high to buy. If you buy it now you'll have an initiation price that's too high. However, it is imperative that you make this trade. The initiation price simply won't have the kind of significance you suppose it will have after the trade is made."[32]

The Turtles were not to wait for a retracement. There was no statistical justification to think like that. If they were trading soybeans at $8.00 and they went to $9.00, the Turtles were taught to buy them at $9.00 rather than wait for them to retrace to $8.00. They might never retrace to $8.00.[33]

How would the Turtles have acted if they'd received a buy signal for Google for the first time at $500? They would buy. Get on board now was the thinking. Dennis always came back to the scientific method, saying that when you have a position, you put it on for a reason and you've got to keep it on until the reason no longer exists: "You have to have a strategy to trade, know how it works and follow through on it."[34]

TurtleTraderThePhilosophy

There is a flip side to this mentality, however. For example, on Wednesday, November 22, 2006, Google opened the day at over $510 a share. Within five days, by Wednesday the 29th, Google was trading at $483, which means Google had pulled back nearly thirty points. When it got to $510, could you know it was going to keep going up or that it was going to go down? You couldn't know either way. What could you do? All you could do was let the price tell you what to do.

Eckhardt was teaching math and rules to manage the emotions felt in the face of uncertainty. He said, "Are you involved in emotional personal memories as opposed to objective knowledge? What I'm advising against is letting factors that are personal, emotional and idiosyncratic to your own history influence your trading."[35]

Measuring volatility was critical for the Turtles. Most people then and today ignore it in their trading.

The question Dennis and Eckhardt always asked was, "How big should you trade based on current volatility?" In other words it's not so much the current price of a given stock or futures contract that is paramount, but rather knowing at all times the market's volatility.[36] For example, it's important to know that Microsoft is at a price level of 40 today, but it's even more important to know Microsoft's volatility ("N") now so you can buy or sell short the right amount of Microsoft based on your limited capital.

Near the end of the breakneck training, Dennis and Eckhardt reiterated the obvious to their newly trained Turtles. The successful students in the class would be the ones who followed the rules and did not deviate. They did not want creative geniuses; It must have been ego-deflating for Turtles once they realized, what Dennis and Eckhardt were looking for was the equivalent of robots.

Investor Bradley Rotter, who has been called the very first investor with Dennis, saw their conundrum:

Applaud the genius of Richard Dennis. The program was well put together. It was focused on discipline. It didn't matter if a trade felt good or felt bad, they had to just [do it]. It was a very, a very

TurtleTraderThePhilosophy

simplistic trend following system that had an aggressive matrix to add to winning positions and subtract from losing positions and all those people who are very successful are those who just followed the formula and did not deviate.[37]

Note: For some readers, chapter 4 will be the only chapter on the Turtle philosophy and rules worth examining. This book has been designed in such a way that you can continue and dive into the "math" that makes up the exact Turtle trading rules in chapter 5, while the casual reader can jump ahead to chapter 6 without skipping a beat.

For those interested in reading chapter 5, the following basic Wall Street terms from Wikipedia.com should be assumed:

Long: One who has bought futures contracts or owns a cash commodity.

Short (noun): One who has sold futures contracts or plans to purchase a cash commodity.

Short (verb): To sell futures contracts or initiate a cash-forward contract sale without offsetting a particular market position. Short selling or "shorting" is a way to profit from the decline in price of a security, such as a stock or a bond. Most investors "go long" on an investment, hoping that price will rise. To profit from the stock price going down, a short seller can borrow a security and sell it, expecting that it will decrease in value so that he can buy it back at a lower price and keep the difference.

Volatility: A measurement of the change in price over a given period.

Futures contract: A standardized contract, traded on a futures exchange, to buy or sell a certain underlying instrument at a certain date in the future, at a specified price. The future date is called the delivery date or final settlement date. The pre-set price is called the futures price. The price of the underlying asset on the delivery date is called the settlement price. The settlement price normally converges toward the futures price on the delivery date. Both parties of a futures contract must fulfill the contract on the settlement date. The seller delivers the commodity to the buyer, or, if it is a cash-settled future, then cash is transferred from the futures trader who sustained a loss to the one who made a profit. To exit the commitment prior to the settlement date, the holder of a futures position has to offset his position by either selling a long position or buying back a short position, effectively closing out the futures position and its contract obligations. Futures contracts, or simply futures, are exchange-traded derivatives.

Market order: A buy or sell order to be executed by the broker immediately at current market prices. As long as there are willing sellers and buyers, a market order will be filled.

Stop order (sometimes known as a stop loss order): The complement of a limit order. It is an order to buy (or sell) a security once the price of the security has climbed above (or dropped below) a specified price, known as the stop price. When the specified price is reached, the stop order is entered as a market order.

Moving average: In finance, and especially in technical analysis, one of a family of similar statistical techniques used to analyze time series data. A moving average series can be calculated for any time series, but is most often applied to stock prices, returns, or trading volumes. Moving averages are used to smooth out short-term fluctuations, thus highlighting longer-term trends or cycles.

5

The Rules

"We have a pretty strict definition of a systematic trader. They basically follow a set series of rules, established in a computer program, that tell you when to buy or sell, how many, as well as when to get out."

Michael Garfinkle,
Commodities Corporation

While the rules taught by Dennis and Eckhardt were not meant as a statistics class, the Turtles did learn some basic statistics including two "errors":

A **Type I error,** also known as an error of the first kind or a false negative, is the error of rejecting something that should have been accepted.

A **Type II error,** also known as an error of the second kind or a false positive, is the error of accepting something that should have been rejected.[1]

If the Turtles made those errors on a regular basis, they would be finished with mathematical certainty. Said another way, they learned that it was better to risk taking many small losses than to risk missing one large profit. The concept of statistical errors was an admission that acknowledged ignorance could be quite beneficial in trading.[2]

At the root of Dennis and Eckhardt's statistical thinking was Occam's razor (a principle attributed to the fourteenth-century English logician William of Ockham).[3] In more contemporary jargon people express it as, "Keep it simple, stupid!" For Dennis and Eckhardt's rules to work, to have some statistical reliability, they had to be simple.

Expectation:
How Much Does Your Trading Method
Earn in the Long Run?

"What can you expect to earn on each trade on average over the long run from your investing decisions or your trading rules?" Or, as a blackjack player would say, "What is your edge?" A first step for the Turtles was to know their edge.

A good analogy is being a batter at the plate in a baseball game, as trades and success rates aren't much different from batters and their averages. Dennis expanded on this: "The average batter hits maybe .280 and the average system might be successful 35 percent of the time."[4]

More importantly what kind of hits did you get in hitting .280. Did you hit singles or home runs? In trading, the higher the expectation, the more you can earn. A trading system with an expectation of $250 per trade will make you more money than a system with a $100 per trade expectation (all other things being equal in the long run). The Turtle rules themselves had a positive expectation per trade because their winning trades were many multiples larger than their losing trades. Expectation (or edge, or expected value) is calculated with a straightforward formula:

$$E = (PW \times AW) - (PL \times AL)$$

Where:

E = Expectation or Edge
PW = Winning Percent
AW = Average Winner
PL = Losing Percent
AL = Average Loser

For example, assume a trading system has 50 percent winning trades. Now, assume the average winning trade is $500 and the average losing trade is $350. What is the "edge" for that trading system?

Edge = (PW × AW) − (PL × AL)
Edge = (.50 × 500) − (.50 × 350)
Edge = 250 − 175
Edge = $75 on average per gain per trade

Over time you would expect to earn $75 for each trade placed. For comparison, another trading system might be only 40 percent accurate with an average winner of $1,000 and an average loser of $350. How would that system compare to the first one?

E = (PW × AW) − (PL × AL)
E = (.40 × 1,000) − (.60 × 350)
E = 400 − 210
E = $190 on average per gain per trade

The second trading system's "edge" is 2.5 times that of the first even though it has a much lower winning percent. In fact, the second system breaks even with a winning percent of 25.9. The first system breaks even at 41.1 percent. Clearly, when you hear the media and talking heads talking about "90 percent winning trades," that talk is misleading. Percent accuracy means nothing.

Look at it this way. Think about Las Vegas. A small edge keeps casinos in business. That's how those monster hotels in Las Vegas and Macau are paid for—by exploiting the edges. Dennis always wanted his trading to resemble being the *house*.

It didn't necessarily matter how little the Turtles lost on any individual trade, but they needed to know how much they could lose in their whole portfolio. Eckhardt was clear: "The important thing is to limit portfolio risk. The trades will take care of themselves."[5]

Trading Your Own Account Tip #1:

You need to calculate your edge for every trading decision you make, because you can't make "bets" if you don't know your edge. It's not about the frequency of how correct you are; it's about the magnitude of how correct you are.

TurtleTraderTheRules

Comparing the expected values of various Turtle and Turtle-style trading money management firms to various stock indexes gives more perspective about the importance of expectation:

Table 5.1: Turtle Trader Expectations from Inception to August 2006.

Trader	Average Winning Month %	Average Losing Month %	Percentage Winning Months	Expectation
Salem Abraham	8.50	(5.77)	55.36	2.13
Jerry Parker	5.06	(3.59)	57.40	1.38
Liz Cheval	12.45	(6.64)	49.62	2.83
Jim DiMaria	4.16	(3.17)	54.34	0.81
Mark J. Walsh	10.06	(7.15)	55.78	2.45
Howard Seidler	6.57	(4.90)	55.56	1.47
Paul Rabar	9.26	(4.89)	52.51	2.54

Table 5.2: Stock Index Expectations from Inception to August 2006.

Market Index	Average Winning Month %	Average Losing Month %	Percentage Winning Months	Expectation
Dow Jones	3.87	(3.85)	58.09	0.63
NASDAQ	4.98	(4.61)	57.75	0.93
S&P 500	3.83	(3.92)	58.37	0.60

The expectation generated by the trend traders generally beats the monthly expectation of buying and holding market indexes. Why? The average winning months of Turtle traders is much larger than their average losing months.

Entries and Exits: "It's Always Better to Buy Rallies"

Everyone wants to know, "How do you know when to buy?" The Turtles were taught to enter trades via "breakouts." A breakout occurs when a market—any market (Cisco, gold, yen, etc.)—"breaks through" a recent high or low. If a stock or futures contract made a fifty-five-day breakout to the upside (long), meaning that its current price was the highest price of the last fifty-five days, Turtles would buy.

If a stock made a fifty-five-day breakout to the downside, meaning that its current price was the lowest price of the last fifty-five days, Turtles would sell short, aiming to profit as the market dropped. In isolation there was nothing special about these simple rules for entry. Philosophically, Turtles wanted to buy a market going up (becoming more expensive) and wanted to sell short a market dropping in price (becoming cheaper).

What about the standard Wall Street refrain of "buy low and sell high"? The Turtles did just the opposite! And unlike most people's understanding of the markets, pro or beginner, the Turtles actively aimed to make money by "shorting" declining markets. They had no bias to being long or short.

While breakouts were the reason to enter, those breakouts did not mean a trend would continue by any measure. The idea was to let price movement lead the way, knowing at any time the price could change and go in a different direction. If a market went sideways, back and forth, you could see how and why Turtle price breakouts produced many small losses while they waited for a price breakout that might produce the big trend.

No matter what price is the variable that the great traders have lived and died by for decades. Making trading decisions more complicated than the simple heuristic of "price" has always been problematic. Eckhardt knew it was hard to do much better: "Pure price systems are close enough to the North Pole that any departure tends to bring you farther south."[6]

Trading Your Own Account Tip #2:

Now that the concept of using price for your decision-making is clear, stop watching TV! Stop looking at financial news. Start keeping track of the open, high, low, and close of each market you are tracking. That is the key data you need to make all of your trading decisions.

TurtleTraderTheRules

Trading Your Own Account Tip #3:

You need to be able to wrap your arms around the concept of "shorting" a market. Or said another way, you have to relish the opportunity to make money in a decreasing market. Shorting was never unique to the Turtles; they just did it effectively.

System One and System Two: The Two Turtle Systems

The Turtles learned two breakout variants or "systems." System One (S1) used a four-week price breakout for entry and a two-week price breakout in *the opposite direction of the entry breakout* for an exit. If a market made a new four-week high, the Turtles would buy. They would exit if/when it made a two-week low. A two-week low was a ten-day breakout—counting trading days only.

While the System One entry rule is straightforward, the Turtles were taught extra rules to confirm whether or not they should take the four-week breakout. The extra rules were called "filters," and they were designed to increase the odds that when the Turtles took a four-week breakout signal, it would continue as a potentially big trend.

The filter rule: The Turtles ignored the System One four-week breakout signal if the last four-week breakout signal was a winner. Even if they did not take the last four-week breakout signal, or even if it was just "theoretically" a winning trade, the Turtles still didn't take the System One breakout. However, if the trade before a current four-week breakout was a 2N loss, they could take the breakout ("N" was simply their measure of volatility, discussed in the next section).

Additionally, the direction of the System One four-week breakout was irrelevant in terms of the filter rule. If their last trade was a short losing trade and a new long or short breakout hit, they could take that breakout and get in.

But this filter rule had a built-in problem. What if the Turtles skipped the entry breakout (since the last trade was a "winner") and that skipped breakout was the beginning of a hugely profitable trend that roared up or down? Not good to be on the sidelines with a market taking off!

If the Turtles skipped a System One four-week breakout and the market kept trending, they could and would get back in at the System Two eleven-week breakout (see below). This fail-safe System Two breakout was how the Turtles kept from missing big trends that were filtered out.

System Two was the Turtles' longer-term trading system. It used an eleven-week breakout (fifty-five days) for an entry signal and a four-week breakout (twenty days) in the opposite direction for an exit.

Trading Your Own Account Tip #4:

The price "breakout" was Turtle jargon to describe a market that had just made a new high or new low over "x" period. Do traders use other values beyond twenty and fifty-five days for entry? Yes. The selection of these values for your trading will always be subjective. Test or practice these rules on paper and/or trading software (such as wealth-lab.com and mechanicasoftware.com) so you can see the ups and downs and gain confidence. The Turtles typically put half of their money toward each system.

Each Turtle had discretion over which of the two systems, System One (S1) and System Two (S2), Dennis and Eckhardt gave them to use. Mike Carr combined S1 and S2, allowing for more entry and exit points. He was trying to smooth out his trading results.

Jeff Gordon preferred S1, but mixed in S2 for smoother returns. Gordon, like some other Turtles, traded System Three (S3). He said the systems were Dennis's attempt to teach the Turtles that they should follow his methodology and not venture off the reservation, so to speak. Gordon added, "It was do anything you want to do, but don't lose more than $50,000 doing it. Once you crossed $50,000 and one dollar, you were out of the Turtle program."

Dennis called System Three (S3) the dreaded flair account. Erle Keefer saw why S3 was not taking hold, adding, "You could do whatever it was and everybody did it to a small degree, but within about six weeks everybody just canned that account."

It was canned because the Turtles had already lived emotionally losing seven out of ten trades. They knew *that* was the right thing to do. Keefer minced no words: "That was the only way you were ever going to hook the real trend. We saw it work. I don't know anybody that's writing really good books called *Counter Trend Trading to Win*."

Trading Your Own Account Tip #5:

Feel free to experiment on breakout lengths. Do not fixate on specific values. The key will be to accept a breakout value and stick with it consistently. Testing and practice are wise for confidence. Trust, but verify.

It is not surprising that over the years some traders—those who knew the Turtle rules—became obsessed with the specific System One and System Two entry and exit values as if they were the long-lost Holy Grail. Traders who fixate like that are looking at the tree instead of seeing the whole forest. For Turtle trading to work, the simplest of entry rules must continue to work. To get into debates about whether entering on a fifty-day breakout or a fifty-one-day breakout is better is misguided. In reality, a minor change of a variable in any robust trading system should not cause significant performance changes. If it does, you are in trouble.

Jerry Parker uses "robustness" as his guiding precept: "I think it's important to stay fairly simple—not a lot of variables. I think the reason we make money? It's the simple moving average systems. They need to continue to do well."

Parker used the Mount Lucas Management Index to make the point. It is a trend-following index based on a fifty-two-week moving average that goes back to the 1960s. Parker knows that core concept is his edge:

Two-thirds of that is what drives our profits. Our little filters to get in early, to get out quicker, volatility filters, if that is how we're going to essentially generate returns, we're going to be in bad shape. The core simple moving average or breakout systems [are key]. I think making our parameters longer term is important, but the minute it takes too much thinking and too much analysis and too much fancy work, it is going to be . . . a very bad situation.[7]

The market 'gurus' who pretend that a complex approach must be used to make money miss Parker's point about keeping it simple. They want the equivalent of quantum physics for trading rules. That kind of thinking is mental masturbation, or as trader Ed Seykota calls, it "math-turbation."

Consider this September 1995 Japanese yen chart to illustrate the System One price breakout in action:

Chart 5.3: Turtle Entry Example Using Japanese Yen.

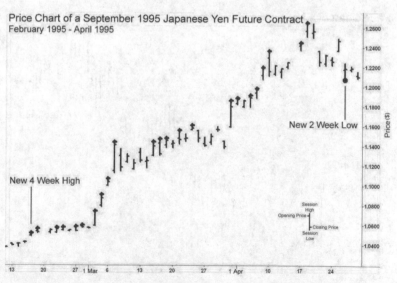

The September 1995 Japanese yen futures made a new four-week high on February 16, 1995. Turtles rules called for an entry on the next trading day. The position was held through all subsequent new highs and exited on a new two-week low on April 26, 1995. Source: Price-Data.com.

TurtleTraderTheRules

The market "broke out" to a new four-week high early in 1995. Then the market moved upward until a two-week breakout in the opposite direction in late April. The Turtles exited.

A great example of this process was seen early in Liz Cheval's career. She bought 350 oil contracts for under $20 a barrel in July 1990 and hung on as prices rose above $40. On October 15, 1990, she started liquidating at $38 a barrel and completed her liquidation at just over $30 with an average exit price of $34.80.[8]

There was no discussion about OPEC, government reports, or other fundamental factors used in Cheval's decision-making. It was all about the price action telling her to enter and exit. It is important to note that Turtles always exited *after* the market went against them, thus having to endure the painful experience of giving back profits. You

Chart 5.4: Turtle Long Entry Example Using Natural Gas.

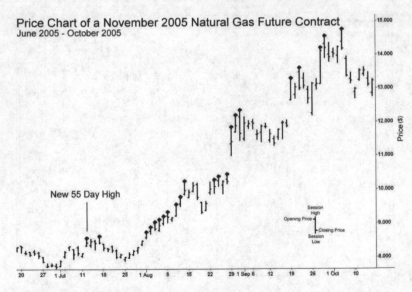

A new fifty-five-day high was made in November 2005 Natural Gas on July 12, 2005. The market continued making new highs until a peak on October 5, 2005. Source: Price-Data.com.

TurtleTraderTheRules

can't pick the bottom and you can't pick the top, so trying to end up with the "middle" of a trend was the goal.

Experiencing that trade made Cheval a believer. She said, "I remember giving back $4 million out of $8 million profit of Rich's money in a few minutes in the silver market in 1987." That lesson helped her to hang on when crude oil dropped from $30 to $25.[9]

Consider another example (chart 5.4), from November 2005 in Natural Gas Futures. Each dot represents a new fifty-five-day high. The first breakout happened in mid-July 2005. There was no way to know entering that breakout that a trend would continue higher, but it did, and the Turtles just followed along making money.

However, that breakout could just as easily have been a loser. In fact, Turtles could have had a string of losers in a row with multiple false breakouts. Phil Lu used to say, "When you have a losing trade, you say to yourself, 'Hey, it seemed like the right thing to do at that time.' " Exactly, following the rules means there will be losses. Trend-following trader Larry Hite has long said, "There are four kinds of bets. There are good bets, bad bets, bets that you win and bets that you lose."

Dealing with and handling losses is not easy. Jerry Parker has lived the struggles of taking losses to win in the long run. He advises:

I used to say we take a small loss, but I think it's better to take an optimal loss. You don't want to take one that's too large and yet you don't want to have your stops so close that you're going to get bounced out. [Just] hang on to the trade. Don't get too excited. If you're not making very much money, that's fine. If you got a little loss, that's fine. If you make a decent profit that turns into a loss, that's fine. Just hold onto it and then really get aggressive when you've been rewarded by a big, huge profit.[10]

December 2006 Eurodollars is yet another good example to illustrate the Turtle rules in action. However, this time the chart shows the opportunity to make money in a falling market. It was a "go short" opportunity. Each dot represents a new fifty-five-day low. The first "short" breakout occurred in February 2006 and the market continued to fall before reaching a low in June.

Chart 5.5: Turtle Short Entry and Exit Example Using Eurodollars.

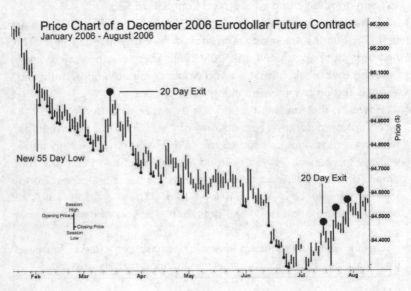

The December 2006 Eurodollars made a new 55-day low, signaling an entry, on February 20, 2006. The market briefly moved lower before making a new twenty-day high on March 16, 2006. Short positions in the market were exited with a loss. On March 29, 2006, the market made a new low and short positions were reestablished. The market continued making new lows before an exit signal, a new twenty-day high, occurred on July 14, 2006. Source: Price-Data.com.

By overlaying the twenty-day breakout exit on the Eurodollar chart, the full trade can be seen in context. An initial "short" breakout occurred in February, with a twenty-day high breakout in mid-March. That forced an exit. That first breakout resulted in a small loss.

However, the market resumed downward in late March and another breakout signal was hit. Turtles got right back in short again. The final exit occurred when a clear twenty-day breakout high was made in July. This is seen on the chart by the slightly larger dot. Profits generated on the second trade covered the loss from the first trade and then some.

That's the process. The Turtles could not afford to ignore the second breakout just because the first breakout resulted in a loss. They had to get back on the horse. The second breakout was the trade they were hoping for, and there was no way to predict it.

It was all a waiting game. Erle Keefer described to me their day-to-day process in rapid-fire summation terms: "First, you use channel breakout theory with a couple of filters. Second, you are going to size your bet by volatility. Third, you are going to have two hard stops on every trade. You are going to have the natural liquidation and you are going to have the firm hard stop. That's what saved everybody. Rich's systems inherently said, 'You got to stay in the game all the time as you never know when trends are going to hit.' "

Random Entries

When a breakout occurred, whether long or short, there was no way to know what would happen next. Maybe the market would go up for a short time and then go down, giving a loss. Perhaps the market suddenly goes higher, giving a nice profit.

Eckhardt witnessed many systematic traders spending great deal of time searching for the "good" places to enter. He cautioned against it: "It just seems to be part of human nature to focus on the most hopeful point of the trading cycle. Our research indicated that liquidations are vastly more important than initiations. If you initiate purely randomly, you do surprisingly well with a good liquidation criterion."[11]

Dennis actually challenged the Turtles to randomly enter the market and then manage their trades after getting in. That was a real Zen moment for many Turtles. If they applied *appropriate* risk management, they could handle the worst that came down the pike once they were in any trade.

Trading Your Own Account Tip #6:

Stop worrying only about how you enter a trade. The key is to know at all times when you will exit.

TurtleTraderTheRules

Risk Management: How Much Do You Bet on Each Trade?

Risk management has many names. You will find it called money management, bet sizing, or even position sizing. It was the very first concept Eckhardt addressed in class and ultimately the most important.

Turtle risk management starts with the measurement of daily market volatility. The Turtles were taught to measure volatility in terms of "daily ranges." It was nicknamed "N" (also known as the Average True Range, or ATR). They were taught to take the maximum of the following for any market to derive "N":

1. The distance from today's high to today's low

2. The distance from yesterday's close to today's high

3. The distance from yesterday's close to today's low

If the result is a negative number, it is turned it into an "absolute value." In mathematics, the absolute value of a real number is its distance from zero on a number line. So, for example, 3 is the absolute value of both 3 and –3.

The maximum value of the three choices is the "true range," or technically the absolute distance (either up or down) the market traveled in a given twenty-four-hour period. The Turtles then took a twenty-day moving average of true ranges. This gave a sample volatility for the last few weeks for each market traded.

Trading Your Own Account Tip #7:

You can determine the average true range for any stock or futures contract. Simply take the last fifteen true ranges, add them up, and divide by 15. Repeat each day, dropping off the oldest true range. Many software packages will do this automatically.

Eckhardt explained the logic behind "N": "We found that volatility is something that can be described as a moving average process. Our

incorporation of a volatility element in our trading—something that tells us how large our positions should be—has both kept us out of trouble during the tough times and allowed us to capture large gains when things are going our way."[12]

The Turtles were taught multiple uses of "N," but first they had to calculate it. Consider this example of "N" calculation:

Table 5.6: September 2006 Kansas City Wheat Futures ATR Calculations Example.

Date	Open	High	Low	Close	TR 1	TR 2	TR 3	True Range	20-Day Moving Average of the True Range
07/03/06	512.00	521.50	511.25	516.50					
07/05/06	517.00	524.00	513.00	521.50	11.00	7.50	3.50	11.00	
07/06/06	521.00	523.50	515.50	518.00	8.00	2.00	6.00	8.00	
07/07/06	510.00	515.00	505.50	506.00	9.50	3.00	12.50	12.50	
07/10/06	508.00	513.00	508.00	511.00	5.00	7.00	2.00	7.00	
07/11/06	519.00	527.50	515.00	524.00	12.50	16.50	4.00	16.50	
07/12/06	523.00	523.00	512.00	518.50	11.00	1.00	12.00	12.00	
07/13/06	510.00	514.00	492.00	493.00	22.00	4.50	26.50	26.50	
07/14/06	494.50	499.50	490.50	497.50	9.00	6.50	2.50	9.00	
07/17/06	501.00	503.50	489.00	490.00	14.50	6.00	8.50	14.50	
07/18/06	491.50	494.50	487.00	490.00	7.50	4.50	3.00	7.50	
07/19/06	486.00	488.00	477.00	486.00	11.00	2.00	13.00	13.00	
07/20/06	489.00	505.00	489.00	501.50	16.00	19.00	3.00	19.00	
07/21/06	500.50	515.00	500.50	505.00	14.50	13.50	1.00	14.50	
07/24/06	502.00	505.50	498.00	499.00	7.50	0.50	7.00	7.50	
07/25/06	503.00	505.00	486.00	489.00	19.00	6.00	13.00	19.00	
07/26/06	489.00	489.50	481.00	481.00	8.50	0.50	8.00	8.50	
07/27/06	482.00	488.00	481.00	485.00	7.00	7.00	0.00	7.00	
07/28/06	486.50	488.00	483.00	484.50	5.00	3.00	2.00	5.00	
07/31/06	484.00	494.00	484.00	492.00	10.00	9.50	0.50	10.00	
08/01/06	490.50	491.00	481.25	481.50	9.75	1.00	10.75	10.75	11.94

If the "N" for corn was 7 cents and the market was up 5.25 cents, then the market was up three-quarters of an "N." That's Turtle jargon. So "N" is a volatility measurement *and* a useful rule of thumb to classify how far a market has trended. Erle Keefer rattled off Turtle jargon: "When we put a bet on, we never said, 'I am putting on a $1,000 bet.' We were taught to think in terms of 'N.' 'I got a one-half N on.' We were taught that way because for most people, if they start to think, 'I've got $34 million in bonds on,' then the concept of money gets into their lizard brain and they start saying, 'Oh, my God!' We learned the correct way to think was, 'How much did the market move today?' It didn't move thirty-one ticks in the bonds, it moved one and one-quarter 'N.' "

The below chart shows "N" plotted below a bar chart of Dell. Notice how "N" can and does change. These values had to be up-

Chart 5.7: Chart Showing Dell Daily Bars with Daily ATR.

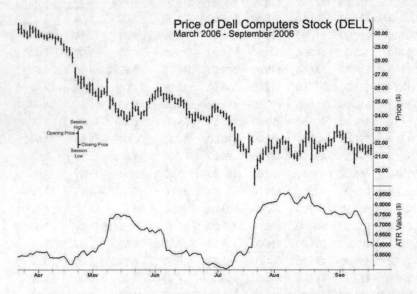

Daily Price Chart of Dell Computers with ATR valued in dollars plotted below. Athe ATR fluctuates as the market moves up and down on any given day.
Source: Price-Data.com.

TurtleTraderTheRules

dated. Eckhardt updated his volatility estimates every day. He said, "That's my routine. Two or three times a year I make an adjustment intra-day."[13]

Once they had a feel for "N," the Turtles were instructed about how much to "bet." They bet a fixed 2 percent of their capital on hand on each trade. If they had $100,000, they would bet (or risk) 2 percent ($2,000) on each trade. Each 2 percent bet of their equity was called a "unit." The "unit" was jargon that they used every day to measure risk.

They had unit limits on any market sector and unit limits on the total portfolio. The unit fluctuated so that every day the Turtles knew how many contracts to have on based on how much money they had in their trading account at that instant.[14]

Trading Your Own Account Tip #8:

Take your account (whatever size it is) and multiply by 2 percent. For example, a $100,000 account would risk 2 percent, or $2,000 per trade. It is always better to bet a small amount initially on any trade in case you are wrong—which can easily be greater than 50 percent of the time. While the Turtles typically used a 2 percent bet, you can reduce your risk and reduce your return by decreasing that number to, for example, 1.5 percent, etc.

The Turtle risk management dictated their stops, their additions to positions, and their equalization of risk across their portfolios. For example, a corn futures contract (a standard corn contract is worth $50 per cent) with an "N" of 7 cents has a risk of $350 (7 cents × $50). If the Turtles received a corn breakout signal (using a 2N stop), they would have had a "contract risk" of $350 × 2, or $700.

Assuming a $100,000 account, they would have had an "account risk" of $2,000 (2% × $100,000). The number of contracts to buy or sell is determined by taking the 2 percent account risk and dividing it by the contract risk. That gives 2.67 ($2,000/$700) futures contracts. Turtles rounded down to the nearest whole number. So when their

TurtleTraderTheRules

breakout signal was hit, they traded two corn contracts for their $100,000 account.

The rules made a corn unit equal to a gold unit equal to a Coca-Cola unit. This was how Dennis was able to trade markets as "numbers" with no fundamental expertise in any of those markets. It was

Table 5.8: Contract Calculation Method Using ATR in $ Terms.

Market	ATR in $	2 ATR in $	Account Risk	Contracts Traded at 2 ATR stop
Corn	$350	$700	$2,000	2.0
Lean Hogs	$420	$840	$3,000	3.0
Japanese Yen	$725	$1,500	$1,875	1.0
Ten-Year Notes	$525	$1,050	$2,000	1.0

how the Turtles were able to trade such a wild cross-section of unrelated markets with only two weeks of training.

However, the Turtles learned another use of "N" beyond a measure of volatility. It was also used as their primary stop (or exit rule, as first mentioned with S1 and S2). The Turtles used a 2N stop. This simply means that their primary stop, or hard stop, was two times the daily "N."

For example, if there was a breakout in corn, and assuming a closing price of $250, Turtles quickly determined their "N" stop. If the "N" was 7 cents, a 2N stop would have been 14 cents. The stop would have been 14 cents behind the entry price. An entry at $250 would have a hard stop at $236 (250 – 14). You would exit if the stop at price level $236 was "touched." No second-guessing. No overthinking. Follow the rules.

Trading Your Own Account Tip #9:

Assume you are trading Google stock and its ATR is 20. A 2ATR (2N) stop would be 40. If you lose 40 points on Google, you must exit, no questions asked.

TurtleTraderTheRules

Chart 5.9: Chart Showing Soybean Daily Bars with Daily ATR.

Daily price chart of May 2004 Soybean Futures shows a smaller ATR at the beginning of the trend. A smaller ATR allows for more contracts to be traded via Turtle money-management rules. By the end of the trend, ATR has expanded greatly, reducing the size of the position you can have on. Source: Price-Data.com.

On the other hand, a small "N" allowed Turtles to trade a larger position or take on more units. Soybean units purchased in August (chart 5.9) at the beginning of the breakout were 2.50 times larger than units that could have been bought at the end of the trend. This example is a great reminder of the relationship between market volatility and unit size: A low "N" value always means more contracts (or shares).

Jerry Parker found that his best trends often start with very low volatility at the initial breakout entries. He said, "If the recent volatility is very low, not $5 in gold, but $2.50 in gold, then we're going to throw in a very large position."[15]

Parker's analysis kept showing that a low "N" measurement at the time of entry was a good thing. He said, "I can have on a really large position. And when volatility is low, it usually means that the market has been dead for a while. Everyone hates the market, has had lots of losers in a row, tight consolidation. And then as it motors through those highs, we get on board."[16]

Unit Limits

It didn't matter whether the markets were futures, commodities, currencies, FOREX, or stocks. One unit of corn, through the Turtle rules, had now roughly the same risk as one unit of dollars, bonds, sugar, or any other market in the Turtles' portfolio.

However, the Turtles could not trade unlimited units. Each unit, after all, represented 2 percent of their limited and finite capital. The Turtles had unit guidelines to keep them from overtrading. For example, they were limited to four to five units for any one market traded.

Thus, trading like a Turtle could leave you with a $100,000 portfolio that might have purchased one bond contract, but a $1 million portfolio might have purchased five. As the bond contracts gained in value, others would be added.[17]

Examples of Initial Risk Determination

The following examples show the basic Turtle trading process in action.

1. Assume a trading account of $150,000, risking 1.5 percent on each trade and seeking to trade Swiss franc futures using a 2N stop. The Swiss franc has a single "N" dollar value of $800.

   $150,000 × 1.50% = $2,250
   2N stop = $1,600
   The number of contracts to trade on this unit is 1.40, rounded down to 1.0.

2. Assume a trading account of $25,000, risking 2.0 percent on each trade and seeking to trade mini corn futures using a 3N stop. Mini corn has a single "N" dollar value of $70.00.

$25,000 \times 2.0\% = \$500$

3N stop = $210

The number of contracts to trade on this unit is 2.38, rounded down to 2.0.

The unit rules make good intuitive sense once the light bulb goes off. However, that light bulb did not turn on immediately. One Turtle described the learning curve: "When somebody says, 'N is volatility and N is your unit size,' I say, 'How do I know the difference between them?' It's really like wrapping yourself around a conundrum, but after a while it was easy. Pretend I am talking to Liz Cheval, 'I have got a half unit on and I am three N up' or 'I have got a half N unit on and I am half N positive.' I totally understand the difference between them. Don't even have to think about it. This is burned into your brain."

Pyramiding: "Adding to Winners"

Once they understood S1 and S2 entry and exit rules, once they understood "N" and units, Eckhardt then instructed the Turtles to pile profits back into winning trades. This maxing out of their big winners was part of what helped to create the Turtles' fantastic positive expectancy, or "edge."

For example, a market bought at a price breakout level of 100 could have additional units added as the market moved through price levels of 102, 104, and 108. Assume a long breakout entry at 100 with an "N" value of 5. Assume that you will add another unit each 1N move. A new unit will be added at 105, 110, etc. Turtles could pyramid a maximum of 5 units. They set their stops at ½N on the first day of trading and from that point forward, 2N stops were used. Then, once the second unit was bought, both stops were brought up to the new unit's 2N stop. As new units were added, all stops were brought up to the stop of the newest unit added.

This process protected open profits, but not to the extent that it would jeopardize catching a very big trend. This thinking also aimed to guarantee that profits would be plowed back into those big unpredictable trends. This was how Dennis and Eckhardt taught the Turtles to "bet their left nut."

Trading Your Own Account Tip #10:

If you want to make Turtle-like money, you will need to use leverage. The key is to always manage your leverage use and not let it get past your limits.

Sample Trade to Demonstrate Pyramiding

This sample trade illustrates how the Turtles pyramided their winning trades.

First Unit

Starting account size: $50,000.

Account risk of 2%, or $1,000 per signal.

Long signal generated in live cattle at 74.00.

1N value is 0.80, 1 point in live cattle is $400, so the dollar value of 1N is $320.

2N value is 1.60, dollar value of $640.

Contracts to trade: $1,000/640 = 1.56 rounded down to 1.0.

Add the next position at 1N, or 74.00 + 0.80 = 74.80.

Stop setting is 74.00 − 1.60 = 72.40.

Table 5.10: Purchase First Unit of Live Cattle at $74.00.

Unit	Entry	No. Contracts	Stop	Profit/Loss	Risk to Original Equity
1	74.00	1	72.40	$0.00	$640 (1.28% of original equity)

TurtleTraderTheRules

Addition of Second Unit

Account value is now $50,320 ($50,000 + unit one gain of $320).

Account risk of 2%, or $1,006.40.

Second position added at 74.80.

1N value remains 0.80, or $320.

2N value remains 1.60, or $640.

Contracts to trade $1,006.40/$640 = 1.57, rounded down to 1.0.

Add the next unit at 1N, or 74.80 + 0.80 = 75.60.

Stop setting on both positions is 74.80 – 1.60 = 73.20.

Table 5.11: Purchase Second Unit of Live Cattle at $74.80.

Unit	Entry	No. Contracts	Stop	Profit/Loss	Risk to Original Equity
1	74.00	1	73.20	$320.00	$320 –0.64%
2	74.80	1	73.20	$0.00	$640 –1.28%
Total		2		$320.00	$960 –1.92%

Addition of Third Unit

Account value is now $50,960 ($50,000 + unit one gain of $640 + unit two gain of $320).

Account risk of 2% or $1,019.20.

Third position added at 75.60.

1N value decreased to 0.70, or $280.

2N value decreased to 1.40, or $560.

Contracts to trade $1,019.20/$560 = 1.82 rounded down to 1.0.

Add the next unit at 1N, or 75.60 + 0.70 = 76.30.

Stop setting on all units is 75.60 – 1.40 = 74.20.

TurtleTraderTheRules

Table 5.12: Purchase Third Unit of Live Cattle at $75.60.

Unit	Entry	No. Contracts	Stop	Profit/Loss	Risk to Original Equity
1	74.00	1	74.20	$640.00	$0.00 –0%
2	74.80	1	74.20	$320.00	$240 –.48%
3	75.60	1	74.20	$0.00	$560 –1.12%
Total		3		$960.00	$800 –1.60%

Addition of Fourth Unit

Account value is now $51,800 ($50,000 + unit one gain of $920 + unit two gain of $600 + unit three gain of $280).

Account risk of 2%, or $1,036.00.

Fourth unit added at 76.30.

1N value remained 0.70, or $280.

2N value remained at 1.40, or $560.

Contracts to trade $1,036.00/$560 = 1.85 rounded down to 1.00.

Add the next unit at 1N, or 76.30 + 0.70 = 77.00.

Stop setting on all units is 76.30 – 1.40 = 74.90.

Table 5.13: Purchase Fourth Unit of Live Cattle at $76.30.

Unit	Entry	No. Contracts	Stop	Profit/Loss	Risk to Original Equity
1	74.00	1	74.90	$920.00	$0.00 –0%
2	74.80	1	74.90	$600.00	$0.00 –0%
3	75.60	1	74.90	$280.00	$280 –.56%
4	76.30	1	74.90	$0.00	$560 –1.12%
Total		4		$1,800.00	$840 –1.68%

Addition of Fifth and Final Unit

Account value is now $52,920 ($50,000 + unit one gain of $1,200 + unit two gain of $880 + unit three gain of $560 + unit four gain of $280).

Account risk of 2%, or $1,058.40.

Fourth unit added at 77.00.

1N value increased to 0.85, or $340.00.

2N value increased to 1.70, or $680.00.

Contracts to trade $1,058.40/$680 = 1.55, rounded down to 1.00.

Stop setting on all units is 77.00 − 1.70 = 75.30.

Table 5.14: Purchase Fifth Unit of Live Cattle at $77.00.

Unit	Entry	No. Contracts	Stop	Profit/Loss	Risk to Original Equity
1	74.00	1	75.30	$1,200.00	$0.00 −0%
2	74.80	1	75.30	$880.00	$0.00 −0%
3	75.60	1	75.30	$560.00	$120 −.24%
4	76.30	1	75.30	$280.00	$400 −.80%
5	77.00	1	75.30	$0.00	$680 −1.36%
Total		5		$2,920.00	$1,200 −2.4%

Turtle stops were adjusted to break even with each 1N market move up.

Position Exit

Live cattle rallies to 84.50 and their exit criteria are met.

Table 5.15: Exit Live Cattle at $84.50.

Unit	Entry	No. Contracts	Exit	Profit/Loss	Gain to Original Equity
1	74.00	1	84.50	$4,200.00	8.4%
2	74.80	1	84.50	$3,880.00	7.8%
3	75.60	1	84.50	$3,560.00	7.1%
4	76.30	1	84.50	$3,280.00	6.6%
5	77.00	1	84.50	$3,000.00	6.0%
Total		5		$17,920.00	35.8%

With this kind of pyramiding, you could have a $300,000 account that was long five units containing Canadian dollars, U.S. dollar indexes, the S&P 500 index, unleaded gas, orange juice, yen, Swiss francs, gold, soybean oil, and cotton. By Turtle trading logic, they would be net long one unit, or 2 percent of the total portfolio.[18]

Risk of Ruin: "Will You Live or Die?"

Aggressive pyramiding of more and more units had a downside. If no big trend materialized, then those little losses from false breakouts would eat away even faster at the Turtles' limited capital. How did Eckhardt teach the Turtles to handle losing streaks and protect capital? They cut back their unit sizes dramatically. When markets turned around, this preventive behavior of reducing units increased the likelihood of a quick recovery, getting back to making big money again.

The rules were simple. For every 10 percent in drawdown in their account, Turtles cut their trading unit risk by 20 percent. For example, if they were trading a 2 percent unit and if an 11 percent drawdown happened, they would cut their trading size from 2 percent to 1.6 percent (2.0 × 80%). If their trading capital dropped down 22 percent, then they would cut their trading size by another 20 percent (1.6 × 80%), making each unit 1.28 percent.

When did they increase their unit sizes back to normal? Once their capital started going back up. Erle Keefer remembered one of his peers saying, "Oh my God, I am down so much that I have to make 100 percent just to get back to even." But that Turtle ended up the year with a nice bonus, because the markets finally started clicking (and trending). Keefer added, "When the statistics finally all work and all those markets start moving, those 'hot wires' can start pulling you up pretty fast from a drawdown."

For example, let's say you are at $10,000 and you keep losing, then you win a little, then you lose a little. You are now down to $7,500. You are probably trading 40 to 50 percent of your original unit size. All of a sudden everything goes back up to $7,800. It goes up to $8,000, and you start restoring unit size. The Turtles could be down eleven months and one week into the year and then in the last three weeks of the year go from being down 30 or 40 percent to up 150 percent. Look at their month-by-month data from 1984 to 1988 (see Appendix). When the markets kicked in, it was a wild ride.

By reducing positions when they were losing money, the Turtles countered the arithmetic progression toward "ruin" effectively.[19] Dennis and Eckhardt's logic makes good conceptual sense, even for non-math novice traders.

Eckhardt did not want the Turtles to worry about linear decreases in their accounts. The slightest exponential curve from a big trend would eventually surpass the steepest linear curve they saw while losing. Discipline, money management, and patience were the only ways it would work.[20]

This day-to-day routine, however, was mundane. Every day they would come in and there would be an envelope with their name on it. That envelope would have their printouts with their positions. It included updated "N" values, too. That's right, the Turtles did not have to worry about the basics of calculating "N." Of course, they learned

94

the hows and whys of "N" from Eckhardt, but the time-consuming calculations were done for them. The Turtles simply picked up their envelopes and checked to make sure their positions and orders were all as they were supposed to be.

Liquidation (Exit) Rule Summaries

There were two basic "stops" or exits to get Turtles out of their trades:

1. The 2N stop.
2. The S1 or S2 breakout exits.

The Turtles were instructed to take whichever stop hit first. For example, assume you enter any market. Your 2N stop is quickly hit, and you exit with a small loss. That's easy. On the other hand, perhaps you enter a market and it takes off. A monster trend zooms either up or down. In that case, your S1 or S2 breakout stop would get you out with a profit.

This was stomach-churning. David Cheval lived this process working with his then wife Liz Cheval. He said, "When we have good profits, then we're very aggressive with those profits. We'll risk 100 percent of the profit in a trade if it doesn't follow through based on our system." The Turtles could have had a 50 percent profit in a market, but their stop still might be at their predesignated risk of 2 percent. It was possible for them to lose all of that profit plus the 2 percent.[21]

Portfolio Selection and
Position Balancing

This philosophy applied to *all* markets, meaning as long as liquidity and a selection of quality markets existed (and today there is no shortage of those) and there is some inherent volatility in that market (Turtles need movement after all to make money), any market could be traded like a Turtle.

The Turtles initially traded these markets:

Table 5.16: Markets Traded Initially By Turtles.

30-Year T-Bond	Deutschmark	90-Day T-Bill
10-Year T-Bond	British Pound	Gold
Cotton	French Franc	Silver
Sugar	Japanese Yen	Copper
Cocoa	Canadian Dollar	Crude Oil
Coffee	S&P 500	Heating Oil
Swiss Franc	Eurodollar	Unleaded Gas

Trading Your Own Account Tip #11:

There is no one set portfolio you can trade. Today, traders trade Turtle-like rules across widely differing portfolios (stocks, currencies, bonds, commodities, etc.). It is a primary reason traders have differing performances. There is also no one starting capital number that can be promised as an elixir for all traders. Some start with small money and get huge. Some start with big money and don't make it. You will see in later chapters the other pieces of the trading puzzle beyond these rules that separate winners and losers.

However, it was critical to avoid having one of highly correlated markets. In simple terms, think of correlated markets typically moving together in lockstep. Too many potentially correlated markets in a portfolio and the Turtles increased their unit risk.

For example, the Dow Jones Industrials stock index and the S&P 500 stock index are highly correlated. Both move up and down together. Buying one unit in the Dow and then buying one unit in the S&P is like having two units in either market alone.

Or, assume both Apple and Dell were in a Turtle's portfolio. Both stocks go up and down together like clockwork. Proper Turtle trading strategy would dictate one unit of Apple. However, if one unit of Dell was also bought, since these two stocks have high correlation, this would be essentially trading double the amount of Apple that

TurtleTraderTheRules

Table 5.17: Table to Show Correlation Effect Between Portfolios.

More Risk (Highly Correlated)		Less Risk (Loosely Correlated)	
Longs	Shorts	Longs	Shorts
Corn	Gold	Soybeans	Gold
Soybeans	Silver	Japanese yen	Five-year notes
Japanese yen	Ten-year notes	Live cattle	Sugar
	Five-year notes		Crude oil

should be traded. To trade both stocks was to take twice the risk you should take.

Look at table 5.17. Notice that both columns in each table have the same number of markets. They could easily have the same number of units. However, the "More Risk" table has more markets highly correlated to each other. Corn and soybeans, gold and silver, and the two note contracts are all highly correlated. Essentially, Turtles would be trading only four markets. The "Less Risk" table shows a broader grouping of markets with less correlation. For example, historically the Japanese yen and crude oil do not move together.

The Turtles were also taught that combining long and short units into their portfolio offered further diversification. In fact, when they combined long and short units, Dennis and Eckhardt discovered that they could actually trade more overall units. This was how they were able to load up on so many positions. While they appeared overleveraged in others' eyes, Dennis and Eckhardt had the Turtles safely under risk management (unit) guidelines.

Consider another portfolio example. Assume it is long units in corn, feeder cattle, gold, and Swiss francs, for a total of four long units. Also, assume it has short units in British pounds, copper, and sugar, for a total of three short units.

To calculate the total Turtle unit risk, you would take the smaller number and divide it by two. Then you would subtract that number from the larger number. In this example it would be 4 − (3/2), giving 2.5 units of risk. This is how the Turtles added more units without adding more risk.

Why did the Turtles diversify so much? There was no way they could

TurtleTraderTheRules

Table 5.18: (2) Charts That Demonstrate Long/Short Rule Calculations.

Example One: Long/Short Rule		Example Two: Long/Short Rule	
Longs	Shorts	Longs	Shorts
Corn (1)	Wheat (1)	Coffee (3)	Crude oil (4)
Live cattle (3)	Sugar (2)	Natural gas (1)	Australian dollar (3)
Cocoa (1)	Ten-year notes (1)	Soybeans (2)	
Swiss francs (2)		S&P 500 (2)	
Total: 7	Total: 3	Total: 8	Total: 7
Total units of risk: $(7-(3/2)) = 5.5$		Total units of risk: $(8-(7/2)) = 4.5$	

predict which market would trend big, nor could they predict the magnitude of any trend's move. Miss only one big trend and their whole year could be ruined.[22]

That was it. Boom. Two weeks of training, at the Union League Club, was done. With those rules in hand, they entered Dennis's office space in the old Insurance Exchange building next to the Chicago Board of Trade. They took his money and started trading.

However, the Turtles were given one more mandate that superseded all the philosophy and rules: Practice. Sure, it might sound clichéd, but it was reality. To put it in perspective, many people see winners like Tiger Woods and make innumerable excuses about why he is great and they are not: "He started learning golf as a toddler." "He is a natural athlete." "He earned his titles during a time when golf was lacking top-notch competition."

The truth? Woods is great because he has the discipline of practice ingrained in him. Look at the tape of him on Johnny Carson when he was three or four years old. Practice, practice, practice—all the time. Woods is famous for saying, "No matter how good you get you can always get better and that's the exciting part." That mentality is mission critical for both golf and trading.

Medicine is yet another field where skills develop as a result of repetitive training. Research shows time and time again that medical students are often clumsy at their first tries at performing even such basic procedures as finding a vein to tap for blood work.[23] However,

their process of focusing on repetition and discipline consistently pro-
duces many competent doctors with long and successful careers.[24]

For the Turtles there was going to be nothing glamorous—just as
with doctors practicing to find a vein. At the end of the day, their training was surely not what they expected (of course how could they have
really known what to expect?). But they never truly got a "secret"
sauce. As one Turtle put it, "Richard didn't quite give us the Holy Grail.
There's no single magic element." Magic or not, once the Turtles
finished class they immediately went to work. However, before they
started making big money, there were rough patches.

6

In the Womb

"It's possible to train people to perform to a certain level in chess, but if this training does not promote self-education and a philosophical attitude, then the trainees will be little more than performing seals."

Nigel Davies,
Daily Speculations

How many Turtles were there? The number of Turtles is in dispute. Dennis and Eckhardt not only included people selected from want ads in the training room, they also invited an assortment of colleagues who were already working for them. Other people in the office entourage, who were close enough to pick up the essential concepts of what they were teaching, ended up exposed to the Turtle rules.

Take, for example, Mark Walsh. Walsh was not an official Turtle, but someone who has traded like a Turtle for twenty years. With a track record of better than 20 percent average annual performance, he is an equal to Turtles who managed money for clients since 1988. Sam DeNardo, a generally accepted Turtle, didn't want his definition of the Turtle club violated: "I love Mark Walsh, I've known him for a long time but he wasn't really a Turtle . . . And I think the Turtles, the real Turtles, feel strongly about keeping the group true to what the list was."

DeNardo also argued against Craig Soderquist as a Turtle even though the *Wall Street Journal* had referred to him as one: "Soderquist was somebody involved in Rich's life at the time who maybe got a couple guys' notes from the meetings." However, Robert Moss, head of Richard Dennis's trading-floor operations in New York from 1984 to 1988, stated without a moment's hesitation that Soderquist was a Turtle. Moss's job was to execute daily for C&D Commodities thousands of futures contracts across New York trading pits. He would know.[1] Yet Jeff Gordon, a verified Turtle, disagreed with Moss, saying that the Turtles were only those who traded Dennis's money.

Clearly, many people, official Turtles or not, learned the methods simply because they were close to the action in the C&D offices. It was easy to see that once Dennis and Eckhardt started the training phase of their experiment, it was similar to the informal seminars Dennis and Tom Willis had held in the 1970s. Training was open to a much wider circle than Turtles hired via the ad would have preferred.

The refinements and distinctions as to who was and who was not a Turtle went right to the heart of what was to become a serious competition. They might have all been told they were equal, and perhaps they were initially, but this was no game. Millions of dollars were on the line.

The Office Environment

Within the offices of C&D Commodities, the Turtles were Dennis's pet project. They were viewed as worker bees freeing him up for bigger-picture political initiatives.[2] Robert Moss said that they were "essentially a stable of 'little Richards,' no pun intended."

That stable had very little in personal oversight once they were trained. Russell Sands, for one, was surprised at the complete lack of supervision. He noted, "We might have seen Rich, Bill, or Dale once a week on a Friday afternoon for two hours." According to Sands, they would walk in and say, "How did you guys do this week? Anybody have any questions?" That was it.

If one of the Turtles did not follow the rules, Dennis and Eckhardt, who reviewed their daily statements, would call up and ask for an explanation. Sands added, "But aside from that, there was no mentoring; there was no supervision, there was nothing. We were totally on our own." It was, "Here's the money, keep a journal, write down every trade you took and why you took it." The Turtles would become more famous and successful over time, but in the beginning there was no fanfare.

The working conditions were Spartan. Dennis provided them with a large trading office sandwiched between two floors in the Insurance

Exchange building. It was furnished with metal desks and chairs. The most basic amenities, such as a coffee machine or TV, were missing. There was a bookcase with trading books that hardly anyone ever read. Eventually a Ping-Pong table was brought in.

The Turtle seating arrangements were reminiscent of grade school. They were seated two by two, with six-foot-tall dividers between the cubicles. The informal, no-frills environment was typical of the way Dennis ran his business and his life. Mr. Anti-Establishment was passing his attitude down to his students.

This attitude left others in the building wondering what the Turtle office was up to. After all, they had all kinds of downtime trading as trend traders. They would go days without trading. On top of that, there was no dress code. They used to show up to work in the summer in cut-offs and T-shirts.

A Harvard MBA worked side-by-side with a recent high school graduate. A Jehovah's Witness played Ping-Pong with a blackjack player from Eastern Europe. Jewish and Christian students were mixed into one diverse office.

Consider Anthony Bruck, a wiry and fashionable Chicago socialite and artist. He reminded some of Andy Warhol. He'd come to work dressed in skin-tight black clothes. Bruck, like Jim Kenney, was a friend of Dennis before the experiment started.

Erle Keefer loved the wild diversity of what was almost a mini United Nations: "You had people who didn't have a college degree, then people who had doctorates. Anthony Bruck had a doctorate in linguistics. Actually, I think that probably helped him to be a good trader because you had to think about it analytically and conceptually."

Mike Carr was a terrific demonstration of Dennis's eclectic hiring policy. He couldn't spell "future" (as in trading futures), so to speak, in the beginning. Carr, like other newbie Turtles, had to be shown a chart and how to read it. He was living proof that you did not need a Harvard MBA to excel.

Even more unusual was the inclusion of Lucy Wyatt. For years, people who were aware of the Turtle story have assumed that there was only one female Turtle, Liz Cheval. But it turns out that there were two.

Wyatt was a friend of William Eckhardt's. Jim DiMaria noted:

"While the rest of us were like Turtles and that's what we were and that's what we did, she would kind of come and go. She did actually have a desk . . . in the room. I guess maybe that's the Turtle barometer . . . you have a desk in that room."

Off the record, several Turtles who'd been hired through the screening process commented that having Dennis employees and friends in the room trading as Turtles caused strife. One said, "The regular Turtles, so to speak, wondered how in the hell were they ever picked for this program. The ones not picked via a screening process just didn't have the mental horsepower for it." All one Turtle could remember about Wyatt was that she was always doing her nails.

Mike Cavallo said that Wyatt had been Eckhardt's girlfriend. He noted, "She was in the room with us. So of the people, if you were going to say who was a Turtle and who wasn't, she would have been considered to be the least likely to be called a Turtle."

Did Wyatt trade? Apparently yes. Many people who hear the Turtle story make excuses for why they could never fit in. Wyatt made it clear that anyone *could* have fit in with the Turtles.

Wildly differing political views did not keep Turtles from fitting in, either. Jerry Parker and Richard Dennis, for example, were political opposites. Mike Shannon painted Parker in extreme terms: "[He was] about as right-wing conservative as you can get and we had people in there who were more liberal than Rich by a long shot." Shannon got a kick out of the political diversity crammed into the one-room office. He said, "Jerry was far right and at the time I was more far left. We would really lock horns once in a while on certain political and social issues. He is so far right. It's just unbelievable. I just never really took him seriously in that regard." However, Shannon did take Parker seriously as a trader, saying, "He's very good. But the funny thing is with all of that, when it came to the actual trading and discussing the systems and methodologies, we were all on the same page. No matter what the political background or social background, we all tried to cooperate as much as possible."

These political differences were no small matter. Jeff Gordon learned this firsthand at a dinner before the 1984 presidential election. Everyone knew Mondale was Dennis's guy. Dennis started going around the table asking everyone who they were voting for. One by one, they all said, "Mondale." They were all his guests, and Dennis was one of the richest guys around. However, when it was Gordon's turn he said, "Gary Hart." Gordon knew he had just upset the trading king of Chicago.

However, far more important than any political differences were the commonalities. Mike Cavallo saw all the Turtles as extremely bright, but viewed the group as an interesting mix of competitive and easygoing people. He believed that the great majority of the Turtles could have a day filled with total disasters yet still be pleasant.[3]

In hindsight, it's hard to know for sure if the Turtles were like what Cavallo described or if they ultimately became like that as a result of their unique situation. No one was going to make waves when a rich guy was giving out millions to a group to trade with an incentive plan to make their own millions. That kind of opportunity kept mouths closed.

The Turtles, however, didn't immediately realize that they had been given the "golden goose" for making millions. Since they had to hit the ground running, they did not have time to test the rules Dennis had given them. They had to trust Dennis and Eckhardt implicitly.

Erle Keefer, hired in the second Turtle class, was in the minority with his desire for a "proof of concept." Like his mentor, Keefer remained skeptical: "You said I learned about the golden goose, but I didn't have a computer program, hadn't seen printouts, hadn't seen proof of concept. You know what I mean?"

As time went on, some Turtles did test the rules Dennis gave them. This effort changed the direction of the Turtle program. Still, initially, the Turtles executed their trades based on the rules they had been taught. They were making big money doing so. In fact, all were now making more money than they ever had in their lives. At that moment, everyone associated with C&D Commodities was certain that they had proven nurture trumps nature—even if no one outside of the firm knew this yet.

A Boring Trading Strategy

The Turtles experienced what the term "free time" really meant. There simply was no trading if a market didn't move. Not trading when there was no market movement was, in fact, one of the most important rules of all. No trending market, no profit. No market moves, no calling Robert Moss to place trades.

These long periods of doing nothing would be considered useless by today's hyperactive crowd, in love with checking stock quotes every minute. However, the Turtles would have had no need for hot tips from the likes of Jim Cramer of *Mad Money* or CNBC's David Faber's latest "breaking" news story.

Today, people gobble up dozens of trading infomercials and nightly advice from everyone under the sun on what to buy and sell. All of this was useless to the Turtles. Today's get-rich-quick crowds have created a whole culture of traders afraid of missing something. They obsess about analysis about what the markets have done or are going to do—even if it has no direct connection to their trading decisions. The Turtles, on the other hand, were perfectly content to do nothing when the rules said to do nothing.

The Turtles would come in every day already armed with their war plans so that they didn't make bad decisions in the heat of the battle. Stare at the screen and it's going to say, "Do something, trade me." All top traders today work like hell to develop a trading philosophy. They convert that philosophy to rules. After that, they stand back and see if their rules act as expected. If you build a system that gives you an entry and exit, tells you *how much* to bet along the way and adjusts to your current capital and current market volatility at all times, no more analysis is needed.

The Turtles did not fight this boring state of affairs. However, everyone handled downtime differently. Jerry Parker, for example, played electronic baseball until he had figured out all the tricks. Does that mean Parker was goofing off and not trading properly? No. Far from it. Parker was always prepared. Self-discipline meant doing nothing until the time came to do something. Parker knew what role they played in Dennis's life when he said that Dennis ran the training "because he wanted to have a certain chunk of money traded using systematic rules" while he went on and tried out new techniques.[4]

But for now, their trading was all about downtime. It was for the Turtles a deliberate process of following about thirty markets, waiting to do something. They didn't trade foreign markets at the time; many of those were yet to be invented. Their basket of markets was not very active.

The Turtle think tank did have occasional undercurrents and personal biases, particularly when it came to Liz Cheval. This was Chicago trading in the early 1980s, and some Turtles thought sexism was an issue. The fact that some Turtles may not have taken Cheval seriously was not easy to deal with. Michael Shannon said, "Between guys hitting on her and guys shunning her and stuff, it kind of made her somewhat ambivalent to the whole Turtle process."

Cheval appreciated the fact that she was getting a great education in the program, but she may have had some residual animosity toward other Turtles. Shannon added support: "A lot of people just underestimated her. You have to remember this was the '80s. How many women commodity traders did you know at the time?" Even though they were the Turtles, it clearly did not mean they were all behaving with the decorum of choirboys.

Jiri Svoboda used his inordinate amount of downtime for other ventures beyond trading. He was always trying to figure out ways to beat the house. This, however, was not gambling in the way most people think of it. His view was all about understanding the odds and making money.

Svoboda had no problem leaving the office for two or three months at a time. Other Turtles made sure his trades got placed properly once Svoboda had worked out all of his if/then contingencies. In turn, he then spent much of his time in Las Vegas developing systems that could read cards being dealt at blackjack tables.

This behavior was fine within the parameters of the experiment, because Dennis himself had created the atmosphere of "get the job done and I don't care where you are physically." By giving Turtles his rules, his money, his brokers, and his ATRs (the computed daily volatility for each market, or what they called "N"), Dennis had taken away much of the day-to-day routine the Turtles would have been experiencing had they been trading entirely on their own.

The trading day unfolded with the Turtles tracking their group of markets. If one or more of those markets generated an entry or exit signal, they picked up the phone, called to the trading floor, and made the trade. Then they would wait for the market to move one way or the other before picking up the phone and calling the floor again.

The Turtles were on their own *Survivor* island. They marked all of their charts and made all their calculations on loose-leaf paper. If they wanted a *Wall Street Journal*, they had to buy it. Dennis of course would have paid, but he was a technical trader, not a fundamental guy. There was no reason to study the *Journal* every day.

Think about how many people in 2007 read the *Wall Street Journal* daily from start to finish searching for fundamental insights. Consider how many people scan annual reports or crop reports online. Not the Turtles.

Everything they did was basic. The Turtles would actually write down their orders for the next day and make a carbon copy. They would leave the carbon copy behind, in case they couldn't make it in the next day. That way their orders would still be executed properly. Jim DiMaria laughed, "People don't even know what carbon paper is anymore."

Beyond the day-to-day office idiosyncrasies, the physical locations of the Turtles would soon change dramatically. For that first year they were all in the same office, but after that some left. Mike Cavallo was in the office for one year before he moved home to Boston to continue working for Dennis long distance. Russell Sands was gone after the first year, too—he left the program completely.

Their office environment was slowly changing as time went by. Jim DiMaria said, "At some point, half the people, like Jerry Parker, moved back to Virginia (his home). So those of us Chicago people who wanted to stay, we moved to a smaller office. But the dynamic was gone at that point."

Early on, when everyone was together in Chicago, there were bonding moments as they labored in the trenches with little outside guidance. They were not expert traders out of the gate—far from it. To begin with, almost all the Turtles were in their twenties or late teens. It wasn't long before the first-year class was down 50 percent each on average six months into the program. If you think some of them were panicking, you're right.

Still, out of those early volatile performance swings came personal anecdotes that put their daily grind into perspective. September 1985, for example, was a difficult learning moment. The "Group of Seven" finance ministers made a concerted effort to weaken the U.S. dollar. Over the weekend they changed their policy on the dollar. All of the currencies quickly gapped a couple of hundred points higher. Some of the Turtles were short.

Jeff Gordon, who had exited his positions, remembered that Tom Shanks was still short. He said, "You have to imagine, here we are, managing millions of dollars, we come in [Monday], we have these positions and the market is so much against you. We have large positions, we've just lost a horrendous amount of money, through no fault of our own." Gordon was pointing out that Shanks was following Dennis's rules and that by following those rules exactly, he had incurred significant losses.

Even though the Turtles were given precise rules. Dennis's weakness for discretionary decisions rubbed off on his students. In theory they all had the same rules for selecting markets to trade, when to enter and exit, and how much to buy and sell. However, there were ongoing incidents of exceptions to the rules.

One of those exceptions involved a cocoa trade. Erle Keefer vividly recalled it: "Cocoa is going out the roof. We generated the whole move because we were allowed to add on. We had the whole market. The guys on the floor knew it was Rich's traders, but they just kept the market going. We push it up another ten points and they add on. We are shoving that through the roof and when our buying dried up, the market collapsed. We all got stung hard because honestly we were loaded. Phil Lu was the only one who didn't have any cocoa positions."

During the Turtle program, Dennis had a policy that one day a year all Turtles would individually go to lunch with him. They got to trade with Dennis for the day, so to speak. When Phil Lu came back from his day with Dennis, he thought Dennis was unhappy with him. Dennis wanted to know what caused Lu not to take the cocoa trade. Lu's decision to not take the trade clearly was against how they had been trained.

Lu had a reason. Each day the Turtles had to write down their contingencies for the day. Lu, who never really had the intense trader drive, simply had two pages on his computer listing his if/then contingencies, his buy and sell points, for each market each day, and his second page listed cocoa. It turns out that Lu had a rule that if he had two pages and if a trade wasn't on page one, he wouldn't trade it. Cocoa was on page two for him.

Dennis said, "Why didn't you trade cocoa? What told you?" Lu said, "Oh, I only trade stuff that is on my first page and cocoa wasn't on my first page." Lu thought he saw Dennis's face fall. After all, Dennis, ever the curious skeptic, had hoped he was about to learn something new from one of his students.

Lu's trading was a great example of the imprecision within the Turtle world that could and did lead to different levels of performance. It was the type of incident that showed even though the Turtles were doing exceedingly well trading, there were reasons for differing performance numbers.

Dennis's hiring process loaded the experiment up with real characters. Perhaps the most colorful background of any Turtle was that of Mike Shannon.

At one point I asked Shannon if there was anything else to know about the whole Turtle process. He said bluntly and out of left field, "You know that I was a criminal, right?" Before explaining himself, he said his story deserved a disclaimer. First, his transgressions were twenty-five years ago, and second, he is very anti-drug today. He then explained, "Probably about two or three years before I joined Richard Dennis, I was a drug dealer. I used to control about maybe 80 percent of the drug traffic within the Rush Street nightclub scene in Chicago."

Other Turtles confirmed his account, but this unusual story kept unfolding long into the Turtle program. After he had been working for Dennis for fifteen months or so as a Turtle, Shannon was called to testify in a federal drug case for the government. Dennis found out and called him into the office. Shannon thought he was going to be let go when Dennis reached into his briefcase and pulled out a transcript of the trial. Dennis was stern: "Now look, I am not going to fire you if you tell me the truth. Just tell me the truth, what's going on?" Shannon gave up the whole story about his drug-dealing past and his current side gig working for the FBI. Dennis was shaking his head. "Are you done with *them*?" Shannon had no clue whether they were done with *him*.

Shannon was convinced that Dennis was the reason his problems went away. He said, "I was well into the Turtle program and I was a little profitable as well. I think if I was a marginal trader he might have cut me loose." Shannon said that Dennis's political connections ended his nightmare, adding, "So, I have no criminal record."

Another Turtle said about Dennis's handling of Shannon, "Rich grew up around a lot of pretty tough guys, being in the trading business and everything else. Rich knew that there was always another story. By his nature Rich is an amazingly forgiving person."

Throughout the Turtle blowouts, quirky trading decisions, and a federal narcotics investigation, Dennis treated his people right. On one occasion he flew the entire C&D entourage to Las Vegas to see the rock band Blood, Sweat and Tears (he was a 1970s music aficionado, after all). Even though he might have led an outwardly frugal life, Dennis was generous to everyone he came in contact with.

The Group Dynamic

The Turtles were exposed to ideas with tremendous power, but those ideas did not come without a price. Human nature was always at play. It was one thing to practice applying Dennis and Eckhardt's rules on a blackboard, but learning how the rules performed in live action was critical for confidence.

In this sense, the Turtles' training had unmistakable parallels with the U.S. Army Rangers' training regime. The Rangers work under the assumption that extraordinary performance can't come from rehearsing under ordinary conditions. Elite troops can be forged only from extraordinary challenges that force them to draw upon emotional and physical reserves *they never knew they possessed*. Trading for Dennis was the same. The Turtles had been taught how to handle their worst-case trading scenarios and to feel confident in any trading situation but it wasn't easy.[5]

Gaining confidence, whether Turtle or Ranger, involved a setting. The Turtles were in an empty office learning their way; the Rangers were in a physical training pit learning theirs. Both groups always had the eerie feeling that someone was watching over them. In a way the

Turtles and Rangers were both trapped, though voluntarily. They had signed over their lives to people they didn't know with the expectation that those people would subject them to pain.[6]

Of course, the Turtles did not endure the physical pain of Ranger School, but they certainly endured psychological pain while they gained confidence in their ability to trade. Whether intentional or not, the Turtle office environment fostered a tribelike atmosphere.

And many Turtles saw their group, or tribe, dynamic as crucial while they were in the womb trading Dennis's millions. Erle Keefer felt the psychological need: "The reason we all needed to stay together, especially in the beginning, was we literally made all our money in a normal year in about a three-week period. The rest of the year, most people were down minus 30 percent. And then the markets all clicked in and we had bullets to fire because of Rich's money management scheme. You can go from minus 30 percent down to a plus 150 percent up in three weeks with no trouble at all."

Slaving away together as comrades-in-arms was important because they were getting the crap kicked out of them on a day-to-day basis, with lots of small losses and very little positive reinforcement. When the big trend came it was great, but they still had to patiently wait for it to happen.

Imagine sitting there day after day with a multimillion-dollar trading account funded by a guy who is Chicago's trading royalty. And imagine that the account appears to be slowly dwindling away, little bit by little bit, even though you are doing what you are supposed to do. There was self-doubt. There was concern. The group dynamic helped the Turtles alleviate stress and reassure each other that they were all doing the right thing.

As time passed, though, the Turtles saw Dennis's system making huge amounts of money from big trends. They finally had the psychological assurance of "I know this works in my gut, and you can't take that away from me."

However, even with the tribelike atmosphere, even with the Ranger parallels, even with learning in their guts what it really meant to trade like Dennis, as evidence accumulated, it showed that the group process had ultimately turned out *not* to be significant. That's because the "Turtle trading tribe" was ultimately undermined by an unexpected threat: competition and jealousy. Liz Cheval addressed the rivalry head on when she declared, "At the end of the day, the numbers are there in black and white. Either you made money or you didn't."[7]

The Turtles would soon learn that trading for Dennis over the four-year life of the program was more complicated than the black-and-white world described by Cheval. The Turtle trading experiment was about to become an experiment inside an experiment, with newly confident Turtles just as quickly burdened with self-doubt.

7

Who Got What to Trade

"It's interesting where the truth ultimately ends up. What you read on the front of the newspaper and what really happens can often be the difference between black and white."
Anonymous Turtle in interview

When the Turtles first started working together the atmosphere was pretty carefree. After all, they had been selected and trained by the trading king of Chicago. But their complacency was short lived. In just a few months they became the equivalent of insecure earthlings being analyzed from afar—just like in an old *Twilight Zone* episode. The initial experiment of nature versus nurture was one thing, but now there was another experiment underway, intentional or not.

Money was mother's milk in a Turtle's world. Since without Dennis's money to trade, there would be no Turtle program. But soon the Turtles learned that there was little rhyme or reason when it came to how much money each of them got from Dennis to trade. This was no small matter; it made the difference between making millions or not. Again, the movie *Trading Places* comes to mind, with the scene in which Billy Ray exclaimed, "The whole thing was an experiment, fool! And you and me were the guinea pigs! They made a bet over what would happen to us!"[1]

Sam DeNardo, a first-year-class Turtle, who received a $1 million allocation from Dennis but rationalized away the smaller amounts given to second-year-class Turtles. He thought Dennis figured he didn't need to risk as much with the second-year class: "He started those guys up with different amounts. It would have been nice to know at the time how fast he wanted us to go, how aggressive, or how conservative. I think that was part of what he was trying to discover."

The outside world was hearing that the Turtles had it made in the shade, but behind the scenes Dennis was making unequal allocations to his students. His action created tension within the ranks, but no one was about to complain openly. After all, they, were making more money than they ever had before. Yet being a Turtle was clearly a double-edged sword.

Jeff Gordon, discerned overall friction before allocations even became an issue. He saw some people in the Turtle program as being there only because of a previous acquaintance with Dennis, while others were hired through the ad. Dennis referred to the people who had had a connection with him as a "control group." Gordon said, "They were just chosen for other reasons."

Gordon and several other traders thought the people like him (those who had been hired and screened from the want ads) were superior traders. Dennis thought there was no difference. This was small potatoes to the real office tension to come.

With different amounts of money being allocated, the Turtles started to earn wildly different amounts. Mike Cavallo, for example, was one of the early leaders. He described everyone as doing well initially, but said that then in the spring of 1984 they all got crushed.

At that point, midyear, when the Turtles in the first class were all in the red, Dennis came in and said that they were all trading well. He then increased their equity. This made no sense to the Turtles. They were shocked. They were down big, and Dennis was going to give them more money?

Cavallo could not believe it: "I might have thought he'd say, 'Well, I think the program has been a failure. I'm going to close you down.' Instead, he increased equity especially for a few of us that he thought who were trading the best. I was one [along with] Curt [Faith] and Howard [Seidler]. I guess we were trading the best at that time." The word "best" made little sense when comparing Turtle performance data (see Appendix). They were all going up and down as a group in general.

Over time, however, the ones who perceived unfairness in the disparate allocations became frustrated. Erle Keefer said some Turtles spoke up vociferously about the allocation of money. He recalled, "You've got guys like Curt Faith and Mike Cavallo who go down to minus 50 percent, minus 70 percent and not only are they given a reload, but they're given even more money."

They all sat in the classroom together. They all learned the same rules. They then went to the office together and initially all received the same amount of money to trade. Almost out of the gate everyone started to lose, but some of the biggest losers were given even more money to trade.

Many Turtles thought Dennis was subjectively guessing who was going to be a great trader, as opposed to letting the actual trading results dictate greatness. The rub for many was that Dennis and Eckhardt always argued that trading should be based on true logic. Now some saw Dennis allocating money in a "losing game" fashion, meaning they could not understand why he was not using the scientific method in his trading allocations just the way he had taught the Turtles to do in their trading.

More and more frustration boiled over at how herky-jerky the allocation process had become. In 1986, for example, the money management business as a whole had a very difficult year. Jeff Gordon was quick to point out his success: "I produced plus 65 percent that year without a double-digit drawdown."

How did Dennis reward Gordon in terms of an allocation for the next year? Dennis decreased his allocation and his incentive fee. It seemed to resemble a science experiment: "Add acid to base and note the reaction." However, it was Dennis's game, and he alone had the right to make the rules.

Gordon was frank about his ultimate difference of opinion with Dennis and the eventual outcome: "He didn't like my risk control. Well, he was the guy making the decisions. Did I appreciate that? No, because I knew how I had done. On a reward-to-risk basis I was wiping everybody else out." Dennis's act of lowering Gordon's incentive fee, which no matter his allocation meant less profit, was not interpreted well: "After that I wasn't terribly enthusiastic about remaining in the Turtle program. I wasn't providing Rich what he wanted. I left the program in July of 1987."

But Gordon had a problem, however. Like all Turtles, he had signed a contract to trade exclusively for Dennis for five years. If he quit the program, he could not trade for others. Gordon knew what he was up against. "You didn't want to get into a lawsuit with somebody who has $200 million," he said.

Dennis did not care whether Gordon had a "decent" risk-adjusted return. Dennis wanted big rewards—absolute returns. It is not surprising that Dennis cut Gordon prematurely. Given Dennis's strong philosophical underpinnings ("follow my rules"), and given the fact that Dennis and Gordon had political differences (Gordon supported Hart in the 1984 presidential race, not Mondale), this appeared to be as much about butting heads as about making money.

But Gordon was not alone. Echoing similar concerns, Jim DiMaria addressed allocations as well: "I think the first year [Turtles] were all given the million-dollar trading limits to start. Then in the second year, there were eight of us. I think three were given a million, two were given $600,000, and three were given $300,000. I was one of the $300,000 ones, which is fine. It was still a job. I was a little surprised, but we did get a draw."

Dennis and Eckhardt matched DiMaria's prior $18,000 salary, but the Turtle allocation process was a mystery. DiMaria said, "Everyone sort of believed in 'the market is never wrong' and 'technical versus fundamental,' but then when the money distribution went out, it was like there was no correlation between who got the money and what the performance was."

DiMaria was at the bottom in equity and near the top in performance. That type of discrepancy continued throughout the whole program. Adding fuel to that fire was the common knowledge that, one turtle was soon getting twenty times what others got.

It bears repeating: The Turtles all had the same rules and the same training. At the same time their earnings were based on an incentive structure tied to their total account value, and some Turtles were trading millions while some were trading thousands. That's a formula for internal strife. Conversation after conversation regarding allocations peeled away the rivalries and ill will below the surface.

As time marched on under Dennis's roof, it became apparent that the *one* Turtle who got the largest allocation of all was purportedly not following Dennis's rules as taught. Almost every Turtle brought all discussions back to Curtis Faith, who had perhaps half the money in the program at one point. DiMaria was blunt: "His trading was pretty erratic. He'd have great months, but he took enormous risks to get there."

In 1989, the *Wall Street Journal* described Curtis Faith as "the most successful Turtle." The article included a chart showing the performance numbers of fourteen Turtles, but conspicuously absent from the chart were Faith's performance numbers. Only in the text of the article was there mention of "trading records" showing that Faith made about $31.5 million in profits during the Turtle program.[2]

However, if you look at the big picture this headline was problematic. If Faith was trading the most money, and hence earning the most from incentive fees, then the *Wall Street Journal* was in severe error by saying he was the most "successful" Turtle. To appreciate the imbalance between Faith and the other Turtles, consider an example: Trader "John" is given $20 million to trade and trader "Mary" is given $20,000 to trade. They both get a 15 percent incentive fee and both produce plus 50 percent returns. It can't be said with a straight face that John is unilaterally more successful.

During research, I found a chat forum posting with what appeared to be an inside view of the Turtles' allocations. The post reiterated the $31.5 million that Faith purportedly made, but also said that the entire Turtle group "made around $100 million." This chat forum posting emphasized that Faith had made 30 percent of the total. It concluded with faulty logic, "What Jerry Parker made 5 years later trading a much larger equity base is not relevant."

That posting conveniently left out the critical fact that Faith was trading upward of twenty times the equity base of other Turtles. In other words, Faith made more because he was trading more. But there are no performance numbers demonstrating that he was the best-performing Turtle.

However, as long as the risk Faith was taking was within the parameters, this was not considered a big deal. DiMaria was quick to correct that view: "No, not within the parameters. That was sort of the standing joke. There were parameters and then there were Curtis parameters. He just got to do whatever he wanted. It's as if the whole thing was decided on 'who knows what?' criteria. Who were going to be the good traders and who weren't? And returns be damned. It was totally fundamental. It was, 'Mike Cavallo, he's like the smartest guy in the program. We got to give him a lot of money.' I was at the other end of the spectrum. Maybe because I was a control person and they thought I wasn't going to be anything."

Faith saw it differently, saying there was a certain amount of variability when they were taught the S1 and S2 trading systems. He saw his subjective choices as key to his success. Faith was also the most openly competitive in his public statements about his experience. It could be that when Faith said he wanted to beat everyone in the room, he was motivated by his lack of a college degree (Jehovah's witnesses do not advocate college as part of their religions practice). Or he simply may have had a healthy "I will show them" chip on his shoulder.

At first blush, DiMaria's initial comments could have been "sour grapes." However, they weren't made purely out of self-interest; he saw other Turtles getting the short end of the allocation stick. He said, "George Svoboda was an absolute genius and probably had the potential to be the best trader of all and might be." However, as the program went on, many Turtles saw that the correlation between trading success and the amount of money they were given by Dennis as not very good.

Yet DiMaria added, "I think at the end of the first year I was one of the top performers, if not the top performer. My bonus was like $10,000 when other people were getting $600,000. I had a kid and all and it was tough. It was very, very difficult."

Twenty years later, the regret of not being given the opportunity to trade a larger account for Dennis still comes across in DiMaria's voice. There was a touch of Rodney Dangerfield's "no respect." However, it is worth noting that today DiMaria has a continuous month-by-month track record dating back to 1988. That's a twenty year track record in stark contrast to Faith's lack of performance numbers over the last 20 years.

While many Turtles like DiMaria thought Dennis was playing favorites, Mike Cavallo bluntly disagreed. He thought allocations were all performance driven. In 1984, Dennis decided that trading grains wasn't worth his time anymore. He gave those grain accounts to Howard Seidler, Faith, and Cavallo to trade.

Talk about even more tension. Everyone in the room knew about these grain accounts. They all knew they created the potential for trading much larger, with the chance to earn much more through incentive fees. Cavallo agreed: "I would say, sure there was some jealousy. I think it's just human nature. People are in this great job that's so much better than anything they've ever done, so much fun, and so lucrative, and who are now making six-figure incomes for the first time, get jealous of the people making seven-figure incomes."

Although no one knew to the penny what other Turtles were making, it was obvious some were trading much more money than others. Everyone was worth basically the same when the Turtles started. Then, within eighteen months to two years, a few Turtles were millionaires and many were not, but all the while everyone was generating very similar returns. This was tension personified.

Cavallo also saw more than just allocation issues at play. He witnessed some Turtles who were less confident in their trading. There were Turtles actually imitating other Turtles. He saw a few trying to piggyback others' trading orders.

However, in the end, it all kept coming back to allocations. For instance Jerry Parker was not happy about being allocated such a small amount either. Parker thought he was trading just as well as the Turtles who were getting the big allocations. The performance numbers support that. At one point in 1986, Parker was trading $4.2 million for Dennis. Then, in 1987, he was trading $1.4 million. Parker made plus 124 percent for 1986 and plus 36 percent for 1987.

Erle Keefer said that politics was the reason why Parker received smaller allocations from Dennis. Keefer said that Parker believed that, too. He said, "Jeff Gordon and Jerry are the political polar opposites of Rich. Jerry was about the biggest polar [opposite]."

Dennis was giving positive reinforcement in the form of larger allocations not only to Turtles who were willing to take bigger risks, but also apparently to those with whom he had become closer friends. Parker was a Republican. Obviously, he wasn't Dennis's favorite Turtle.

Parker may have been the first Turtle hired, but Dennis was still a human being. Keefer added, "He still had his favorites. Curt was a favorite. Mike Cavallo was a favorite. Then you look at some other people and you say, 'Why did they get less money?' Maybe they just didn't want to pull the trigger on big numbers?"

Parker was by no means the only Turtle whose allocation was cut back after big performance runs. Many other Turtles with seriously eye-popping performance had their money under management slashed. Liz Cheval, Paul Rabar, and Mike Carr all had their allocations cut.

The fear of not knowing what to expect next was a constant in the Turtles lives. Turtles would get calls without explanation to increase or decrease 20 percent of their account size. They scratched their heads, wondering what was going on. Some Turtles joked that perhaps they were in a cruel psychological experiment. Others seriously considered the possibility that they were being filmed like Jim Carrey in the *Truman Show.*

Mike Cavallo, who viewed the allocation process as a meritocracy, did end up having some questions, too. He thought Dennis was partly awarding trading aggressiveness, placing bigger bets with Turtles he thought were trading better, but even Cavallo could not understand Dennis's decision-making logic when it came to Faith. He said, "It seemed like Curt was trading too aggressively and too riskily and yet was getting rewarded for it. He was making the most, although probably not on a risk-adjusted basis. So at the time, it was just sort of puzzling. I'm not particularly a jealous person, so I wasn't too worried about it."

Cavallo knew Dennis had become very successful as a very young man by taking big risks. The implication was that Faith was Dennis's chosen one. Others said the C&D brain trust were enamored with the fact that Faith was so young.

It became increasingly apparent that the whole subject of allocations issues was just an entry into the central sticky issue of the program: favoritism. The disparity began almost out of the gate. There was a heating oil trade only weeks after the Turtles' initial training in 1984. The Turtles were supposed to be trading much smaller sizes. They were supposed to be trading "one lots" or just one futures contract.

Faith apparently traded much larger and made more money than all of the other Turtles. Cavallo thought Faith had exceeded what they were allowed to trade, but he also thought an arguably reckless or "go for the jugular" attitude may have elevated him in Dennis's eyes.

It kept coming across loud and clear from assorted Turtles: Faith's trading didn't reflect what they'd been taught. Cavallo, the Harvard MBA, was brutally honest: "It wasn't at all what we were taught. In fact, you could say it was slightly counter to what we were taught." Even though Cavallo was making millions and was easily considered a top-grossing Turtle at the time, the fact that Dennis gave more and more money to Faith perplexed him. Cavallo had no ax to grind in talking about Faith. In fact, years later he served on the board of directors of a firm Faith had started.

Why was Cavallo concerned about Faith's style of trading? He worried that Faith was risking so much that he could ultimately be ruined (as in mathematical risk of ruin). From that first day of class Eckhardt had pressed home the point of managing risk, but many Turtles saw it almost immediately being ignored by one of their own.

DiMaria, who was only eighteen months older than Faith, saw everyone playing by the rules during the program except Faith. He said, "That would go to position sizing, markets traded . . . he was the special boy wonder. So he could do things that the rest of us couldn't. He probably doesn't realize that. Did he have special rules ahead of the game, or did he change the game and then ask if those new rules were okay?"

Jeff Gordon was the first to broach Faith's religion. He said, "Curtis was a Jehovah's Witness. A person of faith, a religious person, someone who you'd think would have morals. I am not saying that Curtis does not have morals or religious convictions. But when it came to handling Richard Dennis's money, Curt could have cared less if he lost it all. That's how he conducted himself. The fact of the matter is, in retrospect that appears to be what Rich wanted. Rich wanted people who would be really aggressive."

The most remembered and controversial trade in the program was that 1984 heating oil trade. All the Turtles were trading $100,000 in the first month, and Faith made much more money pyramiding than the others. Dennis loved it. Gordon was shocked: "It was actually kind of strange because Curtis started getting personal calls from Rich, and he would come in the morning and say, 'Hello, well Rich and I were talking last night and he said, 'da da da.' Nobody else was getting these calls."

Faith saw the 1984 heating oil trade differently, saying that he bought three futures contracts per the rules and quickly added the maximum twelve contracts he was allowed. Heating oil went straight up, and all of the Turtles had big profits.[3]

But Faith, said he saw something odd in the other Turtles' trading. He said he was the only Turtle to have "on" a full position. It was Faith's view that every single other Turtle had decided for some reason to not trade the system as Dennis and Eckhardt had taught them. He wondered if they had even been in the same class with him.[4]

Because this was a very volatile trade, the price of heating oil soon plummeted. The Turtles began to exit. Faith believed that the right thing to do was to hold on (and not exit) as heating oil dropped. Soon it began to rise again, surpassing the previous high. Faith was apparently the only Turtle with all twelve contracts "long." He said, "We had all been taught exactly the same thing but my return for January was three times or more than the best of the other Turtles."[5]

Mike Cavallo and Russell Sands both reinforced the point that Faith had a helping hand that other Turtles did not have. They said Dennis guided Faith at the liquidation point on this trade. It appeared that Faith was in a special "no fail" setup to which the other Turtles were not privy.

Was all of this tension designed by Dennis just to see how other Turtles would react? Or was Faith getting extra ongoing instruction because he and Dennis had become friends?

Mike Shannon connected the dots in very human terms: "I think some of the Turtles had different motivations for doing what they did. I did it because I just found at the end of the day, I just truly enjoyed the experience. You take guys like Jim Kenney and Anthony Bruck, I think their view was a little bit more artistic. Curt Faith, on the other hand, was driven by his father. His father was a Jehovah's Witness and he had to pay a tithing to the church. It was like his dad was a stage mom almost . . . [He] would come up and we'd look at this guy and some of their beliefs are just a little bit off the wall."

Now, Mike Shannon was no angel, but his words revealed a real-world picture of the goings-on in the office. The bottom line: Given the millions Faith was trading, given the clear allocation discrepancies, given the clear discontent, this drama over allocations and extra assistance was just as much a part of being a Turtle as the rules they were taught.

Shannon was sympathetic when he described the situation: "[Curtis] made no secret of it. Look, he wasn't running around giving us copies of [Jehovah's Witness brochures] or anything bizarre like that . . . He was pretty upfront about it. He would say, 'The church I belong to and blah, blah, blah and all that.' "

Perhaps Richard Dennis had become a father figure for the young Faith. Shannon added, "Rich really likes Curt a lot."

The Performance

The personal and perhaps subjective descriptions of what was taking place are fascinating, but the bottom line is performance data. Sol Waksman of Barclays Performance Reporting was the only person I could find with copies of the Turtles' month-by-month performance while they were under Dennis's umbrella.

Table 7.1: Annual Turtle Performance.

	1984	1985	1986	1987
Mike Cavallo	14%	100%	34%	111%
Jerry Parker	−10%	129%	124%	37%
Liz Cheval	−21%	52%	134%	178%
Stig Ostgaard	20%	297%	108%	87%
Jeff Gordon	32%	82%	51%	11%
Mike Carr	24%	46%	78%	49%
Jim Melnick	102%	42%	160%	46%
Howard Seidler	16%	100%	96%	80%

	1985	1986	1987
Phil Lui	132%	129%	78%
Tom Shanks	18%	170%	146%
Jim DiMaria	71%	132%	97%
Brian Proctor	55%	116%	185%
Paul Rabar	92%	126%	78%
Mike O'Brien	99%	135%	78%

Source: Barclays Performance Reporting (www.barclaygrp.com).

Nothing illustrates the life of a Turtle while working for Richard Dennis better than the monthly ups and downs of the raw performance numbers. Consider the performance of three Turtles, Mike Cavallo, Jerry Parker, and Liz Cheval, during 1985 (more Turtle performance numbers are in the appendix).

Table 7.2: 1985 Month-by-Month Performance for Mike Cavallo, Jerry Parker, and Liz Cheval.

Date	Mike Cavallo ROR	Jerry Parker ROR	Liz Cheval ROR
Jan-85	24.45%	2.51%	26.70%
Feb-85	−12.49%	18.92%	23.07%
Mar-85	55.73%	−8.77%	−20.29%
Apr-85	−15.39%	−20.38%	−27.80%
May-85	4.50%	17.52%	72.49%
Jun-85	2.50%	−10.30%	−22.48%
Jul-85	53.75%	61.05%	29.21%
Aug-85	−20.62%	1.18%	−18.77%
Sep-85	−34.21%	11.25%	−26.93%
Oct-85	−5.09%	14.61%	−6.60%
Nov-85	39.52%	20.99%	46.98%
Dec-85	22.82%	−2.46%	20.04%

VAMI (Value Added Monthly Index): An index that tracks the monthly performance of a hypothetical $1,000 investment as it grows over time.
ROR: Rate of return.
Source: Barclays Performance Reporting (www.barclaygrp.com).

I found the omission odd that Sol Waksman did not have Curtis Faith's numbers from inside the Turtle program. Faith said that his performance numbers were not available because he never constructed an approved track record for his years trading Dennis's money, preventing him from giving his exact Turtle performance numbers.[6]

However, how was it even possible that Faith could be trading so much more money than other Turtles? Dennis had a lot of money, but not an infinite amount. Other Turtles said money was being taken from their accounts and given to Faith's account.

Interestingly, once Faith's account got really big, things apparently went south. One Turtle saw Faith losing much of his gains in a 1987 silver trade; it was his contention that all of the money Faith had ever made for Dennis may have been lost on that one trade.

Other Turtles talked about this silver trade, too. One said that Faith didn't exactly follow the system because he had "gotten a feel for it." When silver finally spiked down from a big run-up, he saw Faith as the last trader actually trying to exit.

Faith admitted that he was in error. In the EliteTrader.com chat forum, he said it was his single worst mistake trading: "I was holding 1,200 contracts of Comex Silver, yep the 5,000 ouncers for 6,000,000 ounces for Richard Dennis's account. This along with 500 contracts of Comex Gold. Rode it all the way up and almost all the way down accounting for a whopping −65 percent drawdown in the account. The equity swing on the high-move day for the account from the high to the low was something ridiculous, like $14 million."

At the end of the day there was no way to verify the exact amount Faith lost on that silver trade, and there was no way to verify Faith's exact $31.5 million profit figure while working for Dennis either. In trying to do so, I talked with reporter Stanley Angrist who wrote that 1989 *Wall Street Journal* article nearly twenty years ago. He told me that he had no way to verify Faith's earnings. He received that $31.5 million number from Faith himself.

While this silver trade may have been one of the final behind-the-scenes sagas within the Turtle experiment, it certainly wasn't the last one. Once the idea of taking too much risk and not following rules was on the table, it was as though a dam broke. David Cheval, Liz Cheval's former husband, saw more than one Turtle in the first year ignore the rules and take excessive risk. He said, "I also believe that Rich increased the stake of several traders because they blew out the initial stake — not necessarily because they were the top traders."[7]

Curtis Faith disagreed saying that it wasn't really possible to blow out the initial stake. He said that if the Turtles lost 50 percent on a closed trade basis they would not have money to trade."[8] Fifty percent was not a cutoff point. Turtles clearly breached that, and the data proves it. However, when it comes to allocations there will always be a mystery, with assorted inconsistencies as everyone protects their real or perceived reputations twenty years later.

That said, the allocation story had an ending. Sam DeNardo zeroed back in on allocations as he saw the second-year group of Turtles becoming destabilized. They were concentrating a lot on "How come you got $50,000 where I got $200,000?" or "Why did you get $600,000?" He saw them worried that they had done something wrong in Dennis's eyes. DeNardo even tried to ease tensions by writing Dennis a letter to warn him that there was destabilization in the Turtle ranks. "They were fighting amongst each other," he said.

Keefer also sent a brief letter to Dennis questioning his allocation formula. He believed that if Dennis had done nothing more than give an equal allocation to all Turtles, for example $5 million, he would have made much more money. He said, "I'm quite certain that it didn't endear me to Rich a whole lot when I wrote the paper saying, 'Here's how the logic of asset allocation should be in this kind of a game.'"

Keefer, who thought Dennis deserved a Nobel prize for his real-world work in harnessing volatility in his trading models, lamented the allocations aspect of the program: "You've got somebody that's got an awesome trading system and he's following really rigidly good protocols about trend trading and then he just literally blows it up on asset allocation."

It was DeNardo, however, who got punished for questioning allocations—he got cut from the program. Dennis interpreted his letter as trying to make excuses for his losses. DeNardo said he followed the rules, but not always: "I remembered buying sugar when I should have been selling it. I just said, heck, 'I'll buy some.' Well, I get called in for that. 'You shouldn't do that. It's counter trend.' Well, I never did it again. Let me tell you, *they knew what you were doing.*"

The Memo

While Dennis and Eckhardt always knew what the Turtles were doing, it turned out that the two mentors didn't always know what *they* were doing. During all that downtime of waiting for the markets to trend, four Turtles from the second class (Tom Shanks, Paul Rabar, Erle Keefer, and Jiri "George" Svoboda) formed a small group to do trading research. They wanted to validate their rules instead of just playing by them.

While the rest of the Turtles may have been reading the sports pages and playing Ping-Pong, this group spent their time building a systems testing platform. Doing that took them a year. The results of their research project shook the program. They determined that Dennis had everyone taking far too much risk.

The Turtles had all been trading according to rules taught by Dennis and Eckhardt and were making millions, but the research team, using original Apple computers, blended the S1 and S2 trading systems (see chapters 4 and 5) together and found that instead of a worst-case −50 percent drawdown, they were consistently getting a worst-case −80 percent drawdown.

Paul Rabar intuitively figured out the problem occurred when both systems (S1 and S2) got the entry breakout signal at the same time. At that moment they were putting on too much risk.

Dale Dellutri had somewhat arrogantly always said to the Turtles, "If you guys ever invent anything bring it to us." Dellutri was clear that he never really expected that to happen, so turning over this new research was going to be a delicate matter. Dennis and Eckhardt's attitude was, "We know this trading cave, and we know it better than anyone else." And given the success they had had, why not think that way?

However, the research team had determined the guys in the cave were off by a factor of 100 percent, and they told Dellutri. Soon afterward, Dellutri came out and ordered everyone to reduce their position sizes by 50 percent going forward.

On the heels of Dellutri's order came the official memo from Dennis dated April 23, 1986. It said:

Real-world drawdowns far in excess of theoretically expected values have caused us to reassess the linkage between theory and fact regarding how big to trade. It seems that we have misconstrued the theoretical data so that you have been trading as much as twice as big as we thought. The good news is that this has been true throughout the whole trading program—your profits were doubled, but at the cost of a doubling of the risk. We must be living right.[9]

Dennis went on to reiterate what Dellutri had already told them: They would soon have to cut back their trading by 50 percent. He wanted to turn the Turtles' risk-taking back to what they expected it to be when they started the program. While this order did not change the rules for the Turtles, it meant they would be trading less money now. Instead of trading a $1 million account, they now traded that account as if it were a $500,000 account. Essentially, they were just massively de-leveraged.

Egos must have been bruised when those four Turtles beat Dennis and Eckhardt at their own game. They had been trading by these rules for years, teaching them to others, making millions, and then suddenly their trainees proved the rules were wrong. However, even after the cutback in their leverage, the Turtles kept performing. This was tension.

Some Turtles thought there was a certain side of Dennis that felt as if he had created a bunch of Frankensteins ("My God, I'm competing against the people I trained!"). To top it off, during this period the Turtles were actually outperforming Dennis as a group.

Many Turtles thought they were doing better because they'd been taught good habits. Some thought Dennis had kept bad habits from the days when he was in the pit. Mike Shannon added, "He would not get angry, but he'd become hyper-critical about the certain execution of trades that would make sense if you're standing in the pit, but really wasn't as hyper-relevant if you were trading off the floor. He was always worried about 'skid' and we certainly were concerned about it as well." But for some reason, not getting great fills on his trades (what the industry calls "skid") was an ongoing (and perhaps irrational) bone of contention for Dennis.

For a man who taught logic and the scientific method to his students, it was amazing to hear that he worried too much about arguably inconsequential issues. He may have been feeling the tension when he once wondered outloud if he had a fatal pressure point: "I really am a contrarian at heart, and that's really probably not good if you're a mechanical trend follower."[10]

Bad omen.

8

Game Over

"If Rich would not have traded against our positions, which I know
he did at times, he'd have made even more money."
Anonymous Turtle from interview

In early 1988, the big political news was that the Soviet Red Army was
withdrawing from Afghanistan. In the business arena, Kohlberg Kravis
Roberts & Co. had just completed their then record leveraged buyout
of RJR Nabisco (surpassed only in February 2007 by Blackstone Group's
purchase of Equity Office). The Turtles had their own current event to
deal with when Dennis suddenly pulled the plug.

It was over. Dennis sent a fax telling the Turtles that the program
had been scuttled. Dennis, who was managing money for clients, too,
had two public funds with Michael Milken's Drexel Burnham Lam-
bert. They closed down with big losses. The reason for the Turtle program shutdown has never been officially defined, but Dennis's
performance numbers painted a sobering picture:

The game changed for Dennis when his losses were 55 percent in
April 1988. Not only was his public fund performance beyond terrible;
his father had recently died. One Turtle attributed the program's clo-
sure to "family issues." They were tough times for sure. However, April
was not a terribly tough performance month for the Turtles. They typically lost 10 to 12 percent each for that month (see Appendix). Their
losses were nowhere near the size of Dennis's losses.

That said, the shock of having the plug pulled threw the Turtles for
a loop. Jim DiMaria was bewildered at the Turtle program's abrupt
ending: "All of a sudden it's over. That's how fast it was. They came in
Monday morning and said, 'Friday, we're done.' I was like, 'Oh, better
get a job.' " Some argued that his heavy losses forced Dennis out of the
game, but DiMaria said personal trading losses didn't force his hand.

Table 8.1: Richard Dennis Trading Performance:
January 1986–December 1988.

Date	VAMI	ROR	Yearly ROR	Amount Size
Sep-87	7343	−15.29%		$159.2M
Oct-87	6330	−13.79%		
Nov-87	6474	2.28%		
Dec-87	6572	1.51%	16.12%	$135.9M
Jan-88	6736	2.49%		
Feb-88	6635	−1.49%		
Mar-88	6623	−0.19%		$113.0M
Apr-88	2948	−55.49%		
May-88	2977	0.98%		
Jun-88	3009	1.10%		$40.0M

VAMI (Value Added Monthly Index): An index that tracks the monthly performance of a hypothetical $1,000 investment as it grows over time.
ROR: Rate of return.
Source: Barclays Performance Reporting (www.barclaygrp.com).

DiMaria said that it was Dennis's money, and he just didn't want to do it anymore.[1] Other Turtles said in no uncertain terms that the program was ended as a consequence of the Drexel meltdown.

Dennis himself simply declared that he was retiring. He announced that he would move full time into political causes. He wanted to take the wind out of what he thought were efforts to make "liberal" a dirty word. He quickly plunged headlong into libertarianism. To him, libertarian ideals, which stressed individual rights, were a tonic for society. However, others were not buying his political posturing. They felt the big trading losses had pushed him into politics.

When it came to discussing his rocky trading for the Drexel funds, Dennis laid partial blame on his clients. They did not understand the nature of his trading style and when the drawdowns started, they lost faith in him. He could never understand why his clients (either now or back in the early 1980s) lacked his steely resolve. He also wondered why Drexel's administrative people let him down. When they came to see him he said, "What the hell are you doing?" As a floor trader, Dennis had been down more than 50 percent a few times. He asked Drexel, "Didn't anyone tell these people what they were getting into?"[2]

Clearly, the marketing people sold only the "good times" to the clients invested in the Dennis-managed Drexel funds. That said, Dennis was the trader; he was the one with whom the buck stopped, not the brokers selling him to the masses. However, the Drexel fund's troubles did not immediately discourage the former "Prince of the Pit." He was confident even at his worst moment: "What should give investors confidence is the overall record I've compiled in my 18-year career."[3] An eighteen-year track records mean little to clients when you lose 55 percent in one month.

Drexel executives have proved perennially unwilling to comment on the chain of events that led to the unraveling of Dennis's fund back in 1988. Former Drexel executive Richard Sandor had a good natured response to me when I asked if he would comment on what happened; he said "not in a million years." Not a surprising reaction from one of the more prominent names in Chicago trading.

However, Dennis himself was not as reticent, and he addressed his hard times head on: "I wouldn't trade a public fund now even if it were a cure for cancer."[4] He was angry. He felt the risks of trading with him were fully disclosed in printed materials, and said, "I found out the hard way, by going through the courts that disclosure documents tend not to mean anything. The way our court system is structured, you can make ignorance work to your advantage, by saying, 'I didn't understand the risks and this shouldn't have happened.' "[5]

For someone famous for being sanguine about losses, it was surprising to hear Dennis voice frustration. Many had no sympathy. He was once the boy wonder. He was the guy who'd made hundreds of millions. He was the guy giving money to politicians to spread his influence. His career competitors, those he won money from in the zero-sum game, were not feeling his pain.

Lawsuits soon followed as his former clients in the Drexel funds argued that Dennis had deviated from his own rules. Eventually, U.S. District Judge Milton Pollack agreed to a settlement in which nearly six thousand investors shared $2.5 million and got half of Dennis's trading profits over the next three years. Under the settlement, Dennis and his firms did not admit any wrongdoing.[6]

Even in the midst of losing and being understandably angry about nonstop lawsuits, Chicago's living legend still managed to wax philosophical about what he was going through: "The sad truth is the legal system is so porous that even reflections of things gone and settled have liability that they shouldn't. If I say one day I had a headache and didn't take an aspirin, I guess someone could call me into court for that." Dennis believed that at any time, the vast majority of trading results were determined by uncontrollable factors. He felt that was the case in this period.[7]

Uncontrollable? Dennis's students did not lose 50 percent in April 1988; he did. While followers of Dennis routinely thought his Turtles were an overly risky group because of his trading record, the Turtles' trading strategy was *not* the same strategy their teacher was using. His losses were not the result of pure trend-following trading, and there is no way to know exactly what he was doing differently.

Larry Hite, a founding father in the hedge fund industry and someone at the beginning of the now multibillion-dollar British-based Man hedge fund, wasn't sure what Dennis was doing at the time. He said that Dennis's trading did not make sense, since there was no one market move that should have caused his losses.

Like Hite, David Cheval appreciated what Dennis had been through but questioned his decision-making at a time when his peers were doing quite well: "The fact that Richard Dennis made a fortune from a small opening stake is admirable. The issue is whether he followed his system when he took public money. I believe his drawdowns and volatility were far in excess of those experienced by the Turtles during the same period. Trust me, I admire what Richard Dennis achieved. However, I do believe he is human and open to criticism."[8]

Mike Shannon, who was there to witness the chaos, was alarmed along with other Turtles at Dennis's risk-taking. Shannon said that the Turtles always knew what Dennis's positions were because of position limits. The Commodity Futures Trading Commission (CFTC) had limits designed to keep any one trader from trading too much of any one market.

However, there was another reason for the Turtles' knowledge of

Dennis's trading positions: He was an open book. When Dennis was trading the Drexel funds, Shannon said the Turtles were allowed to trade one, possibly two, units of the S&P 500 stock index. Shannon said Dennis was trading ten or fifteen units of S&Ps. He said the Turtles couldn't figure out why Dennis was overtrading when he had stressed time and time again that overtrading would kill you: "We calculated one day that his risk was probably one hundred times greater than the risk we were taking."

That Dennis was possibly taking risks over and above his Turtles by a factor of 100 simply made no sense. He knew enough to make his students do the right thing, but had a difficult time disciplining *himself*. Both his achievements *and* shortcomings were in plain sight.

Amazingly, even though Dennis was losing money on his own trading decisions, his Turtle trading hedge, in the form of his students' great performance, was keeping him in the black. How much money did he make off of the Turtles' trading over those four years? He did not blink, in answering, "Tons. I think they grossed $150 million and we made $110 million. We started out paying them ten percent. Why not? Why give them a lot—it was our money, we took all the risk."[9]

However, while Dennis was bowing out of the game, his Wall Street fame was about to skyrocket thanks to a new book that featured top traders ranging from Bruce Kovner to Ed Seykota to Larry Hite to Paul Tudor Jones.

In the book *Market Wizards*, author Jack Schwager softened the blow to Dennis's tough times by entitling his chapter "A Legend Retires." Schwager's Dennis chapter became a cult classic. He may already have been an underground legend, but this chapter minted the Dennis legend to a whole new audience right at the rockiest time of his career.

With his fame greater than ever, Dennis hit the speaking circuit. He was invited to make appearances at assorted investment conferences. Not since the 1970s had so many people wanted a piece of him. Now that everyone had read *Market Wizards*, they had visions of being selected for the next Turtle class—even if none were scheduled.

Charles Faulkner met Dennis around this time at a Chicago Board of Trade conference in Chicago. He said, "When I read Dennis was appearing on a panel moderated by Jack Schwager, I immediately bought tickets. I had been thinking a lot about what made it hard for traders to follow their system."

Faulkner saw Dennis being treated like a rockstar. Would-be Turtles mobbed him as he left the stage. Faulkner observed that Dennis was wary with so many people wanting something from him.

Later that evening Faulkner was introduced briefly to Dennis. Faulkner, a close observer of human nature, who would himself be profiled in the second *Market Wizards* book, was struck by Dennis's appearance: "I was close enough to notice that his face had the look of someone who was having a tough time of it and generally not taking care of himself. This got me to wondering about what the non-academic, not 'hard work,' requirements might be for successful trading. For here was someone whose success was costing him dearly."

Whether or not Dennis needed a break from the most tumultuous time of his life, his Turtles had graduated. It was time to see if they could continue to win at the game without their teacher. This would be the real life experiment and with no Richard Dennis safety net.

9

Out on Their Own

"The biggest conspiracy has always been the fact that there is no conspiracy. Nobody's out to get you. Nobody gives a shit whether you live or die. There, you feel better now?"

Dennis Miller, comedian

Fame is a drug. It distorts perspective. The movie *Trading Places*, a firestarter for the Turtle experiment, addresses fame when Eddie Murphy's character, Billy Ray Valentine, makes the transition from street hustler to successful speculator.

Jettisoned into the lap of luxury, he is enjoying the good life, reflecting on his fortune while smoking a cigar and reading a *Wall Street Journal* article about *himself*. Coleman, his butler, peers at him admiringly and remarks how well he has done in only three weeks. Billy Ray thinks about it: "Three weeks? Is that all? You know, I can't even remember what I used to do before all this happened to me." His butler smiles back and says, "All you needed was a chance.[1]

The Turtles were also given a chance, but in a heartbeat the security of trading Dennis's millions was gone. One minute they were trading for a moneymaking god and the next minute they were literally on the Street. As it turns out, some of the Turtles foresaw job insecurity with Dennis and were preparing their own version of C&D Commodities. Others were on cruise control, unaware that life under Dennis's cushy umbrella was about to end.

Jim DiMaria regretted the ending, saying that he thought all of the Turtles would have stayed if Dennis had kept the program going. He said, "I would never have left. Unless they made it that I couldn't make money somehow." Mike Cavallo agreed that it had been one great gig, but also said that Dennis shut the program down ultimately due to problems he had incurred from the 1987 stock crash. (Dennis's April 1988 performance was a big reason, too.)

However, just because Dennis pulled the plug on the Turtle program didn't mean his students were headed back to obscurity. Instead, they became Wall Street's newest rockstars. The phenomenon of students surpassing their teacher may not have been envisioned when Dennis created the Turtles, but it is not uncommon in other areas of life. The ascension of assistant coaches from winning sports teams to head coach happens all the time. Winning rubs off, and people want a piece of winners who have associated with even bigger winners.

Clearly, if Dennis had anticipated the Turtles (as a group) would make hundreds of millions of dollars trading for clients after working for him, he never would have shut down the program. Yet how could he have known that once his students were out of school, Turtle-mania would hit? Maybe he should have known. Other trend-following traders were doing well at the time. They were raising millions to trade, without the snap, crackle, pop of the Turtle story.

In fact the Turtles as a group, along with Michael O'Brien, who had long raised client money for Dennis to trade, saw an opportunity in the whole being greater than the sum of its parts. The Turtles were going to use O'Brien as a broker to set up a Turtle fund. They met to discuss trading as a group, but could not agree on the split. Egos were on full display.

Mike Shannon said that since they were probably "the best traders on the planet at the time," it all went to the heads of some Turtles. Some thought they were better than others. However, the Turtles' performance numbers while working for Dennis did not show great performance differences on average.

That said, while most of the Turtles were confused about what to do next, one of them clearly saw the writing on the wall. Jerry Parker went back to Virginia to start figuring out a trading business on his own. One Turtle thought Parker was a "traitor" for going solo so fast when a Turtle fund idea was on the table. But the name of the game was survival.

Parker's desire to go at it alone was the final demise of any effort to create a single Turtle fund. The collective disappointment could be heard in one Turtle's resigned tone: "It never worked out. It should have; it would have been one of the greatest superfunds in history."

Quickly, most of the Turtles filed with the government to trade for clients. Anthony Bruck, Michael Carr, Michael Cavallo, Elizabeth Cheval, Sam DeNardo, Jim DiMaria, Jeff Gordon, Erle Keefer, Philip Lu, Stig Ostgaard, Jerry Parker, Brian Proctor, Paul Rabar, Russell Sands, Howard Seidler, Tom Shanks, Michael Shannon, and Craig Soderquist all had dreams of running the next C&D Commodities. Curtis Faith did not continue trading, saying that he was now *retired* at twenty-three.

Turtles in *The Market Wizards*

While the idea of a group Turtle fund died a quick death, Turtle fame on Wall Street began rolling. When Jack Schwager wrote *The Market Wizards* (1989) and its follow-up, *The New Market Wizards* (1992), his chapters on Richard Dennis and the Turtles made the Turtle experiment accessible to many for the first time.

However, Schwager's Turtle chapter ended up being about the fact that the Turtles kept saying, "No comment." He even titled it "Silence of the Turtles" because they all refused to talk substance with him.

Nondisclosure agreements were one reason why the Turtles wouldn't talk, but another just as significant reason was that they were afraid too much publicity about their techniques would hurt their returns. Just the opposite happened. Their protective stance of "no comment" created an aura of mystery, even if this was unintended. It seemed that everyone who had heard of the Turtles wanted some of their money managed by them. The time was right to capitalize on their good fortune.

They all pursued that good fortune in different ways. Paul Rabar said the key was to get to Wall Street as soon as possible so they knew the Turtles after Dennis were alive, so to speak. Jerry Parker, however, stayed far away from Wall Street, heading to Richmond, Virginia, to explore ventures with Russell Sands. Sands had been trading in Kidder Peabody's Richmond office. It was a good place to be, as Kidder had access to clients interested in traders like Sands and Parker. One Turtle remarked about Kidder Peabody's operations there, "It was two guys sitting down there traveling around the world trying to raise Middle East money to trade. They had office space down there that they had given to Sands and he had been trading their money."

Most Turtles, however, were essentially one-man road shows. For example, when Paul Rabar first started out, people who wanted to invest with him would ask how he traded. Rabar said that if they wanted to invest, they could give him their money. Period. No questions asked. Potential investors would have to meet him at the airport. Some investors probably walked away from what could be perceived as his arrogance, but without a doubt, many were smitten by Rabar's "take it or leave it" attitude. There is a fine line between confidence and arrogance, and Rabar walked it with great success.

Russell Sands and Jerry Parker initially walked that fine line together. Sands, in a classic small-world story, knew Kidder Peabody broker Kevin Brandt from college at NYU. Parker called Sands to ask if he would introduce him to some Wall Street people (read: brokers to help raise money to trade). Since the two guys at Kidder Peabody in Richmond were Sands's friends, he quickly introduced Parker. Sands added, "The guys at Kidder Peabody basically looked at Jerry when they met him and they looked at me and said, 'You guys will make a pretty good team together. If you [set up a firm], we'll give you some seed money to get started.' That's how Chesapeake Capital got started."

Making Dennis's Rules Less "Risky"

With the skids greased by Jack Schwager and the *Wall Street Journal*, all the Turtles should have been able to land on their feet. Yet one of the decisions each Turtle had to make was whether to trade at the level of risk they had been taught by Dennis or dial it back to make it more palatable for clients (go look at the volatility of the Turtle month-by-month numbers again in the Appendix). They had all just witnessed Dennis's Drexel blowup, so theirs was rightful concern.

Jerry Parker, it turns out, was the first Turtle who figured out the importance of using less leverage to appeal to investors, saying, "The bigger the trade the greater the returns and the greater the drawdowns. It's a double-edged sword."[2] At the same time, the Turtle adventure was the learning experience that pushed Parker to reassess leverage choices:

> I lost 60% in one day, although we were still up 140% at the end of the day. I was probably managing $2 million when the program ended in 1988. When I started Chesapeake, I was sure it was not a good idea to lose 60% in one day. So I compromised on my risk, traded smaller, and tried for 20% a year.[3]

Using a ton of leverage (even if it was well thought out) was the reason for huge swings in the Turtles' performance. Parker said, "We were nuts. And then later in the mid 1980s and 1990s, we said, 'okay, let's make +15%, +20%' and we raised a billion dollars.' If you're going to raise a lot of money, people will be very happy with +15% or +20%."[4]

Others in the hedge fund industry were on the same page with Parker's view on leverage. Paul Tudor Jones (not a Turtle), for example, does not think he is a different trader today—except for reducing leverage. His returns have dropped since the 1980s, but his risk-adjusted returns are the same as in his early days. He said, "What's different has been my own personal appetite for risk and volatility. I think that probably happens with a lot of people, as they get older. Everything is a function of leverage, how much of a drawdown are you willing to tolerate, how much leverage do you want to put on. When I was younger, I had much greater drawdowns, much greater drawdown frequency, much greater leverage." (Side note: Jones got into trading after reading an article on Richard Dennis in college; he recalled, "I thought that Dennis had the greatest job in the world.")

Parker simply used Dennis's trading system in a way that was more appropriate for nervous clients. Not all clients always want the early Turtle-trading absolute returns, the big home runs. In general, high returns do not attract as much money from investors as lower-volatility trading (which means less return).

Not surprisingly, Parker's efforts to change how he traded had an impact on other Turtles. Once big institutional investors looking to invest with a former Turtle had Parker, they didn't really need more Turtles—that is, unless they offered something different than Parker.

With Parker covering that piece of many investors' portfolios, the other Turtles had to try and push their individual differences. The problem was that their performance numbers under Dennis showed a near identical group of traders. Many investors thought the Turtles all sat in a room and when a green light went off, they all bought Swiss francs.[5] For Turtles looking to stand out on their own, this was not a good characterization to be making the rounds.

That did not stop the Turtles from trying to distinguish their trading. Michael Carr said that he was now prone to lighten up or take a portion of the profits.[6] But it was more than just their style that the Turtles wanted to differentiate. Stig Ostgaard, in an effort to gain some distance from Dennis, said he traded on behalf of a well-known Chicago commodity trader in the Turtle program.[7] In a stark demonstration of the Turtles' ambivalence Ostgaard wanted to have Dennis on his résumé without having to name him.

DiMaria also distanced himself from Dennis, saying that clients did not want 150 percent returns and double-digit negative months.[8] The challenges for all of the Turtles, in starting their own version of C&D Commodities, were tough. The industry simply did not want Richard Dennis–type volatility.[9]

This is not suprising. The industry is made up of institutional bean counters managing billions upon billions in pension plans. They don't want higher-volatility or higher-return trading. There is no immediate benefit for them even, if it might be the optimal strategy for their pensioners in the long run. Why? Pension fund managers judge themselves by targeting benchmarks. They only worry about aggregate measures of what their peers are doing, which is by and large trading "long" only. With that mandate, Turtle returns are useless.

Even if it was arguably a bad long-term move to cater to clients' desires for less leverage, there was only so much Turtles could do. If a client says, "I want *this*" and Turtles say, "I won't trade *that* way, it hurts compounding," they will not have that client. It was a classic Catch-22.

Parker got it. He was quite willing to compromise the original rules, which was after all was making him super-rich in the early 1990s. But while, the idea of lowering returns by reducing leverage in the hope of reducing drawdown may have been a winning move for Parker, it wasn't for all the Turtles.

In fact, it may have contributed to their downfall. The very nature of what the Turtles had been taught revolved around taking large calculated risks. Reducing the risk level quickly reduced the size of potential returns. In the trading business, big returns are critical. The basics of compounding are always at play. If Turtles were cutting their appetite for risk in year one, they left little or no cushion if their next year's performance bombed.[10]

However, many of Parker's Turtle compatriots were not ready to give up the original high-risk style they were taught. Those Turtles never stopped seeing the benefits to the home-run approach Dennis had taught them.

Sticking to Their Knitting

Unlike Parker and Rabar, Tom Shanks did not pull back from the original aggressive Turtle rules. From his then home office overlooking the Sonoma Valley in California, he was blunt: "There are individual investors who seek high returns and are willing to accept the risk entailed in achieving them."[11]

However, most investors did not want Shanks's Turtles style even though he would eventually knock the cover off the ball. Other Turtles saw Shanks as Mickey Mantle. "He will hit the ball out of the park. It's just you have to stay with him. Unfortunately, money is being controlled by people who don't know the business. They couldn't trade their way out of a paper bag if their life depended on it."

This criticism of people ignoring high-return traders was spot on, but being right does not mean Shanks was on the way to being Parker wealthy. One Turtle could not figure out how an investment with Shanks could not be a small percentage of everyone's portfolio, saying, "If you . . . saw gold go from $350 an ounce to $600 an ounce, you want to be with Tom, because . . . you're going to make a lot more money with someone like him."

This was the original Turtle trading mentality, but it goes straight against people's natural inclinations. Of course, Dennis had taught the

Turtles that natural inclinations are almost always wrong when it comes to making the right market decisions.[12]

Shanks did his best to differentiate himself from other Turtles by declaring at one point that his trading had shifted to 75 percent systematic and 25 percent discretionary.[13] For some investors, the idea that a mechanical "black box" trading system, with trades placed from code executed inside a computer, is foreign. Shanks used the word "discretion" to allay those fears. He wanted to show that he added value to his trading system beyond the hard and fast rules. However, Shanks's use of discretion almost sank his firm in the mid-1990s before he recovered, acknowledging the mistake.

He was not the only Turtle to stick with Dennis's high-risk, high-return style. Liz Cheval was clear: "I felt that people who invested based on my track record deserved the same trading program that produced those results."[14] She added, "Volatility is what creates the high returns investors want from the market in the first place. As always, when assuming risk, investors should look for commensurate rewards. And high rewards don't come without high volatility."[15] Cheval openly admitted that she adjusted the size of her trading positions using Dennis's model for volatility.[16]

With the passing of years, and with the time to reflect on the wisdom of Parker's less leveraged approach versus Shanks and Cheval's high-octane approach, the market of nervous institutional investors made a choice. It liked Parker's choice and frowned on any allegiance to the original Turtle style.

Highly Correlated Traders

However they positioned themselves, whether as less or more risky than their mentor, the Turtles as individuals were the same traders in the eyes of Wall Street insiders. Their trading performance was highly correlated, which meant there was a historical tendency for their performance to move in tandem.[17] Numerous correlation comparisons showed the Turtles trading the same way.[18]

However, it was Tom Shanks's opinion that the Turtles had evolved and developed systems very different from those taught under Dennis. He said, "Independent evolution suggests that the dissimilarities in trading between Turtles are always increasing."[19] Shanks's opinion seemed designed to camouflage the fact that the Turtles were all really competitors.[20]

This spin did not convince old pros on Wall Street. Virginia Parker (unrelated to Jerry Parker), a fund management consultant, saw no mystery in the Turtles, as well she knew that they were all driven by systematic, momentum-based, trend-following models.[21]

Mark Goodman, president of Kenmar Asset Allocation, a firm that invested with the likes of the Turtles, said what none of them wanted to hear: "If you were to put all trend-following models side by side, you would probably find that most made their profits and incurred losses in the same markets. You are not going to find that EMC [Liz Cheval] made it in one market, while Rabar made it in another. They were all looking at the same charts and obtaining the same perception of opportunity."[22]

Whether dealing with initial fame, trading as a less or more risky Turtle, or battling correlation perceptions or negative associations with Dennis, the pressure was on. If there were potential jealousies *inside* the program, imagine the feelings of rivalry building up now with the Jerry Parkers of the world fast approaching a net worth of over $100 million in the early to mid-1990s.

Perhaps the Turtle story would have ended right there. They had all been part of a grand experiment. They all learned to trade well while under Dennis. It had been a good ride. But here is where Turtles separated. Beyond the rules, they still needed something *else* for long-term trading success.

10

Dennis Comes Back to the Game

"He was the toughest son of a bitch I ever knew. He taught me that trading is very competitive and you have to be able to handle getting your butt kicked. No matter how you cut it, there are enormous emotional ups and downs involved."

Paul Tudor Jones,
hedge fund manager, on his mentor Eli Tullis

Whether the Turtles became big winners or losers, the excitement of their fame and money had their former teacher wanting a piece of the early 1990s money pouring into hedge funds. The Turtles' success was 100 percent because of *him*, but now his students were ahead. To trade or not to trade was Dennis's internal debate as he pondered reentry into a now more crowded field to compete against his apprentices.[1]

However, the early to mid-1990s was a tough time for Dennis. He was still unhappy about a class action suit brought against him after the Drexel fund debacle. Plaintiffs chasing him through the courts concluded he was "financially strapped" and "debt-ridden."[2] Dennis poverty-stricken? Doubtful. Was Dennis envious of his students' success? He essentially said so.

Jeff Gordon attempted to get into Dennis's head: "Rich thought he could out-trade his own methodology. How in the world could a methodology that you created with your own knowledge out-trade you?"

Yet Gordon, like so many others who were acquainted with Dennis's 1988 "retirement" and shutdown of the Turtle program, was not sympathetic. He was perplexed. He kept wondering about what could have been: "Let's just say, you taught a bunch of beginners to play chess, then you start playing them and they all start [beating] you. How would you feel? If Richard Dennis had hung up his cleats and just allowed the Turtle program to manage all that money he got from Drexel, they might have $10 billion now. He could be sitting on easy street. We will never know how many hundreds of millions and perhaps how many billions of dollars he might have left on the table because he disbanded the Turtle group."

Dennis must have felt that he had left money on the table, too, because in 1994, along with his brother Tom, he launched a new firm called Dennis Trading Group. No fanfare; just an unlisted phone number and suite number on the door to protect anonymity.

This was not the mammoth operation of C&D in the 1980s (one hundred employees, fifty to one hundred customers, and $8 million in fixed costs), but Dennis still had loyal supporters. "He is a lifelong student of the markets and a brilliant individual. Anything he does is worth paying close attention to," said Sol Waksman of Barclay Trading Group, a consulting firm that tracks fund performance.[3]

While he had taken to calling himself a "researcher" now instead of a "trader," one of the questions Dennis was asked most frequently was, "Why are you doing this? Why step back into the fire again?" Dennis gave all kinds of answers from philanthropy to politics, but when pressed, he came back to his famous students: "I kept picking up the trade journals and seeing how much money they were managing. I thought, 'I know I'm at least as good as some of these people.' So I decided to give it another try."[4]

Still, there were reservations about this comeback. Vic Lespinasse, a floor analyst at the Chicago Board of Trade, saw the pros and cons: "He still has a very good reputation, although it has been tarnished somewhat by the Drexel episode. He's going to have to establish a track record again, but I don't see why he shouldn't do that. I think he's a superstar."[5]

When Dennis was asked to compare his new firm's trading strategy to the Turtles, he sounded less confident than in years past: "The people I trained [Turtles] are succeeding on the ideas they learned from *me*. People might be interested in getting some updated ideas. If yesterday's motto was that the trend is our friend, today it might be that the trend is a harsh mistress."[6]

Just as the Turtles were trying to overcome identity issues on Wall Street and Dennis was staging his comeback, Turtle Russell Sands threw everyone a curve ball.

Russell Sands

Russell Sands lasted one year as a Turtle before leaving for reasons that aren't completely clear. While he said that he resigned, other Turtles said he was "let go." However, that detail was minor in view of Sands's true Turtle legacy: selling Dennis's famous rules.

The selling of Dennis's rules followed shortly after Sands's departure from Chesapeake Capital (the firm he'd created with Jerry Parker). Sands was always honest about why Parker carried more weight in their former firm ("he had the longer and more valid track record"), but at the same time tension was brewing.

For a while they had a close relationship. Every day they were at each other's house. However, Parker soon bought Sands out. What was Sands's version of the buyout? "Jerry got greedy." In all fairness, many hard-working people who make millions are called greedy. Sands could have just as easily been called jealous.

Sands had an explanation for why trading had not gone his way after parting with Parker: "Paul Saunders and Kevin Brandt [Kidder Peabody/James River Capital Principles] came to me and said, 'Russell, why don't you start your own company? We'll give you some money and let Jerry have Chesapeake.' I said fine. This was right after the first Gulf War, when there had been some huge moves in the oil markets."

Kidder Peabody gave Sands money to trade, but the markets did not produce good trends over the next six to nine months. Sands said his trading performance went down to around 25 percent. His clients all ran for the doors. He sounded boxed in explaining his predicament: "Now, I'm basically out of business and don't know what to do next."

In August 1992, a few days after Hurricane Andrew had rocked south Florida, Sands rocked the Turtles' carefully crafted secrecy. The *Chicago Tribune* blasted the story:

> A disciple of Richard J. Dennis, the world-famous Chicago futures trader, is offering to reveal the master's trading secrets to the public for the first time . . . promising to tell all at seminars across the country, including one this weekend in Chicago, for an admission fee of $2,500 a person.[7]

Maybe Sands selling Dennis's rules would have been no big deal in a normal situation, but the secrecy in the Turtles' world was intense. Mike Shannon laughed at the situation in hindsight: "If we were having this interview and it was 1986 or 1987, we wouldn't be talking. We were very guarded about the whole thing and we were intensely proud of what we were back in the day. We felt that there was something really incredibly special going on, that we were part of a special and experimental project. The secrecy alone was just off the charts. We weren't allowed to discuss it according to Richard or anybody that worked for him."

However, Jim DiMaria downplayed the need for even signing an agreement: "It was pretty obvious to me that this stuff should be kept secret . . . the stuff we were taught was their stuff. I was lucky enough that they shared it with me. I didn't feel like sharing it with anyone else."

DiMaria's response was typical of how most Turtles felt toward Dennis. After all, the Turtle experiment was all about making big-time money, and sharing rules for making millions made no sense. So not knowing what the impact of Sands's actions would be, the other Turtles attempted to minimize the importance of Dennis's rules. They wanted the world to know that the rules alone weren't the secret to riches (true point).

As a counterstrike, Sands argued that it was a good business opportunity: "I didn't do anything illegal. I didn't even do anything immoral. I tell people, 'Whatever I say is what Richard Dennis said twenty years ago.' I give him all the credit in the world for it. I didn't come up with these ideas. I'm just passing it on. That's the way it is."

Fifteen years before he was the arguable billionaire he is today, Jerry Parker reacted with outrage against his former partner: "I don't think Russell has anything to say that's worth $2,500."[8] Given that Sands and Parker had been co-workers and friends at one time, his comment was a ninety-five-mile-per-hour fastball at Sands's head.

Liz Cheval then played the "Sands only learned so much" card, saying that it took her about two years to fully grasp and then use Dennis's rules.[9] Other Turtles said that since Sands was terminated from the program after one year, he did not get the "real" system.[10]

Right. Parker and Sands had worked in the same house every day. At that time, Sands knew what Parker knew about the Turtle trading rules. Both shared the same basic knowledge back then. The "doing" part, the reason Parker is huge today, is a whole other story.

Sam DeNardo pulled back the curtain on Sands: "I think he [Sands] was talking to people outside the room about what he was doing. That got him in a lot of trouble. I heard it with my own ears. There was some talk that he was talking to either his mother or somebody about different trades. The word got back to Rich. And I don't know if it was that or his performance that got him cut from the program. He ultimately got cut." Multiple Turtles gave the same basic story.

Sands said he was not fired, but chose to resign. He said, "I'm sure some of them say I quit. I'm sure some of them say I was fired. I'm sure some of them say I had a big mouth and said things I shouldn't have said."

On the other hand the leaflet for Sands's 1992 seminars said he'd co-managed funds with Parker. Parker, said in most cases that Sands merely placed orders at his direction. He thought Sands's prime motivation for selling the rules was to raise money and get back into trading.[11]

Parker thought Sands's actions violated Dennis's training not in a legal way, but in a moral and ethical one. He said of Dennis, "How could we repay him for giving us all this knowledge?"[12] Parker added, "Rich always said that you can't pay attention to books, articles or papers. If it was worth knowing, the people would keep it for themselves and trade."[13]

In the end, maybe Sands had simply embarrassed his Turtle peers so much that they felt they had to respond. The promotional language Sands and his marketing people used to sell the Turtle rules promised: "The Most Powerful, Valuable and Profitable Trading Method Ever . . . Now Revealed in a New Trading Course for Just a Small, No-Risk Investment!" Sands's ads screamed about "A Very Affordable Low, Low Price! 15 straight years of Profitable Trading!"

Playing right into the attacks against him, Sands's marketing pitched, "Listen, there are a lot of people very upset that Russell is sharing these secrets, especially at such a low price. The other original Turtles and their phenomenally successful mentor do not want these priceless secrets revealed. At any price!" It was like a 2007 late-night infomercial from INVESTools.

Eventually, DeNardo offered a more sympathetic interpretation of Sands's teaching: "Everybody else is sort of mad at him for letting the system out of the bag. What else was he supposed to do? Drive a cab?" Erle Keefer gave another reason for the secrecy at any cost: "Honestly, I don't think we were that sophisticated. I just think there was . . . allegiance to Rich."

Dennis's own take on the selling of rules was tight-lipped. He made it clear, however, that a few Turtles had failed: "There were one or two [Turtles] who will remain nameless. The majority was exemplary."[14]

He may have been diplomatic, but his longtime friend and fellow trader Tom Willis, who was and is no fan of Sands, was not: "I've always thought that Rich exemplifies the Christian attitude and behavior more than most Christians I know. He probably doesn't hold a grudge against Russell."

Dennis Retires Again

Soon after the Sands dustup, Dennis staged another remarkable comeback. It would take him through most of the 1990s. While Dennis did not reveal his exact trading systems to the public, his performance data had earmarks of trend-following trading. After returning in 1994, his compounded annual rate of return was approximately plus 63 percent through September 1998. For two years in a row, 1995 (108.9%) and 1996 (112.7%), Dennis had triple-digit returns.[15]

He was still the same high-risk, high-reward trader he had always been. It was his ticket to the Hall of Fame and his Achilles' heel rolled into one. However, this was now the time of Bill Clinton and the dot-com bubble. It was hard to get noticed even with his great performance.

On top of that, many investors were gun-shy about another Dennis comeback. In an effort to allay client fears, he assured everyone that his infamous *discretion*, his inability to not personally interfere with his own rules, had been eliminated. He said the computer was his new friend: "Given what the computer can do today—compared with what it could do only a few years ago, I just can't see how any human could possibly compete on a level field with a well-designed computerized set of systems."[16]

The term "computer" as a marketing hook was old news. In some ways, Dennis was a technophobe in the middle of the Internet revolution (he always said he could not program). Maybe the over-sixty crowd bought in, but no one else on Wall Street breathed a huge sigh of relief just because he'd used the word "computer."[17]

Worse yet, Dennis's critics thought that his strict mechanical trading formula was just a marketing ploy. Dennis rebutted them by saying he had put in checks and balances. He struck a confident tone: "At the end of the day, a trader has to go with what works. I know that mechanical systems work best, and therefore I am quite comfortable that our strategies will continue to be successful."[18]

There was a difference in Dennis's trading strategy this time around: He was religiously applying that same discipline he had taught his students. For example, he was right there in August of 1998 making big money during one of the most historic months on Wall Street. He, like all trend followers, made a fortune in August. "Between the ruble, Yeltsin, and the deep blue sea, it's been pretty crazy," said Dennis with a hint of glee. He was up 13.5 percent in August 1998, giving him a year-to-date return of about 45 percent.[19]

Other traders were sinking like stones in the zero-sum market game at the same moment Dennis was flying high. Wall Street's darling, Long Term Capital Management's (LTCM), for example, imploded at the same time. LTCM lost billions. Chief Executive John W. Meriwether, the legendary former Salomon Brothers bond trader, said in a letter to investors at the time, "August (1998) was very painful for all of us."[20] LTCM and its two Nobel laureates, Robert H. Merton and Myron S. Scholes, padded the pockets of Dennis and other trend-following traders, including the Turtles.

It was a high point for Dennis's trading return, because within a few years of that historic zero-sum win, he was out of the game again. On September 29, 2000, Dennis Trading Group ceased trading and liquidated customer accounts. Burt Kozloff, an investor in Dennis's current fund, laid out the painful truth: "Dennis Trading Group was −50% down in June but then made a slight recovery in July. But we finally broke through the −50% mark to −52%. You still can trade and try to recover when you're down 50%, but you run the risk of falling to −60% or −70%, and there's no turning back from there."[21]

While it was no solace for Richard Dennis, the moment when clients pulled funds from him in the fall of 2000 was a bottom for trend-following traders. In the following twelve months, returns for many of his trading peers zoomed up 100 percent or more in performance. Dennis's clients had panicked at the bottom and paid dearly.

Dennis was once again out of public money management. Meanwhile, his conservative Republican student Jerry Parker was rising even farther to the top in both the trading and political worlds. His story would take the Turtles and their philosophy to a whole new level.

11

Seizing Opportunity

"A good plan violently executed now is better than a perfect plan next week."

General George S. Patton

Imagine driving to Manakin-Sabot, outside of Richmond, Virginia, to see Jerry Parker's office in 1994. The last thing you would have anticipated was an unassuming colonial-style brick and wood building that looked as though it might house a local insurance company or real-estate office. It was situated in a field along a country road. Describing my feeling, upon seeing it, as thunderstruck would be an understatement.

Actually entering Parker's office was like walking into the old, musty office of your neighborhood attorney who at seventy was about to retire. The front-office staff was friendly, unpretentious, and informal.

In contrast to that original office, Parker's new office (opened in 1995, approximately ten miles away) has a far more gracious feeling of Southern gentility and success. From the entrance, two staircases spiral up each side of the room to a top landing area. However, today visitors can no longer stroll in unannounced. Smoked-glass windows, video cameras, and a request for identification are not surprising precautions in today's security-conscious society.

What remains true to Parker's down-to-earth character is that his current office is located across from a 1960s-style strip mall that includes a salon, Mary Lou and Co: Hair, Nails & Wigs. Soccer moms park in the Chesapeake Capital parking lot to pick up their children at the church-run preschool next door. A Turtle is making a fortune in suburban Richmond, and no one is paying attention.

Moreover, one would never guess the financial disparity between Parker and other Turtles from the furnishings of his private office. It is nondescript, almost utilitarian except for a small turtle on his desk. Yet the gap between him and his former partner Sands is arguably now a billion dollars in net worth. The reasons for that are arguably more important to understand than the rules originally taught the Turtles.

The bottom line is that Jerry Parker, Liz Cheval, Tom Shanks, Howard Seidler, Jim DiMaria, Paul Rabar, and their teacher Bill Eckhardt had entrepreneurial skills beyond trading Dennis's rules. They had something extra. The people who excel in any field are people who realize that the moment is to be seized, that there are opportunities at every turn. They're more alive to the moment.[1]

Did Dennis think that in the long run all of his students would be alive to the moment? Back in 1986, long before the Turtles were out on their own, he was asked how he would have reacted to his ad. He responded, "I guess I would've applied. I have no doubt that for the people who got the job it was the best job that has ever come along for them. Obviously, not all 14 are going to be the greatest traders who ever lived, but I think there are two or three who could be really *excellent*."[2]

R. Jerry Parker, Jr., became excellent. A graduate of Ferrum College and the University of Virginia, he is a devoted Christian and family man, who along with his wife home-schooled their three children.

Even though he is comparatively straight-laced, Parker still makes time to kick back and enjoy life, especially sports. He made sure he got good seats at Chicago Bulls games when they were winning championships with Michael Jordan. Today, he still cheers on his University of Virginia Cavaliers basketball team at the new John Paul Jones arena in Charlottesville.

Parker was certainly not considered the success he is today while working for Dennis. He ended his first year trading as a Turtle down 10 percent before regrouping to have three stellar years. But keep in mind that he did not make the most money while working for Dennis, in large part due to Dennis's allotment of allocations, not his performance. Parker may have had some regrets about the way his mentor parceled out money, but those years under Dennis were central to his development.

The confidence he gained while trading for Dennis was his biggest lesson: "The most important experience that led me to utilize a technical approach was the amount of success that I experienced trading Rich's system."[3] What was the critical experience he gained under Dennis? "It's important to live with someone who says, 'It's okay to lose money.' "

Tom Shanks agreed wholeheartedly with Parker about the need for a mentor: "By far, the structure of what I do is based on Richard's systems, and certainly, philosophically, everything I do in terms of trading is based on what I learned from Richard."[4]

Parker and Dennis are still political opposites. Today, Parker is one of the most influential backers of Republican candidates in the state of Virginia. He has contributed over $500,000 to mostly conservative candidates since 1995. While he has ruled out a run for political office so far, his wealth and political power put him on the short list of potential Virginia governors.

Aspects of Parker's politics have universal appeal. He has said, "When there is a tax increase and the result is a surplus, the taxpayers should receive their money back. Just as when you pay too much for something in a store, you get your change back."[5]

Bottom line, Parker's earnings from 1988 through 2006 are the clearest demonstration yet that the story of the Turtles is relevant today. Using his publicly available disclosures and the size of his fund, and assuming a standard fee structure, the best educated guess of Parker's net worth is approximately $770 million.

Table 11.1: Annual Returns, 1998–2006, for Jerry Parker's Chesapeake Capital.

Year	Total	Year	Total
1988	48.91	1998	16.31
1989	28.30	1999	3.30
1990	43.12	2000	5.23
1991	12.51	2001	−7.98
1992	1.81	2002	11.01
1993	61.82	2003	23.08
1994	15.87	2004	4.84
1995	14.09	2005	1.15
1996	15.05	2006	10.90
1997	9.94		

Source: Disclosure Documents Filed with United States CFTC.

That number assumes no reinvesting for twenty years. If 10 percent growth is assumed and compounded annually, Parker's net worth could be as high as $1.75 billion.

What Separated Parker from Other Turtles?

"You had to be *really* smart to be hired by Dennis." It might be comforting to think that intelligence alone accounted for the Turtles' trading success, but that would be an excuse. That said, many of the Turtles were brilliant. So there is no intention here to slight their individual brainpower.

However, a high IQ is hardly the key to success in life, or Enron's hundreds of MBAs from the top schools in the country might have prevented its demise.[6] Intelligence ensures absolutely nothing in the long run; success requires something more.

As it turns out, most CEOs at the biggest corporations didn't attend Ivy League schools. They went to state universities, big and small, or to lesser-known private colleges. Most people, would guess that the percentage of CEOs bearing Ivy League undergraduate degrees is far higher than the actual figure of only 10 percent.[7] So what, beyond pure intelligence, enabled Parker's twenty years of great performance?

The Maginot line, between those Turtles who achieved huge trading success after working for Dennis and those who failed at trading, came down to an understanding and application of entrepreneurial skills. The Turtles had to have trading rules, but without entrepreneurial savvy they were doomed. Nancy Upton and Don Sexton, professors at Baylor University who have long studied entrepreneurs, pinpointed traits possessed by Parker and other entrepreneurs:

1. Nonconformists—lower need to conform indicating self-reliance.

2. Emotionally aloof—not necessarily cold to others, but can be oblivious.

3. Sky divers—lower concern for physical harm, but does change with age.

4. Risk takers—more comfortable taking it.

5. Socially adroit—more persuasive.

6. Autonomous—higher need for independence.

7. Change seekers—like novel approaches. This is different than 99% of all other people.

8. Energetic—higher need and / or ability to work longer.

9. Self-sufficient—don't need as much sympathy or reassurance, but they still need to form networks so self-sufficiency need not be taken to extremes.[8]

We shouldn't underestimate those nine factors. Dennis turned on the lights and supplied the brokers, the money, and the system. With Dennis out of the picture, the Turtles had to answer for themselves as to whether or not they had the ability and the desire to succeed on their own. Their dilemma, whether they knew it or not at the time, could be solved by how well they applied only those nine traits.

Jerry Parker applied the nine traits out of the gate, which some Turtles proved unable or unwilling to do. Parker always had the self-confidence to believe that one day his earnings could rival those of Dennis. Other Turtles, when seeing firsthand Dennis earn $80 million in 1986, may have thought, "That could never be me." A few confessed that they just felt lucky to be a Turtle, and when describing their peers some used words like "timid" or "gun shy."

No one ever described Parker like that. Although he didn't say so directly, he was referencing those nine characteristics of an entrepreneur when he spoke about what it really takes to be a success. He said, "We're not really interested in people who are experts at the French stock markets or German bond markets. It doesn't take a huge monster infrastructure—not Harvard MBAs and people from Goldman Sachs."

Loren Pope, author of *Colleges that Change Lives*, a book extolling the virtues of small liberal-arts colleges, appreciated the deeper meaning in Parker's wisdom: "The Ivies and other A-league schools have a lot of prestige because they're supposed to open doors and lead to successful careers. But parents who expect the Ivies to ensure their kids' success are going to be disappointed. The old-boy network isn't much good in an economy like this. It's *competence* that counts."[9]

Competence is not easy to acquire. Parker saw life as a Turtle as pretty easy by comparison to his solo operation. He recalled, "Trading for Rich, you got in at 7 A.M. and at 2 P.M. you watched the Cubs game." But once he became a money manager for clients he had to raise money, hire people, do research, track his performance, *and* trade. "The degree to which you are successful will be partly because of your buys and sells. But you're also running a business: hiring, making sure you have good accounting and legal and marketing systems in place."[10]

Parker's business acumen came from many sources beyond Dennis. His favorite book, for example, is *Selling the Invisible*, a modern-day marketing bible. But Parker always brought it back to his training under Dennis: "An honest, humble mentor is the best thing going. Learn from other people. Do the right thing every day, focus on what you're doing, and let the cards fall where they may."[11]

After the Turtle program ended, Jim DiMaria had no doubts about the cards falling right for Parker: "Jerry wanted to raise a lot of money. He said it from day one."

Decide What You Really Want

Following the *Market Wizards* books, many Turtles were content to bask in their fame without making the true effort needed to build a solid business. Parker's goal was not to be on the front cover of magazines (although he did once appear on the cover of *Financial Trader* in 1994, leaning against the white picket fence surrounding his suburban Richmond estate). No, what he wanted was "Master of the Universe" profits.

Jonathan Craven was the second person hired at Chesapeake Capital. Today, Craven runs his own trading firm with $20 million under management. He never forgot Parker's core principles. Parker said, "You have to have faith in two things." When Craven asked, "What's that?" Parker said, "God and your system." Craven added, "You have to have faith that your system works. Otherwise, you would get one hour of sleep a night."

What was Craven getting at? Many people think the Jerry Parkers of the world have systems or rules that limit them to certain markets. Upon learning of a trader like Parker, they naively assume he trades only commodities. The reality is that Parker applies Dennis's philosophy to all markets. He seeks to apply Dennis's original principles globally in markets all around the world. He doesn't care what market: Chinese porcelain, gold, silver, markets that exist, markets that don't exist today, and markets that others are making lots of money in that he is not trading.[12]

Craven learned that philosophy of diversity while under Parker's tutelage. The number of markets they traded was always in flux: "We could have sixty-five markets or we could have thirty." Craven was once asked, "Are you always in the market? What's the maximum number of positions you could have on at any one time?" Craven responded. "It all depends. If the markets are going sideways, theoretically zero. The markets are trending up or down? I could have sixty-five positions."

Unfortunately, what Parker does to make money in all those markets is often confused with jargon terms like "managed futures" and "commodity trading advisor." Both are government terms for hedge funds. In many cases traders have been guilty of compounding the confusion, as Parker was quick to admit:

> I think another mistake we made was defining ourselves as "managed futures," where we immediately limit our universe. Is our expertise in that, or is our expertise in systematic trend following, or model development? Maybe we trend follow with Chinese porcelain. Maybe we trend follow with gold and silver, or stock futures, or whatever the client needs . . . We need to look at the investment world globally and communicate our expertise of systematic trading.[13]

Communicating his expertise has always been a challenge. People with trading philosophies that run counter to Parker's have actively spun the word "commodity" as something negative. It can't be said enough, Turtle trend-following is a *strategy*. These traders trade financial instruments across the globe, ranging from stocks to currencies to energies to wheat to gold to bonds to commodities.

Even though Parker has had a great run, he is still fighting the kind of uphill battle that sunk many of his Turtle peers. He knows that people look at systematic and computerized trading with too much skepticism. He said, "I think we've mis-communicated to our clients what our expertise really is. Our methods will work on lots of different markets. The ones that are hot today and the ones that are not hot today."[14] He could have been William Eckhardt in the Turtles' classroom in 1984: There was no change in the message.

The Problem with Fundamentals

Like many top hedge-fund players today, Parker gives back to his community. He donated $500,000 to the University of Virginia for the "Chesapeake Capital Trading Room." It was designed as "a real-world, highly sophisticated trading atmosphere." Bob Webb, who is the Director of The McIntire Center for Financial Innovation at UVA, graciously gave a tour of the facility. With numerous trading desks and large quote screens on the walls, you appreciate where every dollar of Parker's donation went.

Webb, who is a finance professor at UVA, sees the Chesapeake Capital Trading Room as "the ideal environment to illustrate real-time events in financial markets. Students are able to examine the financial markets' reaction to news events. Working there allows them to look at recent changes and explore what factors promoted the changes." Webb says that "students get their feet wet right away. They're able to make *predictions*, based on real events, from the first day of class. They can then look at factors that later cause prices to change, and that helps them to make better decisions."[15]

One business student unaware of Parker and the original Turtle training environment, that office with cube dividers and no TVs, excitedly described the new Chesapeake Capital trading room: "It's fantastic to be able to use the software to look up information about any company. You can get balance sheets, income statements, ratios, growth patterns—just about anything."[16] The irony, of course, is that Parker would never use "just about anything" to make his trading decisions.

The contradictions between Parker and these statements by a UVA professor and student are not intentional. Webb, an accomplished professor simply teaches a philosophy that sharply contrasts with Parker's. For example, consider Webb's view that individuals at the Federal Reserve beyond the chairman can impact financial market prices through their comments. He said, "One consequence is that traders must monitor the comments of a number of individuals at the Federal Reserve System." Webb's advice is plausible to many on Wall Street and Main Street who follow fundamental analysis, but his observations do not line up with the trading approach of the Chesapeake Capital Trading Room's benefactor.

Like his mentor Richard Dennis, Parker wouldn't consider monitoring multiple voices at the Fed to make a trading decision for a nanosecond. Consider, for example, Parker's standard disclosure, "Chesapeake believes that future price movements in all markets may be more accurately anticipated by historical price movements within a quantitative or technical analysis than by fundamental economic analysis."[17] With that kind of clear statement of intent, how did

Bob Spear runs a systems-testing software firm with a program called "Mechanica." He has arguably the most powerful software programs for testing trading systems available to the public.

Two Turtles became his clients over the years: Jerry Parker and Erle Keefer. It was one of Spear's software ads that caught Parker's attention. The ad blared: "Trading Recipes pinpoints winning systems, then supercharges their performance!" The 1994 ad spoke of "money management" (what William Eckhardt called risk management), a rarity then.

Parker didn't know at the time that there was software available to test the Turtle trading systems and money management (see chapters 4 and 5). When Parker first called about Spear's software, Spear knew immediately who he was. He said, "He didn't have to explain to me Chesapeake Capital."

students enjoying the Chesapeake Room at UVA miss understanding Parker's trading style?

Over his career, Parker has repeatedly gone out of his way to educate everyone that technical traders need no particular expertise in the markets they trade, saying, "They do not need to be an authority on meteorological phenomena, geopolitical occurrences or the economic impact of specific worldwide events on a particular market."[18] Parker often borders on exasperation as he fights to get that message across: "If the alternative is massive diversification stocks only, buy and hold, or listen to some analyst with a fundamental point of view. Well, you see what that's got us."[19] That logic can be hard for people to accept. Investors want big money potential along with a sophisticated story that makes sense fundamentally.

And even if investors understand Parker's Turtle style enough to invest, they don't want to watch their account equity going up and down. Even Parker's clients focus constantly on monthly rates of return. They hold him to a high standard, with admonitions like "Don't give back my monthly profit," "I am concerned with all of this monthly data," and "You're behind this month versus last month." Parker said flatly, "It is crazy."

He added, "I think that risk from initial capital, losing 10%, that's a serious thing. If I'm up 50%, now I'm up 40%, that's a whole different thing. But not to clients! Not to the ratios. So we're screwing around with our profitability when we're playing with the market's money, and trying to fine tune the performance table so we don't have what looks like a risky investment, even though it's risky. But a much different risk than the risk on initial capital. So I think it's ridiculous."[20]

Dressing up his performance to make it more palatable to nervous clients is not something Parker likes:

No matter how well we do, I'm always being met with people who are telling me, "doesn't matter how much money you make or how well you do, I just don't like your style. I don't like the style that relies upon price only. I don't like commodities. And it's hocus-pocus." When we're down 20%, my gracious, [they think] we're on our way out of business. I've actually had people calling me on the telephone, [when] maybe we're down −12% and they'd say, "You're never going to come back. You're never going to make money. Forget it." But if NASDAQ's down −40%, that's a pretty good buying opportunity.[21]

The odd truth about fundamental traders is that behind closed doors, they often trade very similarly to Parker. In public they might talk about the NASDAQ down 40 percent as a good buying opportunity, a value play, but for their actual trading they look for trends.

Parker saw this contradiction firsthand when he was purchasing quantitative information from Ned Davis (a well-known analyst on Wall Street). Parker was getting faxes every day, and he would compare Davis's analysis to his own positions. Parker, the trained skeptic, said to the staff at Davis's office, "It looks like a lot of times, almost all the time, my positions are same as yours." They told Parker, "That's true because even with all of our good analysis, if we don't put a trend following component in it, it doesn't do very well."[22]

That said, the most successful Turtle doesn't sugar-coat his style of trading. He addresses the drawbacks head on. When he compares his philosophy to a form of government, he sounds like a down-to-earth Sunday school preacher:

> Trend following is like a democracy. Sometimes it doesn't look so good, but it's better than anything else out there. Are we going to rely on buy and hold? Buy and hope, that's what I call it. Are we going to double up when we lose money? The world is too big to analyze. The fundamentals are too large. We need to aggressively, unrepentantly sell trend following and describe it as it is: a system of risk controls that gets in the right markets at the right times and limits the disaster scenarios.[23]

Hedge Fund Blowups

In Jerry Parker's world, the unexpected eventually happens. If you think the world is tidy, get ready for the hurricane to blow you away. For example, if there's a good side to the 2006 implosion of the Amaranth hedge fund (to the tune of $6 billion), it's the embarrassment suffered by the state and city pension funds that invested in it. And in

Amaranth's case, its name (a mythical flower that never fades) may have held a hidden meaning. The secondary meaning: a pigweed.[24]

And "pigweed" all started with "mean reversion." This term, with its academic overtone, may make some people cringe, but understanding its ramifications lies at the heart of why hedge funds Amaranth and Long Term Capital Management went belly-up.

What is mean reversion? Over the long haul, market prices have a tendency to "revert to the mean." That is, studies have conclusively shown that when stock prices (or any price, for that matter) get overextended to the upside (or to the downside), they eventually fall back in line with averages. However, stock prices do not exactly snap back into place overnight. They can remain overvalued or undervalued for extended periods of time.[25]

That extended period of time is the sandbar that sinks ships. People who bet on markets' behaving in an orderly fashion (arbitrage) are panning for fool's gold. Parker and the other Turtles learned a long time ago from Dennis that the hard thing to do is the right thing to do:

> Mean reversion works almost all of the time. Then it stops and you're kind of out of business. The market is always reverting to the mean except when it doesn't. Who wants a system like we have, "40% winners, losing money almost all the time, always in a draw down, making money on about 10% of your trades, the rest of them are sort of break even to losers, infrequent profits"? I much prefer the mean reversion where I have 55% winners, 1% or 2% returns per month. "I'm always right!" I'm always getting positive feedback. Then, maybe in 8 years, you're kind of out of business, because when it doesn't revert to the mean, your philosophy loses.[26]

Hearing Parker's Southern cadence as he preaches about mean reversion hits home. Consider an example that makes his point: Let's say an investor gives a trader money because his two-year track record shows he made 2 percent every month with no down months. Six years later, that same fund blows up and that investor's retirement is gone because the strategy was predicated on mean reversion. It is human nature to believe in mean reversion, but as Parker says, "it just is a *fatal* strategy of trading the markets."[27]

"Fatal" is the kind of word that grabs you by the throat. "Most of the time" is not a good enough bet. The bottom line: Those hundred-year floods that give mean-reversion traders solace really occur every two or three years—and they can and do wipe out fortunes.

James River Capital

Back in the summer of 1994, the sign outside Parker's offices in Manakin-Sabot, Virginia, listed two firm names: Chesapeake Capital and James River Capital. Since James River Capital smacked of State of Virginia geography, it could have been anything. It turns out that it was actually the new name for the firm that had risen from the ashes of Kidder Peabody's managed futures division.

Jonathan Craven saw how critical James River Capital was to Chesapeake Capital's start. He said, "I met Jerry through somebody I knew at James River Capital. Those guys introduced me to Jerry and I got hired in March of 1990. We were renting space from James River for a long time." Investor Bradley Rotter added, "Jerry Parker did a very wise thing early on in his career. He associated himself with Paul Saunders and Kevin Brandt." What Parker did was wise for good reason. Brokerage firms were the perfect partners to sell the Turtles to the public as something sexy.

On the other hand, Erle Keefer thought Parker's success had an element of rolling the dice: "You would have never picked who, when they left the Turtle program, would be phenomenal or not phenomenal I think it was a crapshoot."

"Crapshoot" is not quite accurate, but Keefer saw an element of randomness in Parker's stratospheric rise: "What if it was another time in history that was for the so-to-speak 'gambler,' then it would be Tom Shanks who would be trading a billion dollars and Jerry Parker would be trading $250 million. I know a couple of other Turtles who didn't want to trade public money. They wanted to drive a race car rather than an aircraft carrier." Keefer saw other Turtles who could have had Parker's level of success. He said, "If Paul Rabar would have got with those guys at Kidder Peabody rather than Jerry, Paul Rabar would be the one that you're writing about as trading a billion or two billion dollars."

However, Keefer was not slighting Parker: "Jerry was at the right place at the right time and what he did is he did not impede himself. I say that in the most positive of ways. Too many of us are presented with an opportunity in life and we hesitate." Exactly. At the end of the day, Parker had to swing and hit the ball hard to win the game. He had to make it happen. Parker whipped the bat through the strike zone with ferocity.

However, don't expect to see Parker on CNBC explaining how to make money on unpredictable disasters. Don't expect to see him on Fox News debating politics with Hannity and Colmes. You have a much better chance of meeting Parker at the local Richmond, Virginia, area Starbucks. The lesson: Be alert when buying your next morning coffee. You just might meet a good trader to handle your retirement money or the needed benefactor for your political run.

12

Failure Is a Choice

"I ran out of gas. I had a flat tire. I didn't have enough money for cab fare. My tux didn't come back from the cleaners. An old friend came in from out of town. Someone stole my car. There was an earthquake! A terrible flood! Locusts! It wasn't my fault, I swear to god!"

Jake Blues,
The Blues Brothers Movie

Understanding why some Turtles were swallowed up in the pressure cooker of ego and expectations while others went on to great success reveals what is necessary to achieve long-term success. Liz Cheval was blunt: "The most interesting thing about the Turtle program was observing who succeeded and who did not."[1] Cheval never expanded publicly about which Turtles fell into which category, but the evidence about which Turtles she was referring to was becoming clear.

Dennis himself acknowledged in a 2005 interview, "You could make the case on reflection that it didn't make much difference who we picked. The people who could sustain trading after the Turtle program did so pretty much according to their abilities. While they were sort of under our control, it didn't make much difference how intrinsically smart they were."[2]

In fact, when referring to intrinsic intelligence, Dennis makes the point that executing a well-designed trading system does not require, intellect as a key factor: "Good traders apply every ounce of intelligence they have into the creation of their systems, but then they're dumbbells in following them. You've got to have a schizoid approach. Work like hell to make it good, and then ignore it like you're a brick wall. President Bush would be a great trader if he had a system."[3]

Others offered a far different view. David Cheval, a peripheral player in the Turtle story, and Curtis Faith didn't buy the "anyone can do it" premise from the man who actually proved it.[4] Faith said: "You can certainly teach trading and trading concepts. You can teach someone to be a successful trader. There were marked differences in the performance of the group. So some people couldn't apply or learn trading. Some took several years to catch on. I do believe that legends are born not made. Decent traders can be made however. So I'm in the nature and the nurture camp."[5]

The Turtle story does not straddle the debate. Dennis proved conclusively that nurture trumped nature. However once the Turtles were out of his program and out into the real world, many tried to capitalize on their fame in an assortment of different ways. Their behavior provided fascinating insights about what *not* to do if making big money making is your goal.

It turns out that Russell Sands was not the only Turtle to dispense Dennis's rules. Curtis Faith, referring to himself as an "original Turtle," started a website in April 2003 that at first promised to give the Turtles' rules away free, provided those who found them useful sent a donation to charity "in honor of Richard Dennis, Bill Eckhardt and the original Turtles."

Faith, without naming him directly, criticized Sands for profiting off the Turtle system: ". . . it always bothered me that some were making money off the work of Richard Dennis and Bill Eckhardt without their consent."[6]

That said there is no evidence that Dennis had anything to do with giving away his rules for charity. When asked about the rules being offered free online, he sounded resigned: "Once I was walking down Michigan Avenue and I heard somebody talking about it. It was pretty clear that they were looking at the stuff and that they thought it somehow had my blessing. What can I do?"[7]

But Faith's charity soon turned capitalistic. In 2006, the website he created switched gears, no longer asking for a charitable donation. The website now charged $29.95 for Dennis's rules. Faith and his firm were doing what he had criticized Sands for. Additionally, while he had criticized Sands for not trading profitably, there was absolutely no evidence Faith was trading successfully either.

When explaining his career ups and downs, Faith referred back to

the money he made sixteen years before as a Turtle: "You're probably thinking, 'What happened to those millions?' More than half
went to taxes, about a quarter went to charity and helping my father
out, and the rest went to start various businesses." He said the biggest
chunk, $2 million, was invested into a software company.[8]

Faith explained in online chat rooms how this software firm (which
later became the focus of an SEC investigation) went bankrupt. He
blamed the firm's implosion on a newly hired CEO. At the time
there were personal issues at play, too: "I went through a divorce and
gave pretty much all of the non-risk assets to my ex. I still loved her,
and we parted on good terms so I gave her the house, porshe [sic], etc.
Long and short of it is that I don't have as much as I once did. I'm not
complaining as I'm still better off than most."[9]

But different characterizations regarding Faith's purported 2003
stock-trading losses, a disgruntled employee, and his personal solvency
were making the rounds in cyberspace. Faith commented on rumors of
his money woes in 2004: "I am not broke. I have had several periods in
the last several years where I was very, very low on cash, but that's not
the same thing as being broke. Even if I had been broke, I'm not sure
it matters as I'm selling software, not advice on how not to ever go
broke."[10]

Shortly thereafter, Faith launched his first trading effort since leaving Dennis in 1988. *Hedge World Daily* ran with a headline describing
Faith's and broker Yuri Plyam's new Acceleration Mercury 4X LP
hedge fund. The new fund's strategy was going to rely on three time
frames: a one- to two-day holding period, another holding period of ten
to fifty days, and a third for months to years.[11]

The pitch? Faith had taken a fifteen-year break from the trading
business and decided to get back into trading in order to take advantage
of breakthroughs in trading technology. He explained why clients
should be excited at the prospects of him managing their money: "Traders used to have to sit in front of the screen all day, but that's no longer
necessary to trade successfully."[12] (It's worth noting that Turtles trading
for Dennis never sat in front of a screen.)

Faith struck a confident tone in a chat room about coming out of
retirement to form new trading pools.[13] Clearly, raising money for Acceleration Capital without Faith's name and his Turtle association

would have been difficult. Dennis and the word "Turtle" were lead résumé points in the firm's disclosure documents (and in assorted news accounts).

While the ambitious Faith spoke of quickly raising a $100 million fund, Acceleration Capital was started with less than $1 million of client money—an extremely small amount for a hedge fund. The fund traded for a short period, accrued significant losses, and was shut down.

Unfortunately, the shutdown was not only due to bad performance. The Commodity Futures Trading Commission, a government regulatory arm similar to the Securities and Exchange Commission, started investigating the fund.

An employee of Castle Trading (Castle and Acceleration were in the same office) named Toby Wayne Denniston was embezzling customer monies from Acceleration Capital. From November 2004 through August 2005, this employee misappropriated $190,883 from the Acceleration's customer account. He was forging checks and concealing his theft by altering the firm's bank and trading account statements.[14] Denniston bought a new BMW and took several trips with his stolen loot. He was ultimately fined $250,000 in an August 2006 order.

Then a January 16, 2007 government order from a related investigation found Acceleration Capital responsible for Denniston's actions. The firm was barred from managing money for clients permanently and fined $218,000. Yuri Plyam was also fined and prohibited from acting as a commodity pool operator (hedge fund term) for three years. The CFTC's investigation (as of June 2007) is still ongoing, consisting of an unreleased collection of 869 depositions, 694 pages of financial records, and 200 pages of trading records.

Faith should have been one of the biggest traders of the last twenty years, but he was clearly missing that *something* Jerry Parker had. Author Jack Schwager, seeing the struggles of some Turtles, reeled in the legend his *Market Wizards* books had created. He told me, "I don't think it was as much of a miracle as it has been popularized. My feeling is that there is no magic here and perhaps no really great talents other than the original founders."

Schwager may have a point with Turtles such as Faith and others who never traded to great success after the Turtle program ended.

However, twenty-year performance track records established by at least six other Turtles and William Eckhardt are without a doubt impressive.

At the end of the day, the Turtles could have all the trading rules in the world, but if some were lazy or poor businessmen, if they lacked motivation or the ability to follow through, their failure at trading—or indeed at any entrepreneurial endeavor—was not a surprise.

But the success or failure of some of the original Turtles does not tell us conclusively whether Dennis's trading wisdom is truly transferable. The Turtle story arguably remains little more than a fascinating corner of investing history, but one without larger implications for the rest of us. The key test is whether the Turtles themselves were capable of passing on the investing knowledge they'd learned, that they'd applied so successfully while working for Dennis.

Fortunately, there is at least one person who provides inspirational evidence of the true transferability of Dennis's trading wisdom. He is rock-solid proof that a hard-working guy with no direct connection to Dennis and Eckhardt could learn to make big money trading—all out of a sleepy small town in the Texas panhandle. If the applicability of Dennis's original experiment to wider society has ever been doubted, skeptics will need another excuse to explain away this second-generation Turtle's success. His name is Salem Abraham.

13

Second-Generation Turtles

> "I have been broke three or four times. But fortunately for me I'm not an MBA, so I didn't know I was broke."
> *T. Boone Pickens*

That second-generation Turtles exist is arguably the most important part of the Turtle story. Ultimately, these "Turtles" present an even more convincing argument supporting nurture over nature than does the success of the original Turtles. They prove that (possibly) anyone can be a Turtle today.

Second-generation Turtles include Mark J. Walsh, Jonathan Craven, John D. Fornengo (originally taught by Eckhardt in 1989), and Salem Abraham, four traders among hundreds of trend followers who all learned Turtle-style trend following secondhand. In turn, they built trading businesses that in many instances far exceeded those of the original Turtle traders.

When Walsh talks about his trading, it's like hearing Dennis and Eckhardt all over again, discussing strength and weakness: "If beans are up 10 cents and corn is down five cents, we buy beans. Some people think to buy corn because it's going to catch up with beans. We take the opposite. We'd rather buy the commodity that's strongest and sell the one that's weakest."[1] Walsh saw Dennis as "generous with his knowledge of the markets. He gave us a solid foundation on which to build a program."[2]

Two other second-generation Turtles are Robert Marcellus and Scot Henry, who run the Richmond Group Fund. Little is publicly known of their organization except that Henry once worked for Jerry Parker and Kidder Peabody (James River Capital). Coincidentally, their home base is in Manakin Sabot, Virginia, near Jerry Parker's.

There are many ways to analyze successful entrepreneurial traders, but "winning" is the starting point. Behind all the talk about teamwork and balance, people still judge trading success by an individual's ability to win big money. True competitors have a remarkable immunity to failure. It's simply not a factor that takes them out of the game even when it happens. They have a single-mindedness and zealous disregard for obstacles. They have indefatigable optimism. Winners pursue the prize because they are sure they can get it. They're less afraid of striking out than of not taking every possible turn at bat that comes their way.[3]

Many of the original Turtles simply did not think that way. Dennis taught his original Turtles only part of what made him successful. There was no way he could teach them the inner drive that had propelled him from the South Side of Chicago to becoming "Prince of the Pit." Dennis was forced by necessity to learn the hard way, just like so many second-generation Turtles.

Of all of the second-generation Turtles, one stands out. When Salem Abraham started trading he had no prior experience with Dennis and Eckhardt, no group of like-minded Turtle traders with whom to share experiences. He hadn't worked for Goldman Sachs or for any other hedge fund. Yet it didn't matter one iota.

With his pleasant demeanor, thick brown hair, and compact physique, Salem Abraham looks younger than his forty years. He could be mistaken for one of his ranch hands, but his Texas drawl and friendly manner mask a steely entrepreneurial drive that goes back generations.

How far away was Abraham from a Wall Street pedigree? He comes from a family of Christian Lebanese immigrants who settled in rural Canadian, Texas, in 1913. His grandfather, Malouf "Oofie" Abraham, sold ready-to-wear clothing out of a suitcase along the railroad before opening a retail store.

Before Abraham was headed down the path to becoming a trader, he attended Notre Dame and planned to marry his childhood sweetheart, Ruth Ann. He was going to start a mail-order business. While he did marry Ruth Ann and while he still lives in Canadian, Texas, it is not the story of his mail-order career that makes people take notice. It is his twenty-year trading performance:

Table 13.1: Abraham Trading Company—Diversified Program (Salem Abraham).

Year	Annual Return	Year	Annual Return
1988	142.04%	1998	4.39
1989	17.81	1999	4.76
1990	89.95	2000	13.54
1991	24.39	2001	19.16
1992	−10.50	2002	21.51
1993	34.29	2003	74.66
1994	24.22	2004	15.38
1995	6.12	2005	−10.95
1996	−0.42	2006	8.88
1997	10.88		

Source: Disclosure Documents Filed with United States CFTC.

I first interviewed Salem Abraham face-to-face in his office in 2005. His world offers instant culture shock. Canadian, Texas, is the epitome of small-town America, but with a big twist. Abraham's success has allowed him to endow his tiny town with amenities unusual in communities several times its size.

Canadian's Main Street (with one stoplight) now has the Cattle Exchange steakhouse and a restored movie theater with a digital sound system. Abraham has spent millions to create this oasis. How was he able to do it?

Meeting a Turtle

Salem Abraham would never have pursued trading if not for a chance meeting with Jerry Parker. It was the spring of 1987. He was at Notre Dame with one semester left, determined to graduate in three and a half years in order to start his mail-order business. Then he attended a family wedding where he met Parker, and his life changed.

Abraham was making casual conversation with Parker (whose wife and Abraham shared mutual first cousins), with no expectation of a life-changing moment at hand. He asked Parker what he did for a living. Parker said, "We figure out the odds and there's certain patterns that we look for. Then we manage our risk and when these patterns happen, you put on certain trades." Abraham incredulously followed up, "The odds are in your favor? You're sure of that?"

When Abraham heard the Turtle story for the first time, he was floored. He recalled, "Jerry told me about Richard Dennis and told me about these guys that he hired to train to trade. He told me that everybody's making money and how much money they've made each year." Abraham, who'd already decided he wanted "to make a living in a little town in Texas," quickly said to himself, "This can work from Canadian. It's right up my alley."

At that moment he saw an opportunity, just as his grandfather had decades before when the railroad was being built. He had never before heard of the Turtles or Richard Dennis, yet he took stock of Parker's career, and without knowing the specifics, immediately shifted his goals in life to pursue trading. No more mail-order business.

Luckily for Abraham, Parker said that if he ever wanted to visit Richmond he would show him some things to point him in the right direction. Abraham called the next week. It never occurred to Abraham that Parker might have been making polite social conversation, never dreaming that Abraham would take him up on the offer.

The thought that he might have been imposing on Parker simply did not occur to Abraham, who later described his mindset at the time: "I think you're kind of young and dumb and you just say, 'He made the offer and that means he really means it.'" When Abraham called, all he could hear was, "Well, ah." At that moment Abraham knew Parker was just trying to be nice to the new relative. But Parker finally said, "Sure, come on out."

Abraham knew the immediate import of Parker living in Richmond and trading out of his home office for his own plans to build a career in tiny Canadian. That bit of knowledge told him that all he needed was a telephone line to potentially be the next Jerry Parker. The self-confidence to instantly switch gears from mail-order business ideas to a trading career was the first sign of a true entrepreneur in action. Abraham was also very fortunate to have grown up in a family of entrepreneurs who would take a chance on his seemingly crazy trading idea.

Those who immediately interpret this to mean Abraham got a free family gift may want to reconsider. It was his responsibility to use his very limited capital wisely. So not surprisingly, he saw "risk management" as the big lesson during their first meeting at Parker's office. Abraham recalled, "Jerry was clearly aware that there were things that were proprietary he couldn't tell me." But he said to Abraham, "Look, this trend-following works, and here's some ideas you ought to think about," and then gave him some risk management concepts to think about. Reflecting on Parker's generosity Abraham, said, "I certainly would never be in the position I'm in without his early help. I would never be where I am now."

At the time Abraham knew nothing about trading. He had no experience, but he started researching after meeting Parker at his office. Back at Notre Dame, he then read everything he could about Richard Dennis and trend followers. He said, "If you want to be successful at something, well, you want to identify who's been successful and what are they doing."

During his last semester at Notre Dame, Abraham touted the success of Dennis to deaf ears. His professors weren't interested. They said Richard Dennis was "lucky." It's not surprising that professors were skeptical, since Abraham was preaching a gospel that went squarely against the notion of efficient markets—the backbone of generally accepted financial truth.

Nor was Abraham the only convert to new success following a conversation with Jerry Parker. Off the record, another trader also spoke to me about Parker's generosity with trading advice. Parker had helped him navigate the waters of setting up his trading firm many years ago. That trader is worth close to $100 million today.

Taking the Plunge

Once Abraham had Parker's initial mentoring, he started researching trend-following trading rules by hand. It was messy. He was marking charts, noting his risk rules and then just keeping tabs every day. "If I would have bought here, sold here, bought here, sold here."

He went to his grandfather with a portfolio of twenty-one markets that he had tested over an eight-month period, and said, "Look, if I had started with a million dollars, it'd be worth $1.6 million at the end of eight months." He was excited to show all the stuff he had been working on. Abraham's grandfather, who at that time was seventy-two, had seen lots of Texas deals. He was skeptical of his grandson's new venture.

His grandfather's skepticism would be hard to overcome and Abraham had to have been pretty tough to take the withering sarcasm that followed. His grandfather said, "What are we going to do? I guess we just package this up and send it to Chicago. They cut us some check, right, dumb-ass? You may think you're a smart kid coming out of Notre Dame, but these guys in Chicago, they're going to chew you up and spit you out. Of all the ways to lose money, why in the hell did you have to pick the very *fastest* way?"

Not about to be dismissed, Abraham explained the wisdom behind his trading philosophy. He said he was going to use good risk management, explaining, "Just because you have a Lamborghini, you don't have to go 160 miles an hour. I'm never going past 30 and I'm going to control risk."

It was obvious where Abraham had inherited his confidence and entrepreneurial zeal. More than just hard business truths had been passed down from generation to generation. Abraham had also been given a moral business compass. His grandfather used to say that if you screw one person, you're done and you are out of business. He wanted his grandsons to always keep their word, number one. But he also wanted them to go above and beyond what's fair, saying, "Make sure, even though that's not the deal." The legendary investor Boone Pickens, a longtime family friend, saw heredity playing a role in Abraham's drive. He had known the family for fifty years and saw them make a great contribution to the Texas panhandle.[4]

Luckily for Abraham, he had grown up around entrepreneurial risk-taking and even participated in some family business deals. He learned the most from the potential deals that went awry. On one oil and gas deal that he learned about from his grandfather, he decided that he would talk to the representative at Shell Oil. Abraham thought they would sell a piece of land to him.

His grandfather knew it was going nowhere, saying, "No way. They've had this for thirty years, forty years we've all talked to them. They won't do anything with anybody." Abraham was not deterred, and said, "This guy at Shell Oil, he's new there. I think he'll do something."

His grandfather responded with some attitude: "Tell you what, if you get that deal done, I will kiss your butt out there in the middle of the intersection under that stoplight right there." Abraham replied to his grandfather, "Pucker up, old man, because it's going to happen." The deal never happened.

However, it was that same entrepreneurial fearlessness that Abraham used to launch his trading career that last semester at Notre Dame. It demanded burning the candle at both ends. He was trading twenty-one markets and taking a grueling twenty-one semester hours. He was cramming, and all of his classes had to be scheduled in the afternoon. He would wake up at 7 A.M. and trade from 7 A.M. to 10 A.M. Then he would put his stops in and go to class. After class he would check to see if his stops had been hit.

The fall of 1987 was no ordinary time, especially for a brand-new trader experiencing historic market volatility. During the last part of September and the first part of October, the interest rates started going straight down. Abraham had come home for fall break on October 19, 1987. He recalled, "The Friday before fall break I made a lot of money. My $50,000 was $66,000 as of Friday. I'm going home and I'm feeling great." Then, Monday morning, the stock market tanked.

These were big events. Things were going haywire. Abraham worried about his positions in Eurodollars. He called up his broker and said, "So where are Eurodollars?" His broker replied, "They're up 250.'" Abraham shot back, "Two fifty, what do you mean, 25?" His broker said, "No, 250.'" Abraham wanted to know if it was as bad as what he was thinking. He immediately knew that that move was in the neighborhood of 10+ standard deviations away from where Eurodollars normally traded.

His $66,000 had dropped to $33,000. But by the end of the day, he considered it all a great lesson. He had learned the significance of hanging in there to play another day. He felt that to survive at this point in his trading career, with his own money on the line, and not blow out, was "okay." He recalled, "The one lesson I was clear on: always know the thing that they say can never happen, can happen."

Abraham took a short break after the 1987 October crash. He was out of the markets for a week or so and then got back in. He traded during November and a little bit of December and then shut down for the year. His account had bounced back to $45,000 from that $33,000 low. He took $1,600 out of his account and went to Jim's Guns, Gold, and Diamonds to buy an engagement ring to propose to his now wife.

Commodities Corporation

Starting in 1988 Abraham wanted to trade full time, but he still had to prove himself to his grandfather. He told his grandfather, "I want to do this on the side. I know we're not that busy. Will you let me do this on the side?" He had $45,000, and his older brother Eddie agreed to put up $15,000. His younger brother Jason put in $10,000 to get the "Abraham brother fund" up to $70,000. He wanted his grandfather to put in $30,000 so he would have an even $100,000 trading account.

His grandfather was willing to play ball, but true to Abraham family ethos there would be a deal. He announced, "Okay, here's the deal. I'll put up $30,000. But if we get down to $50,000, we throw that quote machine out the window and we stop all this trading nonsense."

For a man in his early twenties, Salem Abraham was taking on some serious risk and pressure. And as is often the case, just when he was out of the gate with his $100,000 account for his new trading firm, the bottom dropped out.

The first two weeks of May 1988 were horrible markets. Abraham was downstairs in his office when his grandfather stuck his head in one morning and said, "Where are we today?" Abraham replied, "Sixty-eight thousand dollars." In sarcastic glee, his grandfather said, "Just a matter of *time*," and he walked out the door.

Time never happened. The grain market drought of 1988 hit and Abraham was long soybeans, corn, and wheat. The markets just exploded the second half of May and into June. He was very well positioned and rocked along to serious profit.

How could Abraham have been certain that bigger things were around the corner with the kind of volatility he had seen in his first eight months of trading? Plenty of people would have quit, chalking it up to a failed business venture. In spite of the ups and downs, once he'd shown his grandfather that he was on to a profitable angle, the senior

Abraham came on board in a big way. His grandfather walked in the door one day with a "Dean Witter Principal Guarantee Fund 2" brochure and threw it on his grandson's desk, declaring, "Hey, you did better than these guys did."

Commodities Corporation was the manager of the Dean Witter fund, and they were in the process of raising $100 million and allocating it among eight to ten traders. Commodities Corporation had quite a history. They were a prominent Princeton, New Jersey–based trading incubator (now part of Goldman Sachs following a late-1990s buyout). They were responsible for the early funding (and in some instances training) of hedge fund greats such as Paul Tudor Jones, Louis Bacon, Ed Seykota, Bruce Kovner, and Michael Marcus.

Abraham did not know all that history at the time. He just picked up the phone and called Commodities Corporation. He got Elaine Crocker on the phone late in the day. Crocker, who now runs Louis Bacon's Moore Capital and today may be the most powerful woman in the hedge fund industry, said she would send some information. Abraham doubted Crocker was taking him seriously, because he had only a one-year track record.

But eventually Commodities Corporation got back in touch with him, announcing that they were going to be in Houston and inviting him to meet with them. He jumped at the opportunity and flew to the Houston airport to meet Crocker and Michael Garfinkel.

Abraham had just celebrated his twenty-third birthday before the meeting. Garfinkel did most of the talking. Crocker sat back and watched the discussion. Garfinkel said, "Wow, last month was a tough month. What happened?" Abraham pointed out that during the current month he was up 40 percent.

Crocker started laughing. Not seeing the humor in his response, Abraham asked. "What's so funny about up 40 percent?" Garfinkel, sensing a disconnect, wanted to know what kind of returns Abraham was shooting for. Abraham gave the Turtle-like answer of 100 percent a year. And just like many of the original Turtles were told after leaving Dennis, Crocker wanted Abraham to back off his riskier "shoot for the moon" approach. She and Garfinkel made the same observation Jerry Parker and others had heard: "If you make 30 percent a year, people will beat a path to your door. You need to back off on the leverage."

Commodities Corporation still wanted to see a ten-year simulation of Abraham's system — something he did not have. Their request forced Abraham to learn programming to quickly test his trading system. The pressure was on. It started Abraham down the path of developing a whole new research and programming skill set. It was just one of the many ways he was setting himself apart from the original Turtles.

There was one more consideration in the deal. Commodities Corporation wanted to invest Abraham's minimum account size. Since he had no minimum, he settled on $200,000, rightfully surmising that Commodities Corporation would pony up to a reasonable number. He was right, and they became his first big client.

For a young man with no trading pedigree and no hedge fund experience, this investment was admission to the major leagues. Commodities Corporation invested the next $7 to $8 million in his firm as well. That initial $30,000 investment from his grandfather? It's worth $1.3 million today.

However, even with all that moneymaking success, Abraham was still just a young guy, and his experiences with the establishment questioning his credibility were similar to those of the young Richard Dennis. Reminiscent of Dennis's trip to the bank to cash the $250,000 check was Abraham trying to rent a car at age twenty-five, with no luck since they had recently raised the minimum age requirement. He was managing $15 million, but the Hertz counter was not budging on renting to him. Salem, after attempting to negotiate, tried some attitude: "Do you know that I have people who entrust $15 million with me, and I can buy and sell whatever I want to with this $15 million? You won't loan me a car? A $15,000, $20,000 car for the day?" The lady at the counter was looking him up and down thinking, "Yeah, right, I'm not believing you, punk." Salem added, "I had to call Joe's Rent-a-Wreck."

Dennis and Eckhardt Training

Even people who are knowledgeable about the Turtles do not know about an obscure third Turtle class after the 1983 and 1984 original ones on which the Turtle legend was built. Abraham actually received personal instruction from Dennis and Eckhardt several years after his trading firm was launched. In the early 1990s, Commodities Corporation asked Dennis and Eckhardt to hold a third Turtle class for their stable of traders. Commodities Corporation was giving them money to trade, and part of the deal was that they had to hold a seminar. The seminar was supposed to simulate the Turtle trader experience, except instead of two weeks, it was held over four days.

While Abraham was already trading by Turtle-style trend-following trading rules, and while he found much of the training to reinforce what he already knew ("What I got out of it was a lot of risk management ideas, position sizing ideas, and system analysis ideas."), the classroom experience with thirty students from Commodities Corporation was a memorable part of his education.

However, Abraham saw his learning process as a step-by-step journey, not just a lucky leap: "It's like climbing a mountain. Which step was the most important? Every step is needed to get to the top of the mountain. Each individual step is not that much." This makes him far more the "average guy" than Parker, Rabar, or any of the other original Turtles, who had four years of Dennis covering the overhead costs.

The seminar opened Abraham's eyes though. He was very impressed by William Eckhardt. All of the students had also been given an advance copy of Eckhardt's interview in the *New Market Wizards*. Abraham added, "I went into that meeting thinking, 'Oh yeah, Richard Dennis, he's the guy and Eckhardt is the sidekick' kind of deal." Just as the original Turtles had learned during their training, Abraham discovered that he was wrong: "However when I got through, I really appreciated the math and the objective data. The statistics of this works, this doesn't work. It's all odds. I actually got more useful information from Eckhardt. But of course Richard Dennis is clearly a brilliant trader."

Dennis would basically tell the class, "The system is a nice thing to guide you, but it's okay to set the system aside." Eckhardt was saying something a little different: "These are the odds; it's all a math game." Nothing had changed about the two teachers since the original Turtle experiment.

Eckhardt challenged the Commodities Corporation traders with a series of questions. There were ten questions the traders had to answer within a range. The goal was to get nine of the ten correct. Eckhardt asked, "What does a 747 plane weigh?" The answer could be as big a range as the traders wanted it to be, but the goal was to be 90 percent certain that they were right. It tested their confidence and their ability to estimate. Everyone missed four or five questions. Eckhardt said that the majority of people missed about 45 percent of the questions because they were overconfident in their ability to estimate reality.

Trend trading thrives on that overconfidence. Abraham made this point using the recent surge in the price of oil over the last few years: "What you see in trend following is people's mistaken mindset of what's a high price and what's a low price. It all has to do with a very limited set of experiences. People make assumptions for a small sample size. To think that crude oil could go from $20 to $70, you say, 'that's nuts.' To buy crude oil at $55? That's a hard bet to do when it's never been to $56. Never in the history of the world has it been to $56 and you say, 'It hit $55 today, I'm buying it.' "

Can you imagine buying a market that is making an all-time high, without any knowledge that it will keep going up or come crashing back down? Abraham put the focus where it really counts: "I care about the statistics." He gave me an example. Pretend a physicist walks in with a coin and says, "This coin will always come up 50–50 heads or tails." A statistician, however, walks in and says, "Yes, but I flipped it one million times and 65 percent of the time it came up heads." The Harvard-trained physicist says, "That is impossible; it's a 50–50 coin."

Abraham asked, "Who do you believe?" He had many college professors with plenty of good reasons why that coin should not be coming up heads 65 percent of the time, but at some point you have to say, "I don't know why this coin is coming up 65 percent heads, but I'm willing to bet after a million flips that the 65 percent rate will hold true even when on the face of it, it shouldn't." Abraham added, "Just because I don't understand it doesn't mean I'm not going to bet on it."

Ultimately, Abraham was saying the same thing that Tom Willis had said years before, which was to just trade the "numbers." The empiricist in Abraham was driving at the concept of the unexpected big event; the nexus of his trading profits derived from trading "price." Is the world due for another large unexpected event that will give him a chance to profit? He did not blink: "Yes, but it will be one that we've never seen before. It's always a different one."

Boil the Ocean

Abraham might not be in Wall Street's top ten in terms of earnings yet. He might not be managing a billion-dollar fund at this moment in his life, but he has done exceedingly well. Sitting in his office, filled with evidence of his eclectic interests ranging from oil and gas leasing projects to the restoration of antique books and papers, he has made a life for himself that includes family, friends, and a company of like-minded people drawn from his local community.

His hiring practices come very close to mimicking Dennis's original Turtle hiring process. No one at Abraham's firm has an Ivy League degree. Most employees have backgrounds working at the area's feedlots or natural gas–drilling companies. For example, Abraham hired Geoff Dockray as a clerk from one of those very feedlots. Dockray appreciated the opportunity to work in Abraham's office. He said, "This beats shoveling manure at 6 A.M. in the morning. The financial markets are complicated but they're not as relentless as dealing with livestock all the time."[5]

Maybe it is that down-to-earth perspective gleaned from living in handshake country that gives Abraham a clear perspective. Sitting in the Cattle Exchange steakhouse located in the historic Moody Building, which he owns and where he has his office, he had no doubts that it is his entrepreneurial tenacity: "I think they [the winning Turtles] have a self-confidence or charisma to run a business. There's a drive to go out and do it. Then there is a drive to want to do it. Some people [the losing Turtles] will just say, 'Oh, hey, I made some money. That's all I need.'"

However, if you are going to boil the ocean (in other words, if you are going to use all means and options available to get something done), especially if it is a very competitive and lucrative endeavor, there will be ups and downs. Salem Abraham's experience has been no different. Twice during his trading career, clients left after down or flat performance periods. He regrouped and made new equity highs each time. During trying times, he handled curve balls in his career by working on other ideas to make money. He always focused on his trading, but he also cast a wider net and caught other kinds of fish.

As with trading, not everything works out. One project was a water deal that he almost cut with billionaire T. Boone Pickens ("Couldn't agree on the price"). Pickens and Abraham's ranches are right next to each other in the Texas panhandle (even though they are separated by forty miles, their ranches touch) and they have become friends over the years; Pickens was not shy about praising Abraham's entrepreneurial guts when I talked to him in his Dallas office.

There were other deals that turned out to be big winners. Abraham was humble about them: "I sold water rights to the city of Amarillo. I invested $1.5 million and I got $9 million out. I said to myself, 'That's a cool idea.' Then I did the Chicago Mercantile Exchange deal [CME Initial Public Offering]. I put $1.5 million in, and got about $13 million out. You recognize opportunities where you see them."

This kind of thinking and risk-taking is how to make your first million by age twenty-five—which Abraham did. Still, it's not enough to simply spot opportunities. The confidence to act on them is mandatory. You need a killer instinct. When faced with real life and death, even with chickens and pigs, it is never easy to pull the trigger or snap a chicken's neck, even for dinner. You have to be able to pull the trigger when there is blood on Wall Street, especially if the blood is yours.[6]

Jerry Parker could not have known Salem Abraham would have the prerequisite killer instinct when they first met. Parker was probably thinking, "Okay, this young guy has got a rough idea of what I do. I've given him some pointers. If he's serious, he's going to figure it all out and 'just do it,' but I will be surprised if he hangs around."

Unlike the original Turtles who won the job lottery—who were given the exact winning rules and allowed to practice on Richard Dennis's dime, all in the womblike atmosphere of C&D Commodities—Abraham was on his own from the get-go. He is tougher for it. There is far more to learn from the attitude and actions of this second-generation Turtle than from any one original Turtle.

14

Model Greatness

"Are Turtles grown, or can they be taught? Do they have a magic sixth sense or something? The jury is in, isn't it? They'd be better off having the knowledge implanted than relying on a sixth sense. I think I could take a kid who wasn't my son and say, 'Do this, I'll pay you $50,000 a year, or you're fired if you don't exactly follow it.' He'd beat me every day, every week, every month and every year."[1]

Tom Willis

The Turtle story breaks down into two parts. Part one takes place during the experiment, when the Turtles are on the relatively level playing field designed by Richard Dennis. His experiment proves nurture trumps nature. Part two takes place after the experiment, when the Turtles have to face the real world as individuals and human nature reenters the picture.

While the experiment itself is what made headlines, some people familiar with the Turtle story recognized the greater significance of part two, the experiment's aftermath as Turtles attempt to carry on solo. Larry Hite called me late on a Friday afternoon after we'd had lunch near his Park Avenue office. Hite, who founded Mint Capital and was instrumental in the early successes of the multibillion-dollar Man Financial hedge fund, had more feedback for me about my Turtle book (i.e., the one you're reading now).

"I have been thinking about this new book. . . ." He laid it out: "The people who are very good and long-lasting are tough. If life goes against them, they stick to their game. There is a certain amount of mental toughness to have clarity. Toughness is just the ability to roll with the punches. They don't get disappointed by losses. Some people when they lose, they don't get back up. Think about the Turtles who failed at trading. What did the failures have in common? Maybe the ones who failed just gave up. They were not tough."

Dennis demanded that the Turtles be mentally tough as long as they worked for him, but once he pulled the plug they had to face head on what Dennis was not providing them. Hite saw it. He brought up the memo (see chapter 7) sent out by Dennis telling the Turtles to cut back their leverage by 50 percent. He observed that Dennis had made an error, ignored any knock against his ego, acknowledged the mistake, and fixed it. That was "an act of mental toughness" in Hite's book.

But Dennis did not select his students for strength of character and drive to win, nor did he train them on the fine art of mental toughness. On that level playing field where he covered the overhead, everyone appeared mentally tough. However, it turned out that only Turtles like Jerry Parker, Paul Rabar, and a few others, and later, Salem Abraham, actually shared the same drive and entrepreneurial spirit that Dennis had.

Think about the annual drafts of professional sports teams. They demonstrate this same inability to screen candidates for mental toughness. For example, every year college stars get drafted with much fanfare. Every year at least one significant stud, one "can't miss" prospect, fails. Look how many thousands of great college players never make it to the NFL, NBA, or Major League Baseball. Something separates pretenders from contenders. Innate talent alone is never enough.

The same is true when it comes to making money. Take, for example, the top ten earners in the hedge fund industry for 2005:

1. James Simons, Renaissance Technologies Corp.: $1.5 billion

2. T. Boone Pickens, Jr., BP Capital Management: $1.4 billion

3. George Soros, Soros Fund Management: $840 million

4. Steven Cohen, SAC Capital Advisors: $550 million

5. Paul Tudor Jones II, Tudor Investment Corp.: $500 million

6. Edward Lampert, ESL Investments: $425 million

7. Bruce Kovner, Caxton Associates: $400 million

8. David Tepper, Appaloosa Management: $400 million

9. David Shaw, DE Shaw & Co.: $340 million

10. Stephen Mandel, Jr., Lone Pine Capital: $275 million

Those men got to the top ten by more than rules alone. While not everyone can make Wall Street's top ten (and many of those top ten are trend-type traders), the story of the Turtles is compelling proof that it *is* possible to learn the steps top earners took and replicate their process.

The greater challenge, the real "secret," comes in following the footsteps of those trading entrepreneurs in part two of the story. All of the winners role-model that extra drive — call it self-confidence, toughness, or entrepreneurial passion — that proves it is possible to surmount those biases inherent in human nature that hold the majority of people back.

To cultivate that extra drive, however, requires *deliberate practice*. Berkshire Hathaway's Charlie Munger (Warren Buffet's number two man) has lived it; he has said, "In my whole life, I have known no wise people over a broad subject matter area who didn't read all the time — none, zero."[2] Most people do not want the real work that comes with real success.

Look at Eddie Lampert, too (number six on the top ten). His nurture process had him reverse-engineering Warren Buffett's thought process. He said, "Putting myself in his shoes at that time, could I understand why he made the investments? That was part of my learning process."[3] Second-generation Turtles did the same thing when it came to Dennis.

Further, consider the similarities between the skills of a surgeon and those of a trader. Great surgeons are the ones who are conscientious, industrious, and boneheaded enough to keep practicing day and night for years on end.[4] Once again, nurture over nature.

The bottom line is that the market doesn't care about you personally. It doesn't care about your gender, culture, religion, or race. It's one of the last frontiers where low barriers to entry allow anyone to bet his cash and take a whack at making big money. In the end, traders like Jerry Parker, Salem Abraham, and Richard Dennis are playing a legitimate game that anyone can play.

And you don't have to have been lucky enough to answer a Richard Dennis want ad in 1983 to be a successful trader. Salem Abraham only needed to know that Dennis and his philosophy existed; from that point on, he would figure it out. That is the reason why Abraham is so important to the story. He embodies the stubborn determination and entrepreneurial guts played out over the four decades since Dennis first entered the Chicago pits.

However, the best affirmation of this story's enduring legacy came from Richard Sandor (a legendary figure in his own right, often viewed as a founding father of the financial futures markets) when we shared a few moments at Chicago O'Hare baggage claim in fall 2006. Sandor spoke directly to practicing, winning, and never giving up. Smiling broadly, he said with a glow of admiration and respect as we parted ways, "You do know that Richard Dennis is trading again?"

That simple comment said it all. It solidified my belief that we all have the opportunity to build upon our inborn gifts. Ultimately, the path that led a regular Chicago guy to the top, that led him to teach a handful of beginners to win big and make millions like him and in many ways inspired a generation of Wall Street titans from up close and afar, is a path we can all take.

Afterword

"Inside baseball is a colloquial term in American English referring to 'behind-the-scenes' conversations or dialogue that the average member of the public would have no way of being privy to."
Wikipedia.com

At one time or another four Turtles (so far) have threatened lawsuits over some aspect of my writing about them. Their reaction should immediately put in context how much of a wild ride it was to put together *The Complete TurtleTrader*. It's always satisfying for an author when reviewers like their work, which has been, to my pleasure, the case for *TurtleTrader* during the past months. But for me the experience of getting this book to print might be my favorite story covering the Turtles. Wall Street loves to create moneymaking gods for public worship. Sometimes those gods deserve adulation, and sometimes they don't. Discovering who is deserving and who is not is what makes my job fun. By the time my Turtle research was over a story had been assembled that some Turtles would want deciphered and disseminated while others would work hard to bury with all of the secrecy of a Cold War-era CIA operation.

Plenty of people knew the behind-the-scenes story would be fascinating. Once final drafts of *The Complete TurtleTrader* started making the rounds feedback from one individual in particular struck a chord. Bob Pardo is a seasoned trader. He is also a skeptic, exactly the kind of individual you would want to pore over a book to ferret out the weaknesses.

Pardo confronted me with a number of questions. He postulated why some Turtles did not want Dennis to talk and wondered if there weren't further lessons to be drawn from Dennis's fund management blowups. He also suggested that what smacked of paranoia from some Turtles warranted further exploration.

During an ensuing phone conversation I told him that many of his questions and concerns were part of an unpublished Afterword, but that my publisher had elected to leave it out saying essentially that it was "inside baseball." Upon reflection that was a mistake and perhaps a harder fight should have been fought to include more of the behind-the-scenes drama—especially when to this day *some* Turtles spin a story contrary to the truth.

However, more behind-the-curtain glimpses into the research and writing and research process had definite pros and cons. Would more drama be perceived as petty and inconsequential? Or would these insights reveal missing details of human frailty that further clarified the dividing line between Turtle winners and losers?

In my opinion, especially given the mythical Turtle legend that existed for over two decades, opening up the blinds and letting sunshine in could only help investors *without* Turtle-like access and success to realize that the Turtles were human. If the original Turtles could learn, the ones chosen off the street, anyone could. Yes, the trading rules they were taught were critical, and yes, some were very intelligent, but the human element can't be ignored when analyzing the experiment's results from 1983 to 2008. So after much internal debate, and after the initial printing of the hardcover version, it was clear that an Afterword was needed for the paperback version.

Digging down into the Turtle vault was like entering the matrix filled with unexpected twists and turns that I doubt even the best Hollywood scriptwriters could have dreamed up. It was like a marathon session of Nintendo's Mario Brothers 3 when you enter new worlds where secret clues and hidden meanings pop up each step of the way, but only if you're willing to venture into uncharted territory where there are no guarantees that your risk will pan out.

That being said in 2006 while investigating the Turtle story it seemed attitudes had finally changed and Turtle openness was in vogue. One Turtle said he would be happy to do an interview, "by phone if necessary." Another said that he would be happy to discuss the Turtle experience. Another Turtle only wanted to provide written answers to questions, but at least he was talking. Yet another said he wouldn't mind if the circumstances were right. Ultimately those responses resulted in thoughtful and incisive interviews. Maybe my gut fear was wrong all along. Maybe this was going to be *fun*.

As my research gained steam, a new Turtle I'd never heard of appeared. For example, there was Rudolf Papirnik. Robert Moss, Dennis's trading-floor chief, called Papirnik a Turtle. Papirnik worked for Dennis before, during and after the Turtle program. He definitely had "Turtle knowledge." A known Turtle, Jim DiMaria, backed Moss's contention that Papirnik was a Turtle too.

Moreover, once the Turtles started talking they were quick to express concern that Dennis would be portrayed as their primary if not only teacher. They didn't want me to diminish the importance of Bill Eckhardt to their success. Take Jeff Gordon who was emphatic, "Bill [Eckhardt]. Very smart guy. It seemed like every time he spoke, I learned something. And there are very few people in the world that I have ever met that I can say that about. I was always learning things from him." Time and time again, Turtles kept coming back to the importance of Bill Eckhardt's teachings.

Besides properly crediting Eckhardt, several Turtles gave different versions of the genesis of the original "Turtle" nickname. Mike Shannon contradicted the legend that Dennis named his students after seeing a turtle-breeding farm in Singapore: "Our original name, in the first year of our existence, was the Disciples. Because it was the name, at the time, of a prominent street gang on Chicago's West Side, we agreed to go with the 'Turtle' idea." Accurate? No one else told me that story, but then again Shannon had told me many other things that I later confirmed as true that no one else had told me. On the other hand, Lucy Wyatt Mattinen, one of the two female Turtles, said the name actually traced back to Richard Dennis's fondness for the music of the '60s pop group The Turtles.

Despite the initial cooperation and despite these colorful asides clear resistance to my effort to write a book was slowly taking shape after initial openness. It was soon clear that some Turtles just did not want an objective treatment of their story made public.

Then there were the contradictory interpretations of their confidentiality agreement with Dennis depending on who wanted their story made public and who did not. The agreement signed by all Turtles had long since expired. It's floating around the Net for all to see. But when trying to contact Turtle Philip Lu, who is now working as a college teacher, he threw a curve ball. Through his Edgewood College email address Lu was blunt, "It is my belief that my confidentiality agreement with Richard Dennis is still in force. Therefore I do not give interviews."

Lu is an intelligent man (graduate of Brown). He apparently made millions as a Turtle and is well respected by many other Turtles, but what was with the ludicrous confidentiality assertion? One Turtle sprang to Lu's defense saying that Lu could have been in the same league as Turtles Jerry Parker and Paul Rabar, "Phil actively chose not to take over a certain amount of money. He didn't want to manage a billion dollars."

Turtle Sam DeNardo clearly respected Lu for saying their confidentiality agreement was still intact. "He knows that that system can still work. And the more people that use it, the less effective it's going to be. He probably feels blessed like a lot of us that we've had the experience." DeNardo's contention that widespread dissemination of the Turtle rules would dilute their effectiveness has not been borne out.

However, the desire to keep things silent did not stop with Lu. As I completed my research I sent out final requests for interviews. Turtle Paul Rabar responded by asking: "how did you get my email address?" I never heard from him again. Another Turtle responded bluntly to an interview request saying he was "not interested." Months later that same Turtle appeared to warm up when his assistant asked for a list of those who had agreed to cooperate. When I sent him a detailed list of everyone who had participated, his response was, "no." Unknown to me at the time, the exact list I handed over was then used to contact Turtles who had completed their interviews to persuade them to not talk. That tactic did not work and in fact irked Turtle Michael Cavallo (one of several pressured not to talk after already talking) who told me he thought the story should be out there.

When I asked another Turtle for an interview he replied: "Thank you for keeping me abreast of your project. It is still unlikely that I will participate, given what I know of Rich's and Bill's feelings about it.

However, as I've indicated before, if [Turtle] and [Turtle] participate, I will too. I am confident the result will be a fine effort either way, and wish you the best with it."

That complimentary but odd response said there was strength in numbers. If this group of three participated together, then it would be fine to go against Dennis's and Eckhardt's desire for privacy, although the desires of the Turtle teachers were not known to be fact. After all, access had been granted to Tom Willis—one of Rich Dennis's closest friends dating back to the early 1970s (long before the Turtles)—a man who talked to me about everything.

However, it was apparent that when it came to interviewing them some Turtles used the defense of wanting to "protect Rich"—whatever that meant exactly—as a means to avoid talking. One Turtle who had talked to me chuckled in disbelief that the 'Rich protection' explanation by other Turtles was "bullshit."

There were also an assortment of stories surrounding the scene that could best be described as sex, drugs, and rock 'n' roll. This was the late seventies and early eighties after all, so debauchery among some was not exactly unexpected (and that is not to say all the Turtles indulged). While not all of those stories made this book, let's just say there were some wild characters around.

Jerry Parker

Seeing Jerry Parker's original office for the first time might seem trivial, but for me it still brings back the "aha moment" as if it were yesterday.

Just finding the place was an adventure. While Richmond, Virginia, was only ninety miles from my house and I had a street address, there were no Map Quest turn-by-turn driving directions available back in 1994. A good old-fashioned hard-copy map from AAA was my compass. While it guided me to the general area of Parker's office, I spent another two hours driving around rural Virginia trying to actually find it. Finally, I stopped at a local country bank to ask if they had ever heard of Parker's firm, Chesapeake Capital.

At first my question was met with blank stares, but then one bank teller said that Chesapeake *might* be a half-mile up on the right side of the street. She was right. Upon reflection it was odd that while the teller sort of knew where Chesapeake was located, she had no clue what they did. She was probably making $35,000 a year (nothing wrong with that), but at the same time Parker was literally a baseball throw away making $35 million a year. My first thought was just to shake her and say, "Don't you get who is working down the road? Forget teller jobs, go be an intern for Parker and learn how he makes millions!"

There was no meeting Parker that summer day. All I saw was the lobby and the twenty-something secretary. My first face-to-face meeting with him did not come until December 1995 at Parker's new suburban Richmond office (about eighteen months later). Pestering him for an informational interview finally paid off when his assistant Jonathan Craven responded with the good news that he would see me. Parker's private office was surprisingly barren except for a small glass turtle on his desk (outside the office today there is a large turtle-shaped stone sculpture, the only giveaway). I knew I was nervous but to my surprise, he seemed to be too. Parker asked, "What do you want to do the most?" Without clarification I blurted out "Execution." Parker took that to mean that the broker world was my goal (it wasn't) and he generously responded by recommending that I speak with his execution broker.

Yet before the allotted thirty minutes was up, I did capitalize on the face-to-face opportunity by looking at Parker straight in the eye and asking for confirmation of who had won the Barings Bank sweepstakes earlier in the year. My proffer of a "name" garnered a look of, "I can't believe you just asked me that in my office," but his one-word answer was confirmation. In that instant much of my understanding of trend following trading was solidified. He probably never knew how much he influenced me in that moment.

Later, the broker Parker recommended, Mike Curtis, had me over to his suburban Richmond, Virginia, home for chili. Curtis was a transplanted Chicagoan clearly enjoying financial success in the Deep South. At one point he mentioned that Parker had mentored one of his distant "relatives" in trend following. It would be years before it was clear to me that Curtis was talking about second generation Turtle Salem Abraham.

My path did not cross Parker's again for years and long after the website TurtleTrader.com was established. For this visit Parker, John Hoade (his number 2 man), Keith Byers (his marketing man), his IT guru and I met in his conference room. The furnishings of his sparse conference room gave no indication of what Chesapeake Capital did except for a huge Swiss alphorn leaning against the wall. Its "thank you" engraving to Parker and Chesapeake Capital from a Swiss "concern" spoke volumes about his firm's global reach.

Why was there that second meeting years later to begin with? Chesapeake Capital was a billion dollar fund at the time, but their brain trust still wanted fresh marketing ideas. They were investigating whether the Internet would enhance their business, and if so, how to use it effectively. Our meeting must have given them some good food for thought because shortly thereafter Parker sought to buy the domain trendfollowing.com from me (Parker did buy the domains trendfollowing.net & trend-following.com and still owned them as of July 2008). It was a wise move not to sell, since the domain name trendfollowing.com became the catalyst in launching my first book, *Trend Following*, four years later.

Today Jerry Parker's firm Chesapeake Capital still has no online presence to speak of, but that has not stifled his success. He is still far and away the most successful Turtle by a long country mile. Interestingly, after the release of *The Complete TurtleTrader* in the fall of 2007 we did communicate again, when I invited him to appear in a film documentary (which was featuring many of his peers in the trading world plus two Nobel Prize winners). He respectfully declined. It wasn't that he appeared to have a problem with the message of the film, but rather that having his privacy intruded on by appearing in a film was not his cup of tea.

Liz Cheval and Lucy Wyatt

There were two female Turtles. That was news to many since up to the time my book was published the lone female Turtle had been publicly positioned as Liz Cheval. Lucy Wyatt Mattinen was a Turtle as well. It was other Turtles who were the source of confirming Wyatt Mattinen's Turtle existence. But there was a more detailed backstory and it starts first with Liz Cheval.

Cheval initially responded to an interview request for this book in a civil fashion saying that due to other professional commitments she could not support the project. Then three weeks later, with no provocation or contact, she followed up to say that she would pursue legal remedies if references were made about her. Did she think as a public figure in the trading world, someone quoted in newspapers and magazines, that she could simply decree that her name be left out of a story on the Turtles? Apparently she did.

Soon after news came across my desk that Cheval would be speaking in Chicago at a Managed Funds Association conference. If she would not speak with me, then it was time to go hear her in person and perhaps convince her to ease up and consider an interview.

Dressed in an eclectic black outfit, almost appearing to be a cape, Cheval was very well spoken and confident. At her luncheon speech that day in Chicago Cheval organized her presentation into two parts:

1. Human investment psychology: the ups and downs and
2. The mathematical solution.

For anyone familiar with the Turtles these two big picture points were not a surprise. During her keynote address Cheval also broached the subject of "correlation." She presented a chart to the audience of 'Trader A' and 'Trader B'. They had, in Cheval's lexicon, "Perfect Negative Correlation":

	Jan	Feb	Mar	Apr	May	Jun	Jul	Aug	Sep	Oct	Nov	Dec
Trader A	4%	0%	4%	0%	4%	0%	4%	0%	4%	0%	4%	0%
Trader B	0%	4%	0%	4%	0%	4%	0%	4%	0%	4%	0%	4%
Blend	2%	2%	2%	2%	2%	2%	2%	2%	2%	2%	2%	2%

	Summary Return	Average Return	Standard Deviation
A	24%	2%	2%
B	24%	2%	2%
Blend	24%	2%	0%

The logic behind Cheval's presentation traced back to her time with Dennis. All traders should want as much negative correlation among the components in their portfolio as possible. As long as their portfolio maintains a positive overall return, constantly adding more and more negatively correlated components will decrease the standard deviation (or one way to view "risk").

Her speech reinforced everything my research had uncovered about the Turtles, their training and their beliefs, but I could not get close to her after her speech. So why wouldn't she grant an interview? For one Cheval was never a fan of TurtleTrader.com. She apparently did not like the fact that anyone beyond a "Turtle" could possibly profit from the word "Turtle" (that faulty logic would eliminate just about every member of the media and/or biographer from writing on any subject of any kind). But her push back never really made any sense given that my depiction of the Turtles for all these years was very positive.

There were a few possible reasons that might explain her reluctance. Cheval's first-year 1984 Turtle performance of -20.98% is missing from her current-day performance track record. It was actually Turtle Jeff Gordon who noted the omission in passing during his interview. It was clear that once Cheval began trading for clients in 1988 her track record started with her 1985 performance of +51.65%, not that negative first year.

But as book research neared completion, the animosity Cheval bore toward a Turtle book project accelerated. In the fall of 2006 a jazz music producer in New York City, Charles Carlini, came to me shopping a Turtle film documentary idea (not yet knowing my Turtle book was in the works). He was excited because he had been in contact with Cheval, who was promising access to *all* of the Turtles for his film. All? There was no way that was going to happen.

Given Carlini's lack of detailed knowledge of the Turtles and given Cheval's disdain for a Turtle book project, the film appeared to be a way to get another version of the Turtles out there before my book. What in blazes was her fear of an objective Turtle book? That said, it was crystal clear that a race with people who could trump my book was on. Pressure? Just a little.

One Turtle sarcastically called the drama created the "conspiracy of the stupid." However, in an attempt to bury the hatchet with Cheval, I made a final sincere effort to assuage her feelings. Bottom line, I had no personal gripe with her. Her email response in the form of a peace offering was suspect. My first thought? "Trojan horse":

"Are you the original founder of the TurtleTrader.com website? I know it's changed quite a bit over the years. I think it's a great resource. Just wasn't sure if you were the original founder and if so, and do you have any contact information for Russell Sands and other Turtles? Rich asked me to put together a list for him and I think you have more up-to-date information than I do. I would appreciate a list of email addresses or other contact information on as many Turtles as you have."

It was satisfying to hear Cheval be positive, but it did not seem like a good idea to give out a list of Turtle interviewees to another Turtle (again) and then have them be used to slow down the book. However, once the book was released in October 2007, there may have been another reason for Cheval's negative actions: Lucy Wyatt Mattinen—the other female Turtle.

Little did I know what a tempest was brewing once I declared that there were two female Turtles. Like my book, my December 2007 Turtle exposé in *Trader Monthly* magazine revealed the existence of two female Turtles. When verifying my article content with Cheval, *Trader Monthly* was told by her that she was the only female Turtle. The magazine, however, stood by the notion of two female Turtles and referred to "women" in my article.

While there was no opportunity to interview Lucy Wyatt Mattinen before my book was released, she came calling once it was out. She was incensed that she was described in the book as "doing her nails" by another Turtle (in another article I used the term "manicurist"—which was false). She vehemently denied the descriptions of her. After some time we both decided to sit down for an in-person interview on April 12, 2008—an interview that quickly added more to the genesis for the Turtle experiment and established perhaps how important Wyatt was to the creation of the Turtles.

La Mere Vipere, often called the world's first punk dance club, opened in Chicago on Halsted Street in 1977. It subsequently burned down in 1978. The La Mere Vipere bar was where Lucy Wyatt met Richard Dennis's brother Tom Dennis (also a trader). There is a very good chance the Turtle experiment would never have happened if not for that chance encounter between Lucy Wyatt and Tom Dennis (and that chance encounter surely included the Sex Pistols' Johnny Rotten belting out at least once that night "God Save the Queen").

It turns out that after becoming friends with Tom and Richard Dennis, Wyatt subsequently met Dennis's childhood friend William Eckhardt. Eckhardt and Wyatt then dated off and on, but before the Turtle experiment had officially commenced, Eckhardt taught Wyatt trading and she subsequently made hundreds of thousands of dollars in the early 1980s when she was only a few years removed from her teens. Wyatt told me that Eckhardt had needled Dennis that her success was due to a "woman's intuition." Dennis of course never bought the intuition argument—the fundamental reason for his launching the Turtle experiment. Within a few years the Turtles were picked and Wyatt joined the Turtles in the Turtle room as an original Turtle.

As a side note Cheval's name came across my desk again in 2008. She must have finally been happy with *The Complete TurtleTrader* as she was now eagerly paying Google to have her firm's ad pop up every time someone searched for the term "Michael Covel."

Jiri Svoboda

Along with Wyatt another Turtle who I could not find during the research process was Jiri "George" Svoboda. In turns out that today Svoboda is an accomplished guitarist who plays all kinds of musical styles from Latin to acoustic and Klezmer music. He happens to be the only original Turtle currently with a MySpace.com page. Is he trading still? Turtle Tom Shanks told me that Jiri "George" Svoboda probably has the best returns for any Turtle since 1988. But forget returns for a moment, his online videos are awesome.

When looking at his online YouTube videos while he and a partner played at San Diego State University, it was easy to wonder how many students walking around campus realized that day that the guy playing classical guitar in the courtyard knew more about trading and making money than the entire finance faculty at the university.

There was no finding Svoboda to interview the first time around, and no finding him for my Afterword either, but to my good fortune one individual who had worked for Svoboda (ten years after the end of the Turtle experiment) randomly contacted me in email.

He told me that while he worked for Svoboda they traded two systems very similar to the Turtle system, a slow and a fast system. Some of the parameters had been tweaked slightly due to results from extensive back-testing, but the basic trading rules were the same as in the original Turtle days. At the time this individual was working for Svoboda their trading day started at around 7:00 P.M. Pacific Time because they were trading Australia and Hong Kong markets and needed the next day trades by no later than 5 P.M.:

"We loaded the daily numbers into the programs and about 15 minutes later we had the next days' trades. [Svoboda and partners] were incredibly secretive toward me; it was a very tight-knit group. George and his partners very much valued their privacy. I think that they were worried about notoriety and the loss of personal freedom."

Clearly, many outsiders experienced the Turtles' secrecy and paranoia, but my strangest experiences by far involved the youngest Turtle.

Curtis Faith

A business trip to the U.S. Virgin Islands in 2001 first brought me into contact with Curtis Faith. I welcomed the opportunity to meet another of Dennis's famed Turtles. Faith picked me up at the Frenchman's Reef Marriott on St. Thomas and after squeezing into the backseat of his beat-up sub-compact rental car we took off to the beach for a chat.

First impression? St. Thomas is the Caribbean. It's an island and there is that certain laid back vibe when you hear steel drums nonstop. Oddly, almost immediately I thought I detected an inferiority complex in Faith, but he was a Turtle and judging a book by its cover in this business was not wise. Faith was around 40 years old by then, but appeared older (tired might be the apt description).

Within minutes of meeting Faith the topic of Ayn Rand's classic book *Atlas Shrugged* came up. He and others were trying to build a money management firm called "Galt" Capital at the time—hence the discussion. He said a friend of his had read the 1200 page classic text in a few hours. His statement struck me as a comical exaggeration, but he was clearly serious. A little later, he announced he was launching a new airline (he was using an email address of curtis@galtair.com at the time). Even though my gut said "no way" that this man was launching an airline, he was a Turtle and maybe he was indeed launching an airline called "Galt Air."

That night over dinner, Faith was complimentary to the Turtle-Trader.com website: "Not sure how you assembled it all, but you got it right." However, it was easy to come away from meeting this Turtle with a distinctly different feeling than meeting Jerry Parker, a man known beyond a shadow of a doubt to have found immense success. Later, due diligence on Google turned up Faith's résumé posted online. A famed Turtle, the one who had positioned himself as the most successful Turtle, was looking for *employment*? While I had no immediate proof my instinct told me that this Turtle had not achieved great wealth. Faith was a direct contradiction to the legend of all Turtles making "it."

It turned out that there were a handful of people who had surrounded Faith attempting to piggyback off of his Turtle fame for assorted business purposes. Those people started talking freely to me and confirmed that Faith was allegedly in monetary straights.

I had no further contact with Faith after those few random meetings, but Faith soon offered a different perspective regarding my efforts. In 2003 he announced publicly that, "You won't get any expert advice from the guy who runs TurtleTrader.com. All you will get is the regurgitation of advice from other traders not tempered by the experience of a successful trading career. Paying for advice from this source is a lot like hiring a blind guide."

Once my book *The Complete TurtleTrader* was released in October 2007, Faith was the one Turtle to express angry dissent. With his own book out touting himself as super successful, Faith's need to defend his legend was apparent: "In my opinion, [Covel] is a parasite who lives off of the creation and energy of others instead of contributing something to humanity."

Someone posting under the screen name "Priapus Maximus" (probably Faith) continued: "Mike's [Covel] last book [*Trend Following*] was a sales brochure for his trading course crap and I think it is pretty obvious which book will do better. I'll bet Mike really hates Curtis now."

The zaniness did not end there. As explored in chapter 12, the one trading firm started by Faith in the twenty years since the Turtle experiment ended was a disaster. In trying to investigate that firm with the government, the bureaucratic process to obtain documents was painfully slow. In fact, as my book went to print in early 2007 all of the details of the case were not in. However, shortly after the release of my book the government finally provided the legal depositions involving their investigation and dismantling of this small trading firm Faith co-founded (the firm name was Acceleration Capital).

As a writer you quickly learn that the maxim "truth is stranger than fiction" is of course true, but when the United States government depositions revealed that Acceleration Capital's trading system was simply the venerable Donchian trend trading system, unchanged, it felt like I had uncovered a shell game.

While this firm's cachet was built off the Curtis Faith Turtle trading "legend," Faith's partner Yuri Plyam painted a picture in depositions of Faith missing in action providing no real value to the trading operation. Further, Toby Denniston, an employee associated with Acceleration Capital (see chapter 12), was stealing money from Faith's firm to buy trips, cars, a payment for his gastric bypass surgery, various gifts for his boyfriend and lastly, to start a Barbie doll collection.

Posting these verbatim depositions (which would have been buried forever if not for my Freedom of Information requests), which included the Barbie doll collection story, was just one of many events that put a damper on Faith's assertion that he was the most successful Turtle. Faith responded to the revelations with guns blazing, "When it comes to trading Covel is an idiot." Another post from Faith referred to me as "an idiot shyster." The Faith lawsuit threats started:

"Covel has been duped by his own anger and his own blindness to the possibility that there might be others out there who are not dishonest charlatans. [Covel] cannot fathom why someone who actually was as successful as I was would leave so much money on the table and stop trading. The courts will prove [Covel] the spiteful jealous liar that he is. . . . Fortunately, Covel made these statements in a magazine published in the U.K. That means that I can sue him for libel there. The English have very tough libel laws because they don't like people making things up about the royals. . . . I won't have to worry about Covel anymore after my suit. . . . [Covel is] an asshole who has made himself my mortal enemy despite my many attempts to get him to stop. . . . Mike [Covel's] continuing actions are only going to make it clearer to a jury that he is being malicious. The punitive damages rise every time he posts more bullshit."

Faith, explaining his legal logic, stated that he would "Donate 100 percent of the proceeds of the suit against Covel to nonprofit organizations dedicated to alternate energy research, poverty, and desease [sic]."

Then in the spring of 2008 Faith's childhood friend Tim Arnold spoke up. Arnold confirmed Faith's Jehovah's Witness beliefs, among other things. Arnold and Faith had started a small software firm together, but then Arnold bought Faith out. Following the buyout, and seeking more money beyond the original agreement with Arnold, Faith posted messages in chat forums about more supposed lawsuits. In conversation with Arnold you could tell he was exasperated with Faith. Arnold painted a picture of a Turtle who was hanging on to a reputation from twenty-five years ago, but who had now run very short on cash.

The entire Faith story reminded me of my childhood experiences growing up around bantam roosters. Those roosters would strut around their pen in a desperate need to show dominance, to impress, to scare, to bully, but you always knew if you chased them or yelled "boo" they would run away.

What does all of this dysfunctional behavior have to do with the Turtles? Faith has long positioned himself as the most successful Turtle. The evidence says otherwise. More important, if investors take Faith at his word and make him their role model, they will be guided down a path that meanders nowhere.

Most recently Faith was a volunteer for the Barack Obama presidential campaign. In that effort he posted a YouTube video in December 2007. With what appeared to be a washing machine running in the background, Faith spent four minutes preaching to Barack Obama about how he could win the presidency. Even a casual observer could see Faith had no substantive tie to the campaign. There was an eerie feeling of superiority to his words as though an army of followers was waiting on his every word, including Obama himself.

Conclusion

When *The Complete TurtleTrader* was first released in October 2007 it ran under the radar of top ten sellers except in Singapore. For some reason, and I am still not sure why, the book quickly made The Singapore Straits top ten list for nonfiction. For thirteen weeks it remained right there in the top ten sandwiched in between books by the likes of

Alan Greenspan and Mother Theresa. It was an eye-opener about the randomness of who was gravitating to the story and who was not, but given the immense wealth and trading success of Singapore, perhaps it should have come as no surprise.

On the other hand China, who has seen extreme ups and downs in their main stock market over the last few years, has millions of investors who could clearly have used some Turtle philosophy. Consider a May 2008 excerpt from the *Washington Post* regarding the correction in the Chinese stock market:

"In February, Li, a 25-year-old engineer, jumped from the seventh floor of the building where he worked in the city of Chengdu. His company said he had lost a huge amount on the stock market. On March 30, a 39-year-old former ice cream-shop owner, also named Li, leapt to his death from his apartment building in the inland province of Shandong after losing a third of the $4,500 he had invested. As China's stock markets crashed over the past six months, the Communist government reacted in a way most consumer investors like Wang did not anticipate: It watched from the sidelines. It wasn't until last week, after the Shanghai benchmark index's fall to a symbolic milestone, below 50 percent of its peak in October, that Beijing finally stepped in. Its announcements that it would slash a tax on stock transactions and control volatility by requiring some big block trades to take place off the regular stock market pushed the market up 14 percent. It has fallen again since then, however."

It is safe to say that these investors did not know of the Turtles or their lessons. I kept wondering if all of the energy expended to try to keep assorted Turtle "secrets" locked away had caused some Turtles to lose sight of the big picture—their great inspirational story and tremendous success was nothing to hide from and that a further expansion of the story might actually be a good thing for them and everyone else.

At the end of the day what could really be so damaging about the Turtle story reaching a wider audience? For example, the Turtles who still publicly trade have returned these performance numbers over the first three months of 2008, a period where stock markets were in turmoil:

Jerry Parker: up 11%

Liz Cheval: up 17%

Tom Shanks: up 37%

Paul Rabar: up 13%

Howard Seidler: up 28%

Bill Eckhardt (Dennis's former partner): up 14%

Salem Abraham (second generation Turtle): up 13%

There is no assurance that those performance numbers will continue, as trading as a Turtle is volatile, but the numbers are the numbers. And those are numbers people don't expect when the nightly news and CNBC are yelling something quite different 24/7.

Maybe the Turtle story is too perfect. Maybe for some people it is just not believable. The refusal to accept obvious truths is the biggest obstacle to getting more people to adopt sound investment behaviors. Why? People have always struggled with perceptions of truth. It comes down to a general rule: We believe what we want to believe.

Where Are They Now?

"It's not the uniqueness of the idea that's the key. It's the uniqueness of your ability to implement it."

Anonymous

Salem Abraham, Second-generation Turtle

In 2006, Shaun Jordan (with Abraham Trading) organized a two-day visit for me to Canadian, Texas—Salem Abraham's home and office location. During the visit, Abraham put William Eckhardt's utility theory of risk in perspective with an example.

Assume a coin-flipping game. You have $10 million to your name. For the game, you get to bet $10 million per flip. With this coin you have a 90 percent chance of winning another $10 million, but you have a 10 percent chance of losing $10 million—all of your money. Can you really afford to bet it all, even if the odds are in your favor? No. Abraham clarified: "As an odds guy I go 'That's a great bet.' I will take the bet. But, wait a minute. If the upside is $10 million, the downside is $10 million . . . I've seen guys around here in Texas oil and gas businesses and they go broke. They're great oil and gas guys, but they bet the ranch too many times and lost it."

Anthony Bruck, Turtle Class of 1983

There is no public information about Anthony Bruck except that he is a board member of the AIDS Foundation of Chicago. He is apparently still associated with C&D Commodities. However, it is not clear if C&D Commodities is still an active business or if it is just a collegial association between Dennis and Bruck.

Michael Carr, Turtle Class of 1983

Mike Carr today is a professional writer whose favorite topic is snow-mobiling and winter recreation. He writes snowmobile travel articles for five different magazines as well as a monthly column called "Making Tracks." He has been a dedicated sledder for over twenty-five years and has ridden more than 40,000 miles.

Michael Cavallo, Turtle Class of 1983

Michael Cavallo continued to answer want ads after his work with Dennis ended. By answering one such ad, Cavallo eventually became the United States Chess Federation executive director. He is also a former New York City Junior Chess champion, with a then ranking of 2,142. He at one time reached the level of "master."

Cavallo has also established and funded The Cavallo Foundation, Inc., to assist people who demonstrate moral courage in the workplace, principally whistle-blowers. Recipients have included environmental-ists, scientists, and those fighting racism and sexual harassment. Cavallo is also the father of triplets.[1]

Liz Cheval, Turtle Class of 1983

Liz Cheval declined to be interviewed for this book. Today, Cheval still runs her trading firm EMC Capital.

Jim DiMaria, Turtle Class of 1984

Jim DiMaria likes the way things have worked out over the last twenty-five years. Would he have liked to make more money? Sure. However, there are always trade-offs. He clearly sees those: "Because of the flexibility of trading, if you use technology right, we picked up and moved to France for three years with the kids. So it was great for the family. The kids are native French speakers. We traveled all over the place. We loved it. I think I traded from twenty-three different countries."

Of all the Turtles, DiMaria did the best job of explaining why blow-ups happen in the hedge fund world. He saw the root of the problem with "allocators," the investors with the money who allocate it across a wide grouping of traders: "The biggest single problem with these allocators is they completely confuse volatility and standard deviation with 'risk.' The two are completely noncorrelated. They want Amaranth, Long Term Capital Management, and III [name of a hedge fund that blew up] and that's going to work 95 percent of the time, but when it doesn't, they're broke."

William Eckhardt, Turtle Teacher and Partner of Richard Dennis

The teacher of the Turtles today manages roughly $1 billion for clients. Beyond his trading, he has remained engaged in his own philosophical pursuits. In 1993, Eckhardt's article "Probability Theory and the Doomsday Argument" was published in the philosophical journal *Mind*. His follow-up article, "A Shooting-Room View of Doomsday," was published in the *Journal of Philosophy*. Both articles made arguments skeptical of the Doomsday Argument as formulated by John Leslie.[2] The Doomsday Argument (DA) is a probabilistic argument that claims to predict the future lifetime of the human race given only an estimate of the total number of humans born so far.[3]

Interestingly, in January 2001, Eckhardt Trading Company took over the employment of a number of people previously employed by C&D Commodities. The world of those associated with the Turtles remains small and close-knit.

Curtis Faith, Turtle Class of 1983

Today, Curtis Faith spends a great deal of time participating in online chat forums. He has also been a vocal critic of my telling of the Turtle story. Faith currently lives in Buenos Aires, Argentina.

Jeff Gordon, Turtle Class of 1983

Gordon, now a private investor, gets his greatest thrill from teaching. He and his wife have been teaching chess to children in Marin County, California, for ten years. His Marin Country Day School Chess Team placed first at the Northern California Regional Chess Championship in 2005.

Gordon provides some food for thought about the dreaded "risk" that everyone must cope with at one time or another: "People's attitude about risk was a very important aspect of being a trader. Can that be taught? Well, it can be taught intellectually. Can it be taught so that it is in the gut? I am not so sure about that. I am not saying no, but I am saying that it is hard. If you ever try to change some of your basic attitude towards basic things like risk, there are people who are more comfortable with risk than others. It comes from upbringing. It comes from attitude, life experiences, and being rewarded or being burned from taking risk in the past."

Erle Keefer, Turtle Class of 1984

Erle Keefer was the oldest Turtle hired. He was about the same age as Dennis, thirty-seven years old, when he started out as a Turtle. Describing himself physically he chuckled, "I'm a miniature Rich."

He also may have had the most diverse work experience prior to his Turtle time. He was a founding member of the London International Financial Futures Exchange, serving on the original membership and rules board. He received his undergraduate degree from the U.S. Air Force Academy and flew Air Rescue "Jolly Greens" in Vietnam.

Military service was instrumental in his development. He said, "Combat forces you to be 100 percent 'in the now.' It changes your DNA forever."

Philip Lu, Turtle Class of 1984

In 2006, an interview was attempted with Philip Lu, now working as a college teacher at Edgewood College in Wisconsin. He threw a curve ball. Lu declined to be interviewed because he believed his confidentiality agreement with Richard Dennis (which expired in the early 1990s) was still in force.

Jerry Parker, Turtle Class of 1983

Years ago, at my first meeting with Jerry Parker, before the allotted time was up, I was quick enough (or dumb enough) to capitalize on the opportunity by asking him to confirm who won the Barings Bank sweepstakes when it imploded. He confirmed the winner. That was the type of confirmation that allowed me to write my first book, *Trend Following*. Today, Parker continues on as hands-down the most successful Turtle. He still works out of his suburban Richmond, Virginia, office.

Paul Rabar, Turtle Class of 1984

Paul Rabar, the second most successful Turtle managing money for clients, theorized as to why some Turtles were more successful than others: "Perhaps some of the others have preferred to focus less on business management."[4]

Rabar actually ran his own version of the Richard Dennis's original 1983 want ad in the *New York Times* for new hires. And a recent online search produced not the old ad, but a 2006 one from the *Times*. Whiners making excuses that *they* were never afforded a foot in the door in *their* lifetime, should look harder.

Tom Shanks, Turtle Class of 1984

Tom Shanks appears to have had the most fun as a Turtle. One of his Turtle peers recalled a Las Vegas Turtle reunion years back when Shanks showed up with a well-known sitcom actress on his arm.

Bradley Rotter saw up close the adventurous side of Shanks: "I remember he bought a jet helicopter, and was learning to fly it and wanted to take me out on one of his maiden missions. He said we were going to fly underneath the Golden Gate Bridge. I said as a matter of principle, I try not to fly with traders at the wheel." Rotter turned serious in the next breath. "He is one of the finest individuals that I have ever met. He has unquestionable discipline."

Shanks is proudest of his first client. That investor put in $300,000 in 1988. Despite redemptions of more than $1 million, the client's account has grown, without further additions, to over $18 million.[5]

Michael Shannon, Turtle Class of 1984

Michael Shannon's career after the Turtles brought him into contact with some of Wall Street's biggest names. He worked on a fund with legendary T-bond trader Thomas Baldwin (profiled in *Market Wizards*) and later worked with Dr. Kaveh Alamouti (who would later run money for Louis Bacon). Today, he enjoys a quiet life outside the United States.

Jiri "George" Svoboda, Turtle Class of 1984

Jiri "George" Svoboda is a Turtle mystery. While he did initially register with the National Futures Association (a government-sanctioned regulatory body) to trade money for clients in 1988, the association never actually granted him final registration, presumably because of his 1988 felony convictions for producing false identification documents and making a false statement in an application for a passport, as well as his failure to disclose such felony convictions to the NFA.

Why a fake passport? As an accomplished card counter, Svoboda was presumably searching for a way to play blackjack abroad and get his winnings back into the States anonymously. This circumspect history aside, several of his peers had great praise for Svoboda; one even said, "He's a very practical person. He's an extremely ethical and honest person who lives in a very black and shades-of-gray world." And one Turtle, who declined to be interviewed on the record, was a big fan of Svoboda's: "His performance is probably the best of all of the Turtles since 1988."

The Turtle grapevine did say that Svoboda has, over the years, provided advice to major Las Vegas casino owners on how to stop cheaters. Beyond that, Svoboda remains an enigma—which is probably just how he likes it.

Appendix II

Related Websites

More information on the Turtles and their teachers Richard Dennis and William Eckhardt can be found at:

www.abrahamtrading.com (Salem Abraham's website)

www.daledellutri.com (Dale Dellutri's website)

www.eckhardttrading.com (William Eckhardt's website)

www.emccta.com (Liz Cheval's website)

www.hawksbillcapital.com (Tom Shanks's website)

www.jpdent.com (Jim DiMaria's website)

www.markjwalsh.com (Mark Walsh's website)

www.michaelcovel.com (Michael Covel's website)

www.saxoninvestment.com (Howard Seidler's website)

www.trendfollowing.com (Michael Covel's website)

www.turtletrader.com (Michael Covel's website)

Appendix III

Turtle Performance Data

"In a world of constant change, risk is actually a form of safety, because it accepts that world for what it is. Conventional safety is where the danger really lies, because it denies and resists that world."

Charles S. Sanford, Jr.

Jerry Parker was not the only Turtle to assemble a continuous track record since the Turtle program ended in 1988. Several other Turtles have gone on to have professional trading careers. Their careers are concrete proof of what sticking with a system over the long haul can do for a trading account. Table Appendices 3.1 and 3.2 graphically illustrate the month-by-month processes and performances of Jerry Parker and Salem Abraham. Table Appendix 3.3 illustrates the yearly performance history of Dennis's former partner William Eckhardt and the performance histories of the other Turtles continuously trading since 1988.

Table Appendix 3.1: Annual and Monthly Returns, 1988–2006, for Jerry Parker's Chesapeake Capital.

Month-by-Month Returns with Annual Total Return

Year	Jan	Feb	Mar	Apr	May	Jun	Jul	Aug	Sep	Oct	Nov	Dec	Total
1988	-2.19%	-2.63	-6.89	-10.71	6.93	32.42	-9.41	6.85	2.03	10.65	11.06	7.04	48.91
1989	4.93	-5.42	6.64	-8.82	22.38	-8.28	11.66	-11.75	-2.82	-7.40	3.90	28.56	28.30
1990	0.49	3.37	8.62	4.37	-4.61	1.77	6.25	15.15	0.60	1.86	-0.25	0.11	43.12
1991	-1.29	4.84	2.32	-2.80	0.27	-1.25	-1.75	-3.32	4.39	4.21	-4.68	12.08	12.51
1992	-10.98	-2.86	0.53	-0.44	-3.66	6.52	12.96	3.16	-6.78	5.21	2.27	-1.93	1.81
1993	0.42	15.99	5.86	7.38	0.40	0.98	9.49	5.88	-2.63	-0.06	1.03	5.77	61.82
1994	-3.33	-4.88	0.09	-0.60	9.06	7.02	-1.70	-2.98	3.49	1.97	4.83	2.86	15.87
1995	-3.23	-4.39	8.60	1.45	6.84	0.88	-3.09	-2.66	0.20	-1.11	1.76	9.18	14.09
1996	1.69	-4.26	0.28	10.16	-3.04	3.27	-7.64	0.57	6.47	5.92	6.57	-4.30	15.05
1997	1.86	5.48	-1.24	-2.41	-2.28	1.44	6.24	-7.88	5.06	-2.34	1.70	4.88	9.94
1998	-1.29	6.06	3.65	-2.16	3.62	-0.67	3.03	7.27	-0.59	-3.21	-1.68	1.80	16.31
1999	-2.76	1.90	-2.65	8.42	-8.71	3.57	-4.80	3.37	1.98	-7.88	4.16	8.49	3.30
2000	-0.87	0.92	1.88	-3.80	0.63	-0.99	-3.71	3.90	-7.30	-0.62	7.42	8.80	5.23
2001	-0.43	3.75	4.98	-7.50	-1.43	0.16	-3.06	-3.40	7.15	5.01	-10.09	-1.92	-7.98
2002	-2.11	-1.79	2.43	-3.27	2.26	4.19	2.84	2.55	3.81	-2.63	-1.58	4.31	11.07
2003	6.52	3.61	-8.76	0.29	5.35	-5.65	-1.85	2.42	-2.78	15.48	1.91	6.61	23.08
2004	1.63	5.05	-2.70	-6.05	-0.50	-2.90	-1.86	-3.23	3.50	2.32	8.89	1.53	4.84
2005	-3.82	0.46	-0.92	-3.62	-1.25	3.41	0.45	4.70	-1.10	-4.75	4.33	1.97	1.15
2006	5.54	-0.69	5.37	3.23	-1.47	-0.77	-2.13	-4.66	-1.53	1.38	3.38	3.32	10.90

Source: Disclosure Documents Filed with United States CFTC.

Table Appendix 3.2: Annual and Monthly Returns, 1988–2006, for Salem Abraham's Abraham Trading.

Month-by-Month Returns with Annual Total Return

Year	Jan	Feb	Mar	Apr	May	Jun	Jul	Aug	Sep	Oct	Nov	Dec	Total
1988	4.17%	−2.59	−8.78	−12.35	32.34	71.99	−2.82	3.45	−1.98	8.01	17.83	4.51	142.04
1989	−8.05	−12.64	13.91	−20.08	38.65	−4.40	16.08	−13.84	−7.75	−14.40	10.30	39.52	17.81
1990	3.65	1.81	9.45	12.90	−7.90	2.49	20.08	18.54	8.57	−0.36	0.31	−0.09	89.95
1991	−15.94	1.30	2.43	−13.70	2.94	2.11	−1.52	−6.33	11.61	16.61	−2.09	33.75	24.39
1992	−12.60	−6.00	−5.47	0.31	−5.71	6.58	16.52	1.92	−0.34	−3.31	4.65	−4.54	−10.50
1993	−4.21	6.10	4.57	9.24	4.88	−1.22	6.60	−5.28	1.16	−6.59	3.71	12.83	34.29
1994	−1.45	−4.16	2.87	−8.39	15.01	1.47	0.98	−7.38	5.05	5.43	14.24	1.06	24.22
1995	−7.91	1.24	6.63	4.73	8.22	0.11	−8.75	−5.34	−1.84	−6.67	−0.19	19.11	6.12
1996	−6.85	−13.78	9.66	14.27	−9.41	1.52	−6.30	−3.34	6.03	16.84	2.45	−6.41	−0.42
1997	5.28	9.15	−1.50	−5.16	−1.32	0.38	4.11	−8.08	4.95	−5.37	2.10	7.46	10.88
1998	−0.90	4.09	−4.45	−4.45	2.61	−2.34	−0.83	23.24	−3.33	−11.39	0.94	4.67	4.39
1999	−11.56	13.35	−9.43	7.52	−6.09	−0.68	−0.83	3.12	0.99	−9.57	13.64	8.41	4.76
2000	8.02	−9.05	−4.16	5.48	−2.58	−2.19	−5.26	11.76	−4.53	9.51	8.58	−0.18	13.54
2001	2.28	2.99	15.17	−10.20	5.13	4.47	−2.85	4.89	9.28	4.13	−13.68	−0.50	19.16
2002	−1.73	1.33	−6.62	4.99	1.51	7.75	−3.97	9.86	3.29	−10.19	−1.80	18.41	21.51
2003	24.18	13.18	−4.73	2.02	5.59	−7.06	−4.86	−3.54	7.02	22.09	−0.03	8.69	74.66
2004	0.47	8.38	0.88	−6.22	2.53	1.37	6.74	−12.25	7.84	4.32	2.79	−0.51	15.38
2005	−5.48	−8.95	−1.00	−10.04	1.93	6.66	−12.16	15.74	−5.79	−5.98	14.15	3.96	−10.95
2006	2.56	−1.53	5.71	2.75	−1.70	−2.32	5.26	2.72	−1.51	4.08	2.23	1.36	8.88

Source: Disclosure Documents Filed with United States CFTC.

Table Appendix 3.3

Year	Eckhardt Trading Company—Standard Program (William Eckhardt)	EMC Capital Management, Inc.—Classic (Liz Cheval)	Hawksbill Capital Management—Global Diversified Program (Tom Shanks)	JPD Enterprises, Inc.—Global Diversified (Jim DiMaria)	Rabar Market Research, Inc. Diversified (Paul Rabar)	Saxon Investment Corporation—Diversified Program (Howard Seidler)
2006	1.93%	21.33%	1.66%	5.38%	9.40%	11.66%
2005	8.56%	9.48%	1.24%	−7.09%	−5.78%	−6.25%
2004	4.49%	−13.02%	−8.84%	3.74%	−2.81%	2.59%
2003	15.01%	34.72%	27.59%	9.97%	23.93%	45.75%
2002	11.07%	−2.58%	36.37%	19.89%	24.57%	19.98%
2001	5.34%	14.50%	22.76%	0.13%	0.77%	9.34%
2000	17.94%	17.77%	24.76%	3.99%	1.79%	22.45%
1999	−4.54%	−11.05%	−24.55%	−5.50%	−9.27%	14.84%
1998	27.10%	3.76%	43.72%	10.25%	24.29%	20.60%
1997	46.01%	14.14%	73.51%	9.87%	11.39%	7.09%
1996	47.94%	−2.16%	−27.10%	13.87%	0.66%	21.62%
1995	47.33%	21.86%	−7.86%	19.95%	12.57%	−24.78%
1994	−11.69%	−18.25%	11.48%	21.76%	33.91%	63.27%
1993	57.95%	65.29%	114.26%	23.46%	49.55%	52.56%
1992	−7.26%	−32.50%	17.24%	−18.13%	−4.45%	9.31%
1991		3.21%	−29.92%	9.41%	−5.68%	−19.54%
1990		188.07%	252.61%	50.36%	122.51%	19.46%
1989		−4.15%	56.45%	−6.59%	10.00%	29.51%
1988		124.77%	12.05%	31.27%	90.34%	19.18%

Source: Disclosure Documents Filed with United States CFTC.

Appendix IV

Turtle Performance While Trading for Richard Dennis

The following performance data have never been published. They are the actual Turtle performance trading results while the Turtles traded for Richard Dennis, along with the amount of money they traded each month.

Table Appendix 4.1: Mike Carr Turtle Performance, January 1984–April 1988.

Date	VAMI	ROR	Account Size
Jan-84	986	−1.40%	
Feb-84	1032	4.70%	
Mar-84	1107	7.20%	$1.0M
Apr-84	869	−21.50%	
May-84	971	11.80%	
Jun-84	679	−30.10%	$0.7M
Jul-84	1031	51.90%	
Aug-84	861	−16.50%	
Sep-84	892	3.60%	$1.6M
Oct-84	966	8.30%	
Nov-84	1000	3.50%	
Dec-84	1241	24.10%	$2.3M
1984 Final		24.09%	
Jan-85	1247	−0.50%	
Feb-85	1301	4.30%	
Mar-85	1210	−7.00%	$3.3M

VAMI (Value Added Monthly Index): An index that tracks the monthly performance of a hypothetical $1,000 investment as it grows over time.
ROR: Rate of return.
Source: Barclays Performance Reporting (www.barclaygrp.com)

Date	VAMI	ROR	Account Size
Apr-85	892	−26.30%	
May-85	1030	15.50%	
Jun-85	765	−25.70%	$1.6M
Jul-85	1251	63.50%	
Aug-85	1132	−9.50%	
Sep-85	1087	−4.00%	$2.4M
Oct-85	1266	16.50%	
Nov-85	1637	29.30%	
Dec-85	1809	10.50%	$2.8M
1985 Final		**45.78%**	
Jan-86	1968	8.80%	
Feb-86	3675	86.70%	
Mar-86	3917	6.60%	$6.0M
Apr-86	3659	−6.60%	
May-86	3081	−15.80%	
Jun-86	3087	0.20%	$5.1M
Jul-86	3432	11.20%	
Aug-86	3786	10.30%	
Sep-86	3487	−7.90%	$5.6M
Oct-86	3480	−0.20%	
Nov-86	3296	−5.30%	
Dec-86	3220	−2.30%	$3.5M
1986 Final		**77.98%**	
Jan-87	3513	9.10%	
Feb-87	3228	−8.10%	
Mar-87	3422	6.00%	$3.3M
Apr-87	6043	76.60%	
May-87	6520	7.90%	
Jun-87	5855	−10.20%	$5.4M
Jul-87	6148	5.00%	
Aug-87	5669	−7.80%	
Sep-87	5839	3.00%	$4.7M
Oct-87	4799	−17.80%	

Date	VAMI	ROR	Account Size
Nov-87	4799	0.00%	
Dec-87	4799	0.00%	$1.3M
1987 Final		**49.06%**	
Jan-88	5207	8.50%	
Feb-88	5145	−1.20%	
Mar-88	4471	−13.10%	$0.1M
Apr-88	3849	−13.90%	

Table Appendix 4.2: Mike Cavallo Turtle Performance, January 1984–April 1988.

Date	VAMI	ROR	Account Size
Jan-84	969	−3.10%	
Feb-84	1070	10.42%	
Mar-84	1097	2.52%	$1.1M
Apr-84	829	−24.43%	
May-84	760	−8.32%	
Jun-84	324	−57.36%	$2.0M
Jul-84	605	86.72%	
Aug-84	575	−4.95%	
Sep-84	608	5.73%	$3.9M
Oct-84	791	30.09%	
Nov-84	874	10.49%	
Dec-84	1145	31.00%	$3.5M
1984 Final		**−14.50%**	
Jan-85	1425	−24.45%	
Feb-85	1247	−12.49%	
Mar-85	1942	55.73%	$9.0M
Apr-85	1643	−15.39%	
May-85	1717	4.50%	
Jun-85	1760	2.50%	$8.6M
Jul-85	2706	53.75%	
Aug-85	2148	−20.62%	
Sep-85	1413	−34.21%	$7.8M

Date	VAMI	ROR	Account Size
Oct-85	1341	−5.09%	
Nov-85	1871	39.52%	
Dec-85	2298	22.82%	$8.5M
1985 Final		**100.72%**	
Jan-86	3172	38.03%	
Feb-86	4726	48.99%	
Mar-86	3299	−30.19%	$8.0M
Apr-86	2439	−26.09%	
May-86	2390	−2.00%	
Jun-86	1495	−37.46%	$4.8M
Jul-86	2719	81.92%	
Aug-86	3595	32.22%	
Sep-86	4092	13.82%	$8.1M
Oct-86	3792	−7.33%	
Nov-86	2891	−23.76%	
Dec-86	3071	6.22%	$8.7M
1986 Final		**33.62%**	
Jan-87	3458	12.60%	
Feb-87	2941	−14.95%	
Mar-87	2603	−11.49%	$6.9M
Apr-87	5181	99.03%	
May-87	6995	35.02%	
Jun-87	6995	0.01%	$14.3M
Jul-87	8162	16.67%	
Aug-87	7447	−8.76%	
Sep-87	7961	6.91%	$12.3M
Oct-87	6668	−16.24%	
Nov-87	7023	5.32%	
Dec-87	6487	−7.63%	$3.6M
1987 Final		**111.25%**	
Jan-88	6597	1.70%	
Feb-88	6769	2.60%	
Mar-88	6315	−6.70%	$0.4M
Apr-88	6006	−4.90%	

Table Appendix 4.3: Liz Cheval Turtle Performance, January 1984–April 1988.

Date	VAMI	ROR	Account Size
Jan-84	1004	0.40%	
Feb-84	984	−1.99%	
Mar-84	1019	3.55%	$1.0M
Apr-84	878	−13.83%	
May-84	800	−8.88%	
Jun-84	683	−14.62%	$1.1M
Jul-84	1302	90.62%	
Aug-84	979	−24.80%	
Sep-84	740	−24.41%	$1.2M
Oct-84	656	−11.35%	
Nov-84	579	−11.73%	
Dec-84	790	36.44%	$1.0M
1984 Final		**−20.98%**	
Jan-85	1001	26.70%	
Feb-85	1232	23.07%	
Mar-85	982	−20.29%	$1.0M
Apr-85	709	−27.80%	
May-85	1223	72.49%	
Jun-85	948	−22.48%	$1.0M
Jul-85	1225	29.21%	
Aug-85	995	−18.77%	
Sep-85	727	−26.93%	$1.1M
Oct-85	679	−6.60%	
Nov-85	998	46.98%	
Dec-85	1198	20.04%	$1.3M
1985 Final		**51.65%**	
Jan-86	1600	33.55%	
Feb-86	2948	84.18%	
Mar-86	3635	23.31%	$3.8M
Apr-86	3279	−9.79%	
May-86	3108	−5.21%	
Jun-86	2652	−14.67%	$2.8M

Date	VAMI	ROR	Account Size
Jul-86	2826	6.56%	
Aug-86	3030	7.22%	
Sep-86	3021	–0.29%	$3.2M
Oct-86	2812	–6.92%	
Nov-86	2812	0.00%	
Dec-86	2812	0.00%	$2.9M
1986 Final		**134.68%**	
Jan-87	3584	27.42%	
Feb-87	3251	–9.29%	
Mar-87	3757	15.57%	$3.2M
Apr-87	7826	108.33%	
May-87	7748	–1.00%	
Jun-87	7461	–3.70%	$6.4M
Jul-87	8201	9.91%	
Aug-87	7127	–13.10%	
Sep-87	7603	6.69%	$5.9M
Oct-87	7140	–6.09%	
Nov-87	7254	1.59%	
Dec-87	7819	7.79%	$1.8M
1987 Final		**178.02%**	
Jan-88	8077	3.30%	
Feb-88	8836	9.40%	
Mar-88	8325	–5.79%	$0.2M
Apr-88	6801	–18.30%	

Table Appendix 4.4: Jim DiMaria Turtle Performance, January 1985–April 1988.

Date	VAMI	ROR	Account Size
Jan-85	979	–2.10%	
Feb-85	1229	25.50%	
Mar-85	1093	–11.00%	$0.2M
Apr-85	791	–27.70%	
May-85	1034	30.80%	
Jun-85	809	–21.80%	$0.2M
Jul-85	1348	66.70%	
Aug-85	1300	–3.60%	
Sep-85	1194	–8.10%	$0.3M
Oct-85	1394	16.70%	
Nov-85	1720	23.40%	
Dec-85	1711	–0.50%	$1.2M
1985 Final		**71.12%**	
Jan-86	2129	24.40%	
Feb-86	4451	109.10%	
Mar-86	4919	10.50%	$3.4M
Apr-86	4491	–8.70%	
May-86	4060	–9.60%	
Jun-86	3853	–5.10%	$2.7M
Jul-86	4307	11.80%	
Aug-86	4837	12.30%	
Sep-86	4556	–5.80%	$3.2M
Oct-86	4283	–6.00%	
Nov-86	4005	–6.50%	
Dec-86	3965	–1.00%	$1.9M
1986 Final		**131.68%**	
Jan-87	4524	14.10%	
Feb-87	3669	–18.90%	
Mar-87	4113	12.10%	$1.5M
Apr-87	8677	111.00%	
May-87	8782	1.20%	
Jun-87	8536	–2.80%	$3.1M

Date	VAMI	ROR	Account Size
Jul-87	9125	6.90%	
Aug-87	8057	−11.70%	
Sep-87	8597	6.70%	$2.8M
Oct-87	7832	−8.90%	
Nov-87	7746	−1.10%	
Dec-87	7800	0.70%	$1.4M
1987 Final		**96.74%**	
Jan-88	7769	−0.40%	
Feb-88	8173	5.20%	
Mar-88	7045	−13.80%	$0.1M
Apr-88	6192	−12.10%	

Table Appendix 4.5: Jeff Gordon Turtle Performance, January 1984–April 1988.

Date	VAMI	ROR	Account Size
Jan-84	996	−0.40%	
Feb-84	1028	3.21%	
Mar-84	1021	−0.68%	$0.2M
Apr-84	972	−4.79%	
May-84	920	−5.34%	
Jun-84	847	−7.93%	$0.2M
Jul-84	1118	31.99%	
Aug-84	763	−31.75%	
Sep-84	830	8.78%	$0.3M
Oct-84	783	−5.66%	
Nov-84	764	−2.42%	
Dec-84	1317	72.38%	$1.2M
1984 Final		**31.74%**	
Jan-85	1405	6.63%	
Feb-85	1561	11.14%	
Mar-85	1522	−2.54%	$2.0M
Apr-85	1399	−8.07%	
May-85	1654	18.28%	

Date	VAMI	ROR	Account Size
Jun-85	1465	−11.48%	$1.9M
Jul-85	1867	27.45%	
Aug-85	1834	−1.76%	
Sep-85	1839	0.29%	$1.8M
Oct-85	2032	10.50%	
Nov-85	2357	16.00%	
Dec-85	2398	1.74%	$1.0M
1985 Final		**82.05%**	
Jan-86	2814	17.33%	
Feb-86	3958	40.65%	
Mar-86	3917	−1.04%	$0.9M
Apr-86	3834	−2.12%	
May-86	3821	−0.34%	
Jun-86	3775	−1.18%	$0.9M
Jul-86	3758	−0.46%	
Aug-86	3815	1.52%	
Sep-86	3610	−5.37%	$0.7M
Oct-86	3601	−0.27%	
Nov-86	3601	0.00%	
Dec-86	3618	0.48%	$0.8M
1986 Final		**50.85%**	
Jan-87	3907	8.00%	
Feb-87	3911	0.09%	
Mar-87	3918	0.18%	$0.4M
Apr-87	3961	1.10%	
May-87	3813	−3.74%	
Jun-87	3740	−1.91%	$0.6M
Jul-87	3960	5.89%	
Aug-87	3960	0.00%	
Sep-87	3887	−1.86%	$0.4M
Oct-87	3986	2.56%	
Nov-87	4000	0.36%	
Dec-87	4034	0.83%	$0.3M
1987 Final		**11.49%**	

Date	VAMI	ROR	Account Size
Jan-88	4061	0.67%	
Feb-88	4140	1.94%	
Mar-88	4181	1.01%	$0.4M
Apr-88	4173	−0.21%	

Table Appendix 4.6: Philip Lu Turtle Performance, January 1985–April 1988.

Date	VAMI	ROR	Account Size
Jan-85	951	−4.90%	
Feb-85	1272	33.75%	
Mar-85	1276	0.31%	$0.8M
Apr-85	1088	−14.73%	
May-85	1462	34.37%	
Jun-85	1244	−14.91%	$0.6M
Jul-85	1811	45.57%	
Aug-85	1840	1.60%	
Sep-85	1546	−15.97%	$1.6M
Oct-85	1881	21.66%	
Nov-85	2045	8.71%	
Dec-85	2322	13.59%	$2.0M
1985 Final		132.25%	
Jan-86	2645	13.90%	
Feb-86	5212	97.01%	
Mar-86	5764	10.60%	$5.0M
Apr-86	5603	−2.79%	
May-86	5340	−4.69%	
Jun-86	5234	−2.00%	$4.5M
Jul-86	5364	2.50%	
Aug-86	5831	8.70%	
Sep-86	5324	−8.69%	$4.6M
Oct-86	5304	−0.39%	
Nov-86	5267	-0.69%	
Dec-86	5314	0.89%	$2.0M
1986 Final		128.80%	

Date	VAMI	ROR	Account Size
Jan-87	5653	6.39%	
Feb-87	5371	–5.00%	
Mar-87	6122	13.99%	$1.9M
Apr-87	9802	60.10%	
May-87	9802	0.00%	
Jun-87	9567	–2.39%	$2.9M
Jul-87	10017	4.70%	
Aug-87	9377	–6.39%	
Sep-87	9649	2.90%	$2.5M
Oct-87	8579	–11.09%	
Nov-87	8579	0.00%	
Dec-87	9437	10.00%	$1.2M
1987 Final		**77.58%**	
Jan-88	9842	4.30%	
Feb-88	10156	3.19%	
Mar-88	10156	0.00%	$1.3M
Apr-88	10156	0.00%	

Table Appendix 4.7: Jim Melnick Turtle Performance, January 1984–January 1988.

Date	VAMI	ROR	Account Size
Jan-84	721	–27.90%	
Feb-84	916	27.04%	
Mar-84	591	–35.48%	$1.0M
Apr-84	527	–10.82%	
May-84	967	83.49%	
Jun-84	768	–20.57%	$1.0M
Jul-84	1680	118.75%	
Aug-84	1183	–29.58%	
Sep-84	1398	18.17%	$1.0M
Oct-84	1356	–3.00%	
Nov-84	1370	1.03%	
Dec-84	2023	47.66%	$1.0M
1984 Final		**102.33%**	

Date	VAMI	ROR	Account Size
Jan-85	2124	4.99%	
Feb-85	2606	22.69%	
Mar-85	2030	−22.10%	$1.0M
Apr-85	1602	−21.08%	
May-85	2115	32.02%	
Jun-85	1330	−37.11%	$1.0M
Jul-85	1938	45.71%	
Aug-85	1596	−17.69%	
Sep-85	1535	−3.82%	$1.0M
Oct-85	2032	32.39%	
Nov-85	2769	36.28%	
Dec-85	2877	3.90%	$1.0M
1985 Final		**42.18%**	
Jan-86	4117	43.11%	
Feb-86	7205	75.00%	
Mar-86	7888	9.49%	$1.0M
Apr-86	7943	0.69%	
May-86	7609	−4.20%	
Jun-86	7677	0.89%	$1.0M
Jul-86	8190	6.69%	
Aug-86	8035	−1.90%	
Sep-86	7538	−6.19%	$1.0M
Oct-86	7493	−0.59%	
Nov-86	7493	0.00%	
Dec-86	7493	0.00%	$1.0M
1986 Final		**160.47%**	
Jan-87	8085	7.90%	
Feb-87	7876	−2.59%	
Mar-87	7829	−0.59%	$1.0M
Apr-87	10248	30.89%	
May-87	10074	−1.69%	
Jun-87	9612	−4.59%	$1.0M
Jul-87	10150	5.60%	
Aug-87	10039	−1.10%	

Date	VAMI	ROR	Account Size
Sep-87	11373	13.29%	$1.0M
Oct-87	10908	−4.09%	
Nov-87	10951	0.40%	
Dec-87	10918	−0.30%	$1.0M
1987 Final		45.71%	
Jan-88	11376	4.19%	

Table Appendix 4.8: Mike O'Brien Turtle Performance, January 1985–April 1988.

Date	VAMI	ROR	Account Size
Jan-85	1008	0.80%	
Feb-85	1271	26.09%	
Mar-85	1091	−14.16%	$1.1M
Apr-85	1006	−7.79%	
May-85	1201	19.38%	
Jun-85	1175	−2.16%	$0.9M
Jul-85	1679	42.89%	
Aug-85	1460	−13.04%	
Sep-85	1527	4.58%	$1.6M
Oct-85	1798	17.74%	
Nov-85	1890	5.11%	
Dec-85	1995	5.55%	$1.6M
1985 Final		99.46%	
Jan-86	2247	12.63%	
Feb-86	4417	96.61%	
Mar-86	4632	4.86%	$3.8M
Apr-86	4767	2.93%	
May-86	4802	0.73%	
Jun-86	4761	−0.85%	$3.9M
Jul-86	4955	4.07%	
Aug-86	5117	3.26%	
Sep-86	4767	−6.83%	$3.9M
Oct-86	4657	−2.30%	

Date	VAMI	ROR	Account Size
Nov-86	4649	−0.19%	
Dec-86	4704	1.20%	$1.9M
1986 Final		135.86%	
Jan-87	5046	7.26%	
Feb-87	4854	−3.80%	
Mar-87	5324	9.67%	$1.9M
Apr-87	7162	34.54%	
May-87	7129	−0.47%	
Jun-87	7120	−0.12%	$2.5M
Jul-87	7410	4.07%	
Aug-87	7291	−1.60%	
Sep-87	7417	1.72%	$2.9M
Oct-87	6892	−7.08%	
Nov-87	7366	6.89%	
Dec-87	8390	13.90%	$1.4M
1987 Final		78.35%	
Jan-88	7778	−7.30%	
Feb-88	7265	−6.60%	
Mar-88	6749	−7.10%	$0.4M
Apr-88	5804	−14.00%	

**Table Appendix 4.9: Stig Ostgaard Turtle Performance,
January 1984–April 1988.**

Date	VAMI	ROR	Account Size
Jan-84	990	−1.00%	
Feb-84	1060	7.07%	
Mar-84	980	−7.54%	$1.0M
Apr-84	820	−16.32%	
May-84	740	−9.75%	
Jun-84	580	−21.62%	$0.6M
Jul-84	1060	82.75%	
Aug-84	750	−29.24%	
Sep-84	770	2.66%	$0.8M

Date	VAMI	ROR	Account Size
Oct-84	740	−3.89%	
Nov-84	710	−4.05%	
Dec-84	1200	69.01%	$0.8M
1984 Final		**20.03%**	
Jan-85	1310	9.16%	
Feb-85	1390	6.10%	
Mar-85	1570	12.94%	$1.1M
Apr-85	1130	−28.02%	
May-85	1190	5.30%	
Jun-85	800	−32.77%	$0.6M
Jul-85	2350	193.75%	
Aug-85	2000	−14.89%	
Sep-85	3340	67.00%	$0.7M
Oct-85	3940	17.96%	
Nov-85	4110	4.31%	
Dec-85	4760	15.81%	$1.3M
1985 Final		**296.56%**	
Jan-86	4250	−10.71%	
Feb-86	10780	153.64%	
Mar-86	10741	−0.37%	$2.9M
Apr-86	10611	−1.21%	
May-86	9342	−11.96%	
Jun-86	9082	−2.78%	$2.6M
Jul-86	8732	−3.85%	
Aug-86	9692	10.99%	
Sep-86	9991	3.09%	$2.9M
Oct-86	9622	−3.70%	
Nov-86	9691	0.72%	
Dec-86	9911	2.27%	$1.6M
1986 Final		**108.21%**	
Jan-87	10460	5.54%	
Feb-87	10021	−4.20%	
Mar-87	11670	16.46%	$1.6M

Date	VAMI	ROR	Account Size
Apr-87	19230	64.78%	
May-87	19499	1.40%	
Jun-87	16631	−14.71%	$1.8M
Jul-87	18849	13.34%	
Aug-87	18131	−3.81%	
Sep-87	19400	7.00%	$1.9M
Oct-87	16351	−15.72%	
Nov-87	19660	20.24%	
Dec-87	18610	−5.34%	$0.7M
1987 Final		87.77%	
Jan-88	19040	2.31%	
Feb-88	17330	−8.98%	
Mar-88	16460	−5.02%	$0.5M
Apr-88	14171	−13.91%	

Table Appendix 4.10: Jerry Parker Turtle Performance, January 1984–April 1988.

Date	VAMI	ROR	Account Size
Jan-84	988	−1.20%	
Feb-84	900	−8.87%	
Mar-84	969	7.57%	$1.0M
Apr-84	804	−16.98%	
May-84	753	−6.30%	
Jun-84	619	−17.89%	$0.7M
Jul-84	969	56.56%	
Aug-84	699	−27.85%	
Sep-84	698	−0.15%	$0.8M
Oct-84	654	−6.22%	
Nov-84	582	−11.01%	
Dec-84	900	54.49%	$1.0M
1984 Final		−10.04%	

Date	VAMI	ROR	Account Size
Jan-85	922	2.51%	
Feb-85	1097	18.92%	
Mar-85	1000	−8.77%	$0.9M
Apr-85	797	−20.38%	
May-85	936	17.52%	
Jun-85	840	−10.30%	$0.8M
Jul-85	1352	61.05%	
Aug-85	1368	1.18%	
Sep-85	1522	11.25%	$1.4M
Oct-85	1745	14.61%	
Nov-85	2111	20.99%	
Dec-85	2059	−2.46%	$1.6M
1985 Final		**128.87%**	
Jan-86	2706	31.43%	
Feb-86	5446	101.26%	
Mar-86	5472	0.47%	$4.2M
Apr-86	5265	−3.78%	
May-86	5054	−4.00%	
Jun-86	4921	−2.63%	$4.2M
Jul-86	4898	−0.47%	
Aug-86	5139	4.91%	
Sep-86	4685	−8.84%	$3.7M
Oct-86	4668	−0.35%	
Nov-86	4652	−0.34%	
Dec-86	4627	−0.54%	$1.6M
1986 Final		**124.74%**	
Jan-87	5355	15.72%	
Feb-87	4742	−11.44%	
Mar-87	4815	1.53%	$1.4M
Apr-87	7669	59.28%	
May-87	7529	−1.82%	
Jun-87	6988	−7.18%	$2.0M
Jul-87	7826	11.98%	
Aug-87	6582	−15.89%	

Appendix IV

Date	VAMI	ROR	Account Size
Sep-87	6800	3.31%	$1.6M
Oct-87	6350	–6.62%	
Nov-87	6339	–0.17%	
Dec-87	6328	–0.17%	$1.5M
1987 Final		**36.76%**	
Jan-88	6190	–2.19%	
Feb-88	6027	–2.63%	
Mar-88	5612	–6.89%	$2.1M
Apr-88	5011	–10.71%	

Table Appendix 4.11: Brian Proctor Turtle Performance, January 1985–April 1988.

Date	VAMI	ROR	Account Size
Jan-85	985	–1.50%	
Feb-85	1190	20.80%	
Mar-85	994	–16.50%	$0.2M
Apr-85	699	–29.60%	
May-85	930	32.90%	
Jun-85	624	–32.90%	$0.2M
Jul-85	1113	78.50%	
Aug-85	1109	–0.40%	
Sep-85	1096	–1.20%	$0.3M
Oct-85	1149	4.90%	
Nov-85	1431	24.50%	
Dec-85	1548	8.20%	$1.2M
1985 Final		**54.82%**	
Jan-86	1819	17.50%	
Feb-86	3706	103.70%	
Mar-86	3746	1.10%	$3.7M
Apr-86	3821	2.00%	
May-86	3504	–8.30%	
Jun-86	3508	0.10%	$3.6M

Date	VAMI	ROR	Account Size
Jul-86	3767	7.40%	
Aug-86	4069	8.00%	
Sep-86	3902	–4.10%	$4.1M
Oct-86	3480	–10.80%	
Nov-86	3320	–4.60%	
Dec-86	3347	0.80%	$2.1M
1986 Final		116.17%	
Jan-87	3658	9.30%	
Feb-87	3205	–12.40%	
Mar-87	3817	19.10%	$1.9M
Apr-87	7133	86.90%	
May-87	8410	17.90%	
Jun-87	8646	2.80%	$5.0M
Jul-87	9329	7.90%	
Aug-87	9273	–0.60%	
Sep-87	9486	2.30%	$5.2M
Oct-87	9609	1.30%	
Nov-87	9609	0.00%	
Dec-87	9542	–0.70%	$1.2M
1987 Final		185.10%	
Jan-88	9895	3.70%	
Feb-88	9657	–2.40%	
Mar-88	9764	1.10%	$0.1M
Apr-88	10291	5.40%	

**Table Appendix 4.12: Paul Rabar Turtle Performance,
January 1985–April 1988.**

Date	VAMI	ROR	Account Size
Jan-85	993	–0.70%	
Feb-85	1100	10.80%	
Mar-85	1001	–9.00%	$0.8M
Apr-85	790	–21.10%	

Date	VAMI	ROR	Account Size
May-85	992	25.60%	
Jun-85	839	–15.40%	$0.7M
Jul-85	1505	79.30%	
Aug-85	1495	–0.70%	
Sep-85	1433	–4.10%	$1.8M
Oct-85	1594	11.20%	
Nov-85	1849	16.00%	
Dec-85	1917	3.70%	$2.0M
1985 Final		**91.72%**	
Jan-86	2172	13.30%	
Feb-86	4520	108.10%	
Mar-86	5550	22.79%	$5.9M
Apr-86	4801	–13.50%	
May-86	4590	–4.39%	
Jun-86	4177	–9.00%	$4.4M
Jul-86	4745	13.60%	
Aug-86	5234	10.30%	
Sep-86	4753	–9.20%	$5.0M
Oct-86	4273	–10.10%	
Nov-86	4200	–1.70%	
Dec-86	4330	3.10%	$2.0M
1986 Final		**125.86%**	
Jan-87	4906	13.30%	
Feb-87	4121	–16.00%	
Mar-87	4657	13.00%	$1.8M
Apr-87	9612	106.40%	
May-87	9055	–5.79%	
Jun-87	8566	–5.40%	$3.3M
Jul-87	9516	11.09%	
Aug-87	8688	–8.70%	
Sep-87	9139	5.19%	$3.1M
Oct-87	7220	–21.00%	
Nov-87	7306	1.20%	

Date	VAMI	ROR	Account Size
Dec-87	7716	5.60%	$1.2M
1987 Final		**78.19%**	
Jan-88	7792	0.99%	
Feb-88	8563	9.90%	
Mar-88	7818	−8.70%	$0.1M
Apr-88	7037	−9.99%	

Table Appendix 4.13: Howard Seidler Turtle Performance, January 1984–April 1988.

Date	VAMI	ROR	Account Size
Jan-84	973	−2.70%	
Feb-84	1097	12.70%	
Mar-84	1090	−0.60%	$1.1M
Apr-84	989	−9.30%	
May-84	1049	6.10%	
Jun-84	881	−16.00%	$0.8M
Jul-84	1322	50.00%	
Aug-84	924	−30.10%	
Sep-84	970	5.00%	$2.0M
Oct-84	990	2.10%	
Nov-84	883	−10.80%	
Dec-84	1159	31.20%	$2.0M
1984 Final		**15.91%**	
Jan-85	1214	4.70%	
Feb-85	1580	30.20%	
Mar-85	1401	−11.30%	$3.4M
Apr-85	1266	−9.70%	
May-85	1490	17.70%	
Jun-85	1284	−13.80%	$3.0M
Jul-85	1690	31.60%	
Aug-85	1632	−3.40%	
Sep-85	1658	1.60%	$6.1M

Date	VAMI	ROR	Account Size
Oct-85	1905	14.90%	
Nov-85	2130	11.80%	
Dec-85	2320	8.90%	$6.3M
1985 Final		**100.16%**	
Jan-86	2343	1.00%	
Feb-86	4368	86.40%	
Mar-86	5420	24.10%	$14.4M
Apr-86	4754	–12.30%	
May-86	4459	–6.20%	
Jun-86	4231	–5.10%	$12.1M
Jul-86	4401	4.00%	
Aug-86	4982	13.20%	
Sep-86	4872	–2.20%	$13.5M
Oct-86	4804	–1.40%	
Nov-86	4597	–4.30%	
Dec-86	4547	–1.10%	$7.0M
1986 Final		**95.98%**	
Jan-87	4801	5.60%	
Feb-87	4379	–8.80%	
Mar-87	4668	6.60%	$5.8M
Apr-87	9181	96.70%	
May-87	8961	–2.40%	
Jun-87	8719	–2.70%	$10.4M
Jul-87	9565	9.70%	
Aug-87	9115	–4.70%	
Sep-87	9425	3.40%	$9.9M
Oct-87	6475	–31.30%	
Nov-87	7116	9.90%	
Dec-87	8162	14.70%	$5.0M
1987 Final		**79.52%**	
Jan-88	8236	0.90%	
Feb-88	8219	–0.20%	
Mar-88	7685	–6.50%	$3.7M
Apr-88	7685	0.00%	

Table Appendix 4.14: Tom Shanks Turtle Performance, January 1985–April 1988.

Date	VAMI	ROR	Account Size
Jan-85	941	−5.90%	
Feb-85	1155	22.70%	
Mar-85	935	−19.00%	$0.8M
Apr-85	683	−27.00%	
May-85	765	12.00%	
Jun-85	561	−26.60%	$0.5M
Jul-85	1065	89.70%	
Aug-85	1034	−2.90%	
Sep-85	850	−17.80%	$1.3M
Oct-85	1031	21.30%	
Nov-85	1198	16.20%	
Dec-85	1181	−1.40%	$1.7M
1985 Final		**18.10%**	

Date	VAMI	ROR	Account Size
Jan-86	1629	37.90%	
Feb-86	3052	87.40%	
Mar-86	3125	2.40%	$4.8M
Apr-86	3266	4.50%	
May-86	3063	−6.20%	
Jun-86	3109	1.50%	$4.8M
Jul-86	3330	7.10%	
Aug-86	3470	4.20%	
Sep-86	3345	−3.60%	$5.1M
Oct-86	3238	−3.20%	
Nov-86	3109	−4.00%	
Dec-86	3183	2.40%	$4.2M
1986 Final		**169.53%**	

Date	VAMI	ROR	Account Size
Jan-87	3813	19.80%	
Feb-87	3813	0.00%	
Mar-87	4771	25.10%	$5.1M
Apr-87	8740	83.20%	

Date	VAMI	ROR	Account Size
May-87	9212	5.40%	
Jun-87	9083	−1.40%	$9.6M
Jul-87	9846	8.40%	
Aug-87	9284	−5.70%	
Sep-87	9303	0.20%	$9.5M
Oct-87	7554	−18.80%	
Nov-87	7902	4.60%	
Dec-87	7846	−0.70%	$2.4M
1987 Final		**146.49%**	
Jan-88	7289	−7.10%	
Feb-88	6932	−4.90%	
Mar-88	5740	−17.20%	$0.2M
Apr-88	4976	−13.30%	

Endnotes

Preface

1. David Greising, "Adlai Bankroller Dennis Eschews 'Millionaire' Tag," *Chicago Sun-Times*, August 3, 1986, A3.
2. Andy Serwer, "The Greatest Money Manager of Our Time," *Fortune*, November 15, 2006 (4:07 P.M. EST).
3. Jeffrey Kluger, "Why We Worry About the Things We Shouldn't and Ignore the Things We Should," *Time*, November 26, 2006.
4. Adam Levy, "Brain Scans Show Link Between Lust for Sex and Money," February 1, 2006. See www.bloomberg.com.

Chapter 1

1. Jack D. Schwager, *Market Wizards: Interviews with Top Traders* (New York: HarperCollins, 1993).
2. Jack D. Schwager, *The New Market Wizards: Conversations with America's Top Traders* (New York: HarperBusiness, 1992).
3. Stephen Jay Gould, *The Mismeasure of Man* (New York: W. Norton & Company, 1996).
4. Ibid.
5. Marc E. Pratarelli and Krystal D. Mize, *Biological Determinism/ Fatalism: Are They Extreme Cases of Inference in Evolutionary Psychology*, 2002.
6. Jeffrey Pfeffer, "Only the Bulldogs Survive," *Business 2.0*, September 2006, p. 62.
7. Thomas Petzinger, Jr., "Speculator Richard Dennis Moves Markets and Makes Millions in Commodity Trades," *Wall Street Journal*, November 8, 1983.
8. Jenny Anderson, "Hedge Funds Are Back (Were They Ever Gone?)," *New York Times*, August 4, 2006.

9. Andrew Barber and Rich Blake, *Trader Magazine*, August/September 2006, p.76.

Chapter 2

1. Making Oodles of Boodle, *Time*, June 22, 1987, p. 49.
2. Julia M. Flynn, "Market Turmoil; Trader's Survival Lessons," *New York Times*, October 28, 1987.
3. Manager Profiles, Dennis Trading Group, Inc., BMFR, 4th Quarter (1998). See www.barclaygrp.com.
4. Flynn, "Market Turmoil."
5. David Greising, "Richard Dennis: The Man Behind All That Money," *Chicago Sun-Times*, February 1, 1987, p. A1.
6. See www.philosophypages.com.
7. Kevin Koy, *The Big Hitters* (Chicago: Intermarket Publishing Corp., 1986).
8. Richard J. Dennis, Cato's Letter #6, "Toward a Moral Drug Policy," The Cato Institute, 1991.
9. Douglas Bauer, "Prince of the Pit," *New York Times*, April 25, 1976.
10. Geoffrey Keating, "How Richard Dennis Became a Commodity Trader and Made $102,000 One Year While Remaining Skeptical of Fat Cats," *Chicago Tribune*, November 4, 1973, p. H24.
11. Bauer, "Prince of the Pit."
12. Keating, "How Richard Dennis Became a Commodity Trader."
13. Bauer, "Prince of the Pit."
14. Ibid.
15. Dennis, Cato's Letter #6.
16. Ibid.
17. Holcomb B. Noble and David C. Anderson, Endpaper, *New York Times*, December 26, 1976.
18. Art Collins audiotape interview with Richard Dennis, 2005.
19. Bauer, "Prince of the Pit."
20. Ibid.
21. Thomas Petzinger, Jr., "Speculator Richard Dennis Moves Markets and Makes Millions in Commodity Trades," *Wall Street Journal*, November 8, 1983.
22. Ibid.
23. David Greising, "Adlai Bankroller Dennis Eschews 'Millionaire' Tag," *Chicago Sun-Times*, August 3, 1986, p. A3.
24. Ibid.

25. Donald R. Katz, "Richard Dennis: The Once and Futures King," *Esquire*, December 1986.

26. Jonathan R. Laing, "$200 Million Swinger: Meet Richard Dennis, Commodities Speculator," *Barron's National Business and Financial Weekly*, vol. 66, no. 7 (February 17, 1986), 8.

27. Laurie Cohen, "Farmers Fume Over Prices," *Chicago Tribune*, January 15, 1984.

28. Ibid.

29. Michael Ervin, "Trader Richard Dennis Gets Back Into the Game . . . Again," *Central Penn Business Journal*, vol. 7, no. 2, sec. 1 (September 1992), 12.

30. Ibid.

31. Peter Newcomb, "Would You Play Poker With This Man? Do You Think You'd Win?" *Forbes* (October 27, 1986), p. 324.

32. Kevin Koy, *The Big Hitters* (Chicago: Intermarket Publishing Corp., 1986).

33. Laurie Cohen, "A Rare Trip: Trading Pit to Think Tank," *Chicago Tribune*, July 31, 1983.

34. Dennis, Cato's Letter #6.

35. Laing, "$200 Million Swinger."

36. Ibid.

37. Collins Audiotape interview with Richard Dennis.

38. Ginger Szala, "Once a Trader . . . Profile of Richard J. Dennis, Futures Funds Trader," *Futures*, August 1991, p. 46.

Chapter 3

1. *Trading Places*, directed by John Landis and written by Timothy Harris and Herschel Weingrod. Don Ameche, Dan Aykroyd, Ralph Bellamy and Eddie Murphy, performers. Distributed by Paramount, 1983.

2. Collins audiotape interview with Richard Dennis.

3. Koy, *The Big Hitters*.

4. Keith Button, "A Turtle's Take." *Managed Account Reports*, February 2004, p. 8.

5. "The Billion Dollar Club," *Financial Trader Magazine*, vol. 1, no. 7 (September/October 1994).

6. Stanley W. Angrist, "Winning Commodity Traders May Be Made, Not Born," *Wall Street Journal*, September 5, 1989.

7. Greg Burns, "Financial on the Move: Former 'Turtle' Turns Caution into an Asset," *Chicago Sun-Times*, 1989.

8. Koy, *The Big Hitters*.

9. "The Life Blood of Chicago," *Managed Account Reports*, September 2004, pp. 11–12.

10. Ibid.

11. Button, "A Turtle's Take."

12. Schwager, *The New Market Wizards*.

13. Ibid.

14. Ibid.

15. Laing, "$200 Million Swinger."

16. Ibid.

17. Katz, "Richard Dennis: The Once and Futures King."

18. Adam Hamilton, "Surviving Speculation," December 31, 2004. See www.ZealLLC.com.

19. "Turtles Outperform Industry in a Challenging Year," The Barclay Group (1995), 1st quarter.

20. Ibid.

21. Button, "A Turtle's Take."

Chapter 4

1. http://en.wikipedia.org/wiki/Scientific_method.

2. Ibid.

3. Collins audiotape interview with Richard Dennis.

4. Van Tharp. See www.iitm.com.

5. Collins audio tape interview with Richard Dennis.

6. Ibid.

7. Barbara Saslaw Dixon, "Confessions of a Trend Follower," *Commodities Magazine*, December 1974, pp. 19–21.

8. Ibid.

9. Darrell Jobman, "Richard Donchian: Pioneer of Trend-Trading," *Commodities Magazine*, September 1980, pp. 40–42.

10. Koy, *The Big Hitters*.

11. Katz, "Richard Dennis: The Once and Futures King."

12. Laing, "$200 Million Swinger."

13. "The Whiz Kid of Futures Trading," *Business Week*, 1982, p. 102.

14. Susan Abbott, "Richard Dennis: Turning a Summer Job into a Legend," *Futures Magazine*, September 1983.

15. Collins audiotape interview with Richard Dennis.

16. Abbott, "Richard Dennis."

17. "William Eckhardt: Top Systems Traders," Futures Industry Association. Speech on audiotape, 1992.
18. Ibid.
19. Abbott, "Richard Dennis."
20. "William Eckhardt: Top Systems Traders."
21. Ibid.
22. Ibid.
23. Ibid.
24. Ibid.
25. Ibid.
26. Keating, "How Richard Dennis Became a Commodity Trader."
27. "William Eckhardt: Top Systems Traders."
28. "The Whiz Kid of Futures Trading."
29. Abbott, "Richard Dennis."
30. Kevin, *The Big Hitters*.
31. Laing, "$200 Million Swinger."
32. "William Eckhardt: Top Systems Traders."
33. Koy, *The Big Hitters*.
34. Abbott, "Richard Dennis."
35. "William Eckhardt: Top Systems Traders."
36. Ibid.
37. Bradley Rotter interview.

Chapter 5

1. http://en.wikipedia.org/wiki/Type_I_and_type_II_errors.
2. TASS, "Twenty Traders Talk," William Eckhardt. June 29, 1996.
3. http://en.wikipedia.org/wiki/Occam's_Razor.
4. Collins audiotape interview.
5. TASS, "Twenty Traders Talk."
6. Ibid.
7. Trading Systems Review, FIA Futures and Options Expo Audio, November 8, 2002.
8. Stanley W. Angrist, "Traders in the Slippery Oil Market Bet That Slide Won't Last," *Wall Street Journal*, October 25, 1990.
9. Ibid.
10. Trading Systems Review, FIA Futures and Options Expo Audio.
11. TASS, "Twenty Traders Talk."
12. Ben Warwick, "Turtle Wisdom." Managed Account Reports, Inc., 2001.

13. "William Eckhardt: Top Systems Traders."
14. David Cheval and Patricia N. Gillman. *How to Become a CTA: Based on CME Seminars, 1992–1994*, edited by Susan Abbott Gidel (Chicago Mercantile Exchange, 1994).
15. FIA Futures and Options Expo Audio.
16. Ibid.
17. McRae, "Top Traders." *Managed Derivatives*, May 1996.
18. Ibid.
19. Ibid.
20. Ibid.
21. Cheval and Gillman, *How to Become a CTA*.
22. McRae, "Top Traders."
23. Boris Schlossberg, "Trading House," *Stocks, Futures & Options Magazine*, vol. 5, no. 2 (February 2006).
24. Ibid.

Chapter 6

1. RAM Management Group, Ltd., *Barclays Managed Futures Report*, 2nd Quarter (1998).
2. Ervin, "Trader Richard Dennis Gets Back Into the Game . . . Again."
3. Ginger Szala, "Even Without Dennis, 'Turtles' Still Keeping Apace in Trading Race: Traders Following Methods of Retired Trader Richard J. Dennis," *Futures*, vol. 18, no. 5 (May 1989), 72.
4. Greg Burns, "Rich Dennis: A Gunslinger No More," *Business Week*, April 7, 1997.
5. Brett N. Steenbarger, "Trading the Ranger Way: Training the Elite Trader." See www.BrettSteenbarger.com
6. Brace E. Barber, *Ranger School: No Excuse Leadership* (Brace E. Barber, 2000).
7. Button, "A Turtle's Take."

Chapter 7

1. *Trading Places*.
2. Stanley W. Angrist, "Winning Commodity Traders May Be Made, Not Born," *Wall Street Journal*, September 5, 1989.
3. See www.turtletradingsoftware.com, April 16, 2003.
4. Ibid.
5. Ibid.

6. See www.turtletradingsoftware.com, July 25, 2003.
7. See www.turtletradingsoftware.com, November 14, 2005.
8. See www.turtletradingsoftware.com, February 08, 2006.
9. Richard Dennis memo, April 23, 1986.
10. Collins audiotape interview with Richard Dennis.

Chapter 8

1. Burns, "Financial on the Move."
2. "Dennis Trading Group, Inc: At a Glance," The Barclay Group, 4th Quarter (1998).
3. Julia Flynn Siler, "A Commodity Trader Fares Poorly in Funds," *New York Times*, April 26, 1988.
4. Scott McMurray, "Personal Finance (A Special Report): No Future—Safety in Numbers?" *Wall Street Journal*, October 19, 1990.
5. Michael Abramowitz, "Dennis Faces Doubts After Drexel Debacle," *Washington Post*, September 1, 1991, p. H1.
6. "Judge Approves Dennis Pact," *New York Times*, November 11, 1990.
7. Szala, "Once a Trader."
8. See www.turtletradingsoftware.com, March 14, 2005.
9. Collins audiotape interview with Richard Dennis.

Chapter 9

1. *Trading Places.*
2. McRae, "Top Traders."
3. McIntire School of Commerce, University of Virginia. *McIntire now*, Spring 2002.
4. Trading Systems Review, FIA Futures and Options Expo Audio.
5. Szala, "Even Without Dennis, 'Turtles' Still Keeping Apace."
6. Carla Cavaletti, "Turtles on the Move; Former Students of Rich Dennis; Managed Money," *Futures*, vol. 27, no. 6 (June 1998), 76.
7. See lacm-usvi.com.
8. Cavaletti, "Turtles on the Move."
9. Burns, "Financial on the Move."
10. Jack Reerink, "Turtle Bisque; Money Management Experts Educated by Richard Dennis." *Futures*, vol. 24, no. 5 (May 1995), 60.
11. "Dealing with the Challenge of Unfavorable Markets Strategies and Methods CTAs Apply in Difficult Trading Environments," The Barclay Group, 4th quarter (1993).

12. Ginger Szala, "Trader Profile: Tom Shanks: Former 'Turtle' Winning Race the Hard Way," *Futures*, vol. 20, no. 2 (1991), 78.
13. Reerink, "Turtle Bisque."
14. Elizabeth Anne Cheval, "MFA Journal Encore: Why Choose High Volatility Trading?" *EMC Capital Management*, vol. 9, issue 1 (1994).
15. Cheval, "MFA Journal Encore."
16. "What's in Store for 1991?" The Barclay Group, 1st Quarter (1991).
17. See www.jwh.com.
18. Michael W. Covel, *Trend Following: How Great Traders Make Millions in Up or Down Markets* (New York: Prentice Hall, 2004).
19. Cavaletti, "Turtles on the Move."
20. Reerink, "Turtle Bisque."
21. McRae, "Top Traders."
22. Ibid.

Chapter 10

1. Szala, "Once a Trader."
2. Burns, "Rich Dennis: A Gunslinger No More."
3. Michael Fritz, "Richard Dennis: He's Baaaaaack—A Quiet Return for Futures Exile," *Crain's Chicago Business*, vol. 18, no. 50, sec. 1 (December 11, 1995), 1.
4. "Dennis Trading Group, Inc: At a Glance."
5. Michael Abramowitz, "Dennis Faces Doubts After Drexel Debacle," *Washington Post*, September 1, 1991, p. H1.
6. Fritz, "Richard Dennis: He's Baaaaaack."
7. Laurie Cohen, "Promotion for Seminar on Futures Trading Secrets Not Telling All," *Chicago Tribune*, August 30, 1992, Bus 1.
8. Ibid.
9. Ibid.
10. Ibid.
11. Ibid.
12. Ibid.
13. Ibid.
14. Collins audiotape interview with Richard Dennis.
15. Dennis Trading Group, Inc: At a Glance."
16. Ibid.
17. Burns, "Rich Dennis: A Gunslinger No More."
18. Daniel A. Strachman, "Trader Profile: Back from the Bottom of the Pit," *Financial Trader*.

19. Andrew Osterland, "For Commodity Funds, It Was as Good as It Gets," *Business Week*, September 14, 1998.

20. Peter Coy and Suzanne Woolley, "Failed Wizards of Wall Street," *Business Week*, September 21, 1998.

21. Diane Kruegar, "Managed Money Review: Richard Dennis Closes Shop—Again," *Futures* (November 2000).

Chapter 11

1. David Nusbaum, "Charles Faulkner: Mind Reader," *Futures*, vol. 22, no. 12 (November 1993), 98.

2. Koy, *The Big Hitters*.

3. "Technical vs. Fundamental: How Do Traders Differ?" The Barclay Group, 3rd Quarter (1991).

4. Ginger Szala, "Trader Profile: Tom Shanks: Former 'Turtle' Winning Race the Hard Way," *Futures*, vol. 20, no. 2 (1991), 78.

5. Jerry Parker, Chairman of VCAP. April 18, 2005, www.vcap.org.

6. Malcolm Gladwell, "The Talent Myth," *The New Yorker*, July 22, 2002.

7. Carol Hymowitz, "Nation's Top Chief Executives Find Path to the Corner Office Usually Starts at State University," *Wall Street Journal*, September 18, 2006, p. B1.

8. "What Does It Take to Be an Entrepreneur?" *Under 25*, Summer 1993.

9. Greg Farell, "Does Harvard 'Brand' Matter Anymore? 1980 Grads Reflect on What They Learned," *USA Today*, June 7, 2005.

10. McIntire School of Commerce, University of Virginia. *McIntire now*, Spring 2002.

11. McIntire School of Commerce, *McIntire now*.

12. "Roundtable: The State of the Industry II," *Managed Account Reports, Inc.*, no. 257 (July 2000), 8.

13. "Roundtable: The State of the Industry," *Managed Account Reports, Inc.*, No. 256 (June 2000).

14. Ibid.

15. McIntire School of Commerce, University of Virginia, *McIntire now*. Spring 2001, 17.

16. Ibid.

17. Disclosure Document of Chesapeake Capital Corporation, March 29, 1999.

18. "Technical vs. Fundamental: How Do Traders Differ?" The Barclay Group, 3rd Quarter (1991).

19. FIA Futures and Options Expo Audio, Trading Systems Review, Friday, November 8, 2002.
20. Ibid.
21. Ibid.
22. Ibid.
23. "Roundtable: The State of the Industry II," *Managed Account Reports, Inc.*
24. Allan Sloan, "Amaranth's Wilting Is a Lesson on Hedges," *Washington Post*, September 26, 2006, p. D2.
25. Nathan Slaughter and Paul Tracy, "Profiting from Mean Reversion." See www.streetauthority.com, February 21, 2006.
26. FIA Futures and Options Expo Audio.
27. FIA Futures and Options Expo Audio.

Chapter 12

1. Button, "A Turtle's Take."
2. Collins audioTape interview with Richard Dennis.
3. Ibid.
4. See www.turtletradingsoftware.com, April 12, 2005.
5. Ibid.
6. See www.originalturtles.org, 2003.
7. Collins Audiotape Interview with Richard Dennis.
8. See www.turtletradingsoftware.com, February 13, 2004.
9. Ibid.
10. See www.turtletradingsoftware.com, August 19, 2004.
11. Paul Barr, "New Futures Fund Rolls at Acceleration Capital," *Hedge-World Daily News*. May 20, 2004.
12. Ibid.
13. See www.turtletradingsoftware.com, July 24, 2003.
14. Commodity Futures Trading Commission. See www.cftc.gov/opa/enf06/opa5211-06.htm, August 8, 2006.

Chapter 13

1. Ginger Szala, "Top Traders Who Tamed the Rough and Tumble Markets of 1993," *Futures*, vol. 23, no. 3 (March 1994), 60.
2. Mark Aronson, "Trading Advisor Review: Learning from a Legend," *Managed Account Reports*, June 1997.
3. Diane Brady, "Yes, Winning Is Still The Only Thing," *Business Week*, August 21, 2006.

4. Bill Deener, "Who Is This Man? And Why Is He Trading So Many Futures Contracts Out of Canadian, Texas?" *Dallas Morning News*, September 7, 2003.
5. Simon Romero, "A Homespun Hedge Fund, Tucked Away in Texas," *New York Times*, December 24, 2003.
6. Jim Sogi, "The Killer Instinct." See www.dailyspeculations.com, March 15, 2005.

Chapter 14

1. Art Collins, *Market Beaters* (South Carolina: Traders Press, Inc., 2004), pp. 190–91.
2. Michael J. Mauboussin, "Mauboussin on Strategy: Are You an Expert?" *Legg Mason Capital Management*, October 28, 2005.
3. Ibid.
4. Atul Gawande, *The New Yorker*, January 28, 2002.

Appendix I: Where Are They Now?

1. Don Schultz, *United States Chess Federation President's Letter*, January 17, 1997.
2. See en.wikipedia.org/wiki/William_Eckhardt_(trader).
3. See en.wikipedia.org/wiki/Doomsday_argument.
4. Reerink, "Turtle Bisque."
5. Elise Coroneos, "Trading Advisor Review: Steadying the Ship," *Managed Account Reports, Inc.*, January 2004, p. 15.

About the Author

1. Michael Lewis, *Liar's Poker* (New York: W. W. Norton & Company, October 1989).

Index

About the Author, Michael Covel

"Call me arrogant, cocky, crybaby, whiner or whatever names you like. At least they're not calling us losers anymore. If people like you too much, it's probably because they're beating you."
Steve Spurrier,
University of South Carolina football coach

Taking very little at face value is my modus operandi. In fact, since childhood I've challenged the accepted norms regarding access to the truth. Along the way I've challenged a number of people who have wanted to keep the curtains closed. In this small world, one of the more unlikely people to have asked me, "How do you go about unearthing details?" was Mikhail Gorbachev (This happened at a reception sponsored by Christian Baha, who runs the managed futures firm Superfund).

The former president had been told in Russian that I write about men who trade big money, so when we were introduced he asked me in Russian, "What is it like to write about these men?" Realizing his time was limited, I kept it short: "Very interesting." He waited for the translation. "It must be difficult to get behind the scenes; how do you do it?" I smiled, "Oh, I am very good at digging." He laughed. No translation needed there. He understood my English perfectly.

Walking into the world of Turtles was not planned. It was an unconventional journey. Spring 1994 was the "get your act together, now is the time" year for me. I had just finished an MBA at Florida State, having spent my final semester in London studying international relations.

Back in the States, armed with the so-called prerequisite advanced degree and a deep desire to become rich, Wall Street called. Unfortunately, Virginia, my home state, was not the place to start looking for a mentor or an opportunity that would lead to big money. Most of my friends were products of government workers, not the types looking beyond security or "fitting in."

So, I tracked down one of the few Florida State alums on Wall Street, recently retired James Massey. He had made millions at Salomon Brothers and was memorably portrayed in Michael Lewis's classic *Liar's Poker*:

> [Jim] Massey . . . was John Gutfreund's (the then CEO) hatchet man, an American corporate Odd Job. It didn't require a triple jump of the imagination to picture him decapitating insolent trainees with a razor-edged bowler hat. He had what some people might consider an image problem: he never smiled . . . Trainees feared Massey. He seemed to prefer it that way."[1]

At lunch, Massey did not say a word. After a half hour the conversation was speeding downhill. Astute enough to see my sink- or swim-predicament, I said: "Have I said anything so far that makes you think I am full of shit?"

That got his attention. "Yes, you said you wanted to be the best. You don't want to be the best; you just want to win." Massey, like any good coach, was offering the reminder that winners play harder than anyone else.

As fate would have it, I didn't get hired at Salomon Brothers, but right after meeting Massey, the word 'Turtle' crossed my desk for the first time. Shortly thereafter, in 1996, long before YouTube.com, Google, and millions of blogs, I was there at the start of TurtleTrader.com—a controversial website designed to teach trend following and Turtle trading. It ended up becoming one of the most popular financial websites in the world and was ultimately the start of this book.

One of my goals has always been to make people think twice. That attitude has made me a target, but I was a baseball catcher so I am used to taking the shots. I often face intense reactions because I represent the other side that's never considered. Ten years of digging and reporting have produced my fair share of critics, some legit, some off the wall. I am a messenger and people love to shoot messengers.

At the end of the day, this was not the career direction I'd originally planned as a freshly minted graduate. However, sitting at the nexus of access and insight from some of the best trading minds on the planet has become my singular passion—for now.

For more information: www.turtletrader.com and www.michael covel.com.